CW01649077

Holiday T[illegible]

Katharine Wo[illegible] of Belgian and E[illegible] e, reading Comm[illegible] and literature at Edinburgh University. Following a period as a freelance public relations consultant and freelance journalist she entered the world of travel journalism. An eighteen-month spell touring Europe and North Africa resulted in the book *Europe by Train* (published by Fontana) which she wrote in conjunction with George McDonald and which is one of the UK's top-selling guidebooks. As well as working full time on this series of Holiday Guides, she is currently involved in several projects encompassing every aspect of the travel industry – from backpacking students to round-the-world first-class tours. She regularly appears on radio and TV travel programmes in the UK, USA and Far East, and contributes freelance to several publications, writing on holidays and leisure. In the course of her work she has so far clocked up 48 countries and has travelled extensively in Turkey. She is married and lives in Scotland, with her husband, who works with her on various guides, and young sons, Andrew and Euan.

George McDonald was born in Dumfries and was educated at Fettes College and Edinburgh University. Following a brief spell on the family farm he has since travelled the world, usually as a hobby, but often as a full-time travel researcher. He toured Europe and North Africa with Katie Wood to help research the guidebook *Europe by Train*. Home, when he's there, is Guernsey in the Channel Islands.

Also by the same authors:

The Round the World Air Guide
Europe By Train
Holiday Yugoslavia
Holiday Turkey
Holiday Greece
Holiday Portugal
Holiday Ireland
Holiday Coastal Spain
The Winter Sun Guide

Also by Katie Wood:

European City Breaks
The Best of British Country House Hotels and Restaurants
Holiday Scotland

Holiday TURKEY

Compiled and Edited by
Katie Wood

Head Researcher:
George McDonald

Editorial Assistant: Alastair Dalton

FONTANA/Collins

First published in 1987 by Fontana Paperbacks
8 Grafton Street, London W1X 3LA
Revised 1988, 1989, 1990

Copyright © Katie Wood and George McDonald 1987, 1988, 1989, 1990

Set in Linotron Plantin

The Holiday Guide research team used a
Ferguson Videostar C-Auto-Focus CCR
in the preparation of this guide

Made and printed in Great Britain
by William Collins Sons & Co. Ltd, Glasgow

Conditions of Sale
This book is sold subject to the condition
that it shall not, by way of trade or otherwise,
be lent, re-sold, hired out or otherwise circulated
without the publisher's prior consent in any form of
binding or cover other than that in which it is
published and without a similar condition
including this condition being imposed
on the subsequent purchaser

To Andrew

Contents

Part Two – HOW TO GO

Part Three – WHEN YOU'RE THERE

Part Four – THE COUNTRY

ACKNOWLEDGEMENTS

Thanks are due to the following people who helped bring this guide to fruition: Julie Douglas, our head researcher in Turkey; Harriet Wylie for graphics; Nicola McClymont-Sutherland, researcher in Istanbul and eastern Turkey, and all other contributing journalists; Mrs Kahraman of the Turkish Tourist Board London office; Syd House for his late-night editing; and the many friendly Turks who made our time in their country so enjoyable and rewarding.

In the collating of this guide an Apple Macintosh SE was used. We would like to acknowledge and thank Apple Computers UK Ltd for this piece of excellent machinery, without which it would have been impossible to assimilate all the information in such a short space of time. This computer travelled round the world with us, producing hard copy when needed, and storing the hundreds of pieces of information we found out daily. It has to be acknowledged as the ultimate travel journalist's tool!

WHAT THIS GUIDE IS ABOUT

This book is designed to fill a void which has existed for too long in the travel guide market. Once you have decided where you would like to go for your holiday you will find no shortage of guide books on the country of your choice. You might, however, find it difficult to find a guide which does not assume you are middle-class, middle-aged, and probably American, or at the other end of the scale, a back-packing penniless student.

Catering for the first group there are the 'heavies' such as Fodor, Michelin and Benn's Blue Guide books. These are all very good books, especially if you require a blow-by-blow account of the country's history or you are studying for a degree in Turkish archaeology. At the other extreme there are the '£10 a day' guides which will show you how to cover as much ground as possible with minimum expenditure – providing, of course, you are willing to forgo luxuries like square meals and comfortable beds.

This guide has been written for the vast majority of people, like you, who come somewhere between these two extremes. It is aimed at the fun-loving tourist – which you no doubt are – who usually plans one good holiday a year and wants to make the most of it. It also recognizes that many of you will be in the under 40 age group – young people eager to see the country you have chosen to visit while at the same time having plenty of fun. You will not want to throw your money around, but you might expect the occasional treat – after all, it is a holiday. Our recommendations for hotels, restaurants, entertainment, etc. start at the lower end of the market just to give you some idea of what to budget for.

Turkey is a fascinating country with an increasing number of good, comfortable holiday resorts and a wealth of tourist attractions which make it more popular every year. With so much to choose from we want to be sure that you find the holiday package tailor-made for your needs. This guide looks at all the options available and the pros and cons of the different packages offered by the tour operators. We also consider the options open to independent travellers and supply information which will help you choose between a package holiday and independent travel.

This guide has been written in a light-hearted style, giving you the information we think you will need to ensure that your holiday is enjoyable and problem-free. It should enable you to enjoy Turkey to the full by telling you where to go for what – depending on your particular hobbies and interests. It is not a specialist guide for any one group of people (historians, nature-lovers, watersport enthusiasts, etc.) but it does show you where best to pursue your hobby. We have placed some emphasis on 'sun-worshipping', which many holiday-makers seem to adopt as a hobby in itself, given half the chance, and with four beautiful coastlines, Turkey certainly lends itself to this popular pastime.

This guide will also equip you with enough basic information to enable you to understand and appreciate the country's culture, its history and the various monuments and places of interest you are bound to stumble across. We do not claim to be the ultimate authority on Turkey. What we do present, though, is a stack of information on the country which we have catalogued so that it can be easily referred to. But that doesn't mean we're not interested in what you have to say. Only recently has Turkey's tourist potential been fully recognized, and every year more and more is learnt about this ancient and mysterious country. If you discover anything new and interesting, or feel you can contribute to our research in any way, please write to us so that we can include your recommendations in future editions of this guide.

Part One

BEFORE YOU GO

ENTRY REQUIREMENTS British visitors with a full passport or visitor's passport have been allowed to stay in Turkey for up to three months without a visa. However, it is likely that a visa for visitors to Turkey from the UK will be introduced with effect from 1 November 1989. It will probably be a point of entry formality and not something you need organize in advance, and will cost £20.

POPULATION 52,000,000

CAPITAL Ankara (pop: 3,000,000)

CURRENCY Turkish Lira (TL) (£1 = 3300TL)

POLITICAL SYSTEM Democratic Republic

RELIGION Muslim (Seclusion States)

LANGUAGE Turkish

PUBLIC HOLIDAYS 1 January
23 April
19 May
30 August
29 October

What to Expect

Until the last decade very few British holidaymakers had ever seriously considered Turkey as a holiday destination. Even now, most people are surprised to discover just how much this beautiful and diverse country has to offer. At the mention of Turkey most people conjure up a mental picture of Istanbul with its mystical domes and minarets, but few people know about the coastal resorts, the ski resorts, the thermal centres, the historical and archaeological sites or the scenic beauty of the inland regions.

Since the early 1960s when the Ministry of Culture and Tourism devised a national plan to put the country on the international map, Turkey has gradually built up a thriving tourist industry. It now offers a wide range of reasonably priced holidays in attractive settings. For the British holidaymaker a package tour to Turkey will still cost slightly more than the equivalent holiday in Spain or Greece – where mass tourism makes for more competitive prices – but in return you can enjoy your holiday in a country which is relatively unspoilt. Once you've made the initial outlay for your holiday or your travel, you will find Turkey incredibly cheap. The cost of food, drink, sightseeing trips and entertainment is very low compared with that of most European destinations.

Turkey's tourist industry is centred around Istanbul, Ankara and the resorts of the Aegean and Mediterranean coasts, and it is here that the majority of modern hotels are to be found. The inland regions of Cappadocia, Pamukkale and Konya are now being developed for tourism, but outside these regions Turkey's heartland has little to offer in the way of good hotels. Wherever you go in Turkey you can always find cheap places to stay, but the standard of accommodation sometimes varies greatly. One thing you won't have to suffer in Turkey are the rows of unsightly hotels which mar the coastlines of so many Mediterranean resorts. One of the country's main selling points, apart from its guaranteed summer sunshine, is the friendliness of the Turks themselves. Whether you're touring the country or staying in one place, you'll always be greeted with warmth and hospitality.

Turkey has more than five thousand miles of coastline, but the best beaches are found in the south and south-west on the Aegean and Mediterranean coasts. This section of the coastline, with its white sandy beaches, secluded coves and crystal-clear blue sea, is undoubtedly one of the country's major assets. Resorts like Bodrum, Kusadasi, Marmaris, Antalya and Alanya, which are already popular with tourists from the UK and the USA, are expected to witness a tourist boom during the next few years as more and more tour operators recognize their potential for sailing, watersports and beach holidays. The Black Sea coast is attractive, but lacks the amenities of the Aegean and Mediterranean coasts.

To see Turkey as it really is, you have to move away from the coastal resorts – only then can you begin to experience the diversity of this vast country. Some of the most spectacular scenery can be found in the inland region of south-west Turkey, where the mountains and lush green valleys provide a haven for nature-lovers, and in Cappadocia, famous for its incredible rock formations and underground cities. In eastern Anatolia life goes on pretty much the way it did a hundred years ago, and the austere and unsophisticated lifestyle of the Turkish peasants comes as a sharp contrast to the gaiety and liveliness of the up-and-coming tourist resorts. In the centre of Turkey's modern capital Ankara you'll find few buildings more than fifty years old, while in contrast Istanbul stands as a monument to many past civilizations, which have shaped her into one of the world's most exciting cities.

As far as the country's culture is concerned, you must learn to expect the unexpected. Just as you're becoming used to the modern Western lifestyle you'll encounter some ancient Eastern custom. The country's present culture is a direct result of the reforms introduced by the national hero Kemal Ataturk when he founded the Turkish Republic in 1923. But there are still numerous reminders of Turkey's 10,000-year-long history, and the influence of past eras is very much in evidence. For centuries, the country's geographical position between Europe and Asia made it a battleground for the Roman and Byzantine invaders from the west, and the Seljuk and Ottoman Turks who originated from Central Asia.

The Muslim faith, which is now embraced by 99 per cent of the population, is a significant part of Turkish culture, and, despite the endeavours of Ataturk to promote Western attitudes, many Turkish men still adhere to their Eastern attitudes when it comes to women. However, things are now changing and women travelling alone are less likely to be hassled than they were a few years ago. Outside the cities and tourist resorts, Turks are not accustomed to seeing women alone and a woman who is not accompanied by a man may be hassled more than normal. Women who abide by the basic rules (i.e. dress appropriately in a mosque) and show willingness to respect Muslim beliefs should not have problems. As we've said before, the Turks are a very friendly people, and if you are prepared to respect their customs they will be happy to welcome you.

When to Go

This will vary depending on the region you intend to visit and the type of holiday you are planning. The tourist season runs from the beginning of April to the end of October, and most resorts are at their hottest and busiest in July and August. You will pay most for your holiday from July to mid-September, which is considered the 'peak season' by most package tour operators, but in return you will find everything open and the social scene in full swing.

For the majority of beach and sightseeing holidays spring and autumn are good times to go. The climate in Istanbul and on the Aegean and Mediterranean coasts is ideal for sunbathing between April and June and in September and October – when temperatures are hot but not uncomfortable – and you will find fewer crowds. Central Anatolia is slightly cooler at these times, but just right for sightseeing and touring. Most tour operators offer their cheapest deals in April, with prices rising a little for May, June and October.

If you are planning a watersports holiday you may prefer to visit Turkey in August or September, when water temperatures are at their warmest. But don't worry, if you do decide to go in May, June, July or October, you'll still find the water warm by British standards.

If you are planning a trip to eastern Anatolia and are hoping for warm temperatures, July and August are definitely your best bet as spring and autumn can be fairly cool in this region. Unless you are planning a winter skiing holiday in one of the main resorts, travel is not recommended in this region between October and April as snowfalls can be very heavy and certain roads may be impassable.

The Climate

Coastal Weather

The Marmara, Aegean and Mediterranean coastlines enjoy a typically Mediterranean climate with hot summers and mild winters. The hottest months are July and August, when temperatures are around 29°C or 82°F, and rainfall is relatively low throughout the tourist season. Marmara is Turkey's most humid region with an annual average of 72 per cent humidity.

Temperatures become a few degrees warmer as you travel south from Izmir on the Aegean coast to Antalya on the Mediterranean. Water temperatures also become warmer the further south you go. In the Marmara and north Aegean regions the swimming season is from June to September, but in the south Aegean and Mediterranean you can bathe in warm water from April to October.

The Black Sea coast has a more temperate climate with warm summers and mild winters. Here rainfall is higher than in any other region (almost three times the national average) and the weather is generally less predictable, even in the summer months. The Black Sea swimming season runs from June to September.

While most of Turkey's coastline enjoys mild weather throughout the winter months, with temperatures reaching a low of 8°C or 46°F in January, you can forget serious sunbathing between November and April.

Average maximum daily temperatures, based on Istanbul:

	JAN	FEB	MAR	APR	MAY	JUNE
°F	46	48	52	61	70	77
°C	8	9	11	16	21	25

	JULY	AUG	SEPT	OCT	NOV	DEC
°F	82	82	75	68	59	52
°C	29	29	24	20	15	11

Inland Weather

The climate varies quite dramatically between the western coastal regions and the high altitudes of Turkey's central and eastern heartland. In central and eastern Anatolia the climate is extreme, with hot dry summers, when temperatures can reach 42°C or 109°F, and cold snowy winters. Early spring and late autumn can also be cold and damp, and even in the height of summer the nights can be cool. The weather is at its best in late spring and early autumn.

Average maximum daily temperatures, based on Ankara:

	JAN	FEB	MAR	APR	MAY	JUNE
°F	39	42	52	63	73	78
°C	4	5	11	17	23	26

	JULY	AUG	SEPT	OCT	NOV	DEC
°F	86	87	78	70	57	43
°C	30	31	26	21	14	7

Winter Turkey

SKIING

Most people never even think about Turkey when considering a winter skiing holiday and are surprised to discover there are no fewer than eight ski centres dotted around the country. Turkey is not noted as a great winter sports destination and most of the resorts are under-developed compared to the major European ski centres. Nevertheless, facilities are adequate for the average ski enthusiast, and it does have the advantage of being less expensive and less crowded than a lot of European resorts.

Winter sports resorts in Turkey are generally located in forested mountains of heights between 2000m and 2500m. At present the most popular resort is **ULUDAG**, which is twenty-two miles south of Bursa in the Marmara region. This will soon be rivalled by **SAKLIKENT**, which is located twenty-six miles from Antalya on the Mediterranean coast and is currently being developed as the country's largest ski centre. Other resorts which are reasonably accessible by road or internal flights are **KOROGLU** near Bolu, **PALANDOKEN** near Erzurum, **SARIKAMIS** near Kars and **ERCIYES** near Kayseri.

The skiing season in Turkey runs from November to April, but in the western resorts like Uludag and Saklikent, the snow is at its best between January and March. In some eastern and central resorts, like Palandoken and Erciyes, conditions are good throughout the season.

WINTER SUN

If you want to lie on a beach for two weeks in the middle of December, Turkey is not really the place to go. While temperatures on the Mediterranean and Aegean coasts are quite pleasant during the winter, they cannot really be described as hot. Istanbul is quite a popular sightseeing destination in winter and some tour operators offer two-centre holidays, in Istanbul and resorts on the Mediterranean. It's a nice way to see the country and avoid the crowds, but don't expect big discounts for travelling off-season. In most cases prices are comparable with the summer season, and in some cases they are even more expensive.

Where to Go for What

So often people spend weeks deliberating which country to choose for their holiday destination, then leave the choice of where they stay within the country to either a photo and brief, optimistic write-up in a travel brochure, or to the discretion and persuasive talk of a travel agent (most of whom haven't actually visited the country in any depth anyway). This lottery results, not surprisingly, in many having a disappointing holiday simply because they got the facts wrong on this crucial decision. If anything, the decision as to which part of the country you base yourself in is more important than the choice of country itself, for there is good and bad in every country – Britain, for example, offers a superb holiday destination, but if the visitor were to opt for two weeks in Sheffield when he really wanted a 'get-away-from-it-all' break, he would be sadly disappointed. Don't think that the Turkish equivalents of Sheffield aren't on offer. They are, but you will not know if you've landed in one of them until you've paid over your money and arrived at the resort.

The aim of this section, therefore, is to try to match your needs and preferences with the appropriate destination within Turkey. In order to find you the most suitable resort, we have divided holidaymakers into certain stereotypes. Doubtless most of you fall into several of the categories, but the idea is to find which resorts crop up in the areas you are interested in, and match your needs accordingly.

The following symbols representing the various interests appear throughout the text of the guide as a means of easy reference to spot the places likely to be of interest to you:

The Sun-worshipper 

The Sightseer 

The Socialite 

Healthy Holidays 

The Nature-lover 

The Recluse 

Family Holidays 

The Sun-worshipper

Sun-worshippers are people who like to spend their entire holiday languishing on a beautiful sun-soaked beach with nothing more to do than cultivate a tan and admire the talent. If you fit this description, the advice is to head for either the south Aegean or the Mediterranean coast where you will undoubtedly find the country's most beautiful beaches.

Apart from the hot sun, warm surf and soft sand, which will be high on your list of priorities, both the Aegean and the Mediterranean coastlines offer breathtaking scenery which will provide an idyllic setting for your sunbathing. The Aegean coast comprises extensive sandy beaches, rocky bays and crystal-blue lagoons. On the Mediterranean coast – which is often referred to as the Turquoise coast or the Turkish Riviera – the snow-capped Taurus Mountains provide a dramatic backdrop to the broad, sandy shores and rocky coves.

There are numerous quiet, pretty beaches dotted along the Aegean and Mediterranean coastlines and it would be impossible to mention them all, but here are some of the resorts the dedicated sun-worshipper should look out for:

THE AEGEAN COAST

BODRUM – This is probably the Aegean's most popular resort, and is an ideal place for the sun-worshipper who enjoys the challenge of seeking out his own deserted beach. There is no beach in the town, but the shores of the Bodrum Peninsula are a succession of secluded coves with sandy beaches and clear, warm water. This picturesque port is also well known for its abundance of watersport facilities, and has a lively atmosphere which seems to attract a young, fun-loving crowd.

KUSADASI – This is an increasingly popular resort which combines lovely scenery with good sandy beaches. The best beaches are situated a few miles from the town centre, as are many of the good hotels. The lively resort of Kusadasi overlooks a large sweeping bay which is considered by some to be the most beautiful on the Aegean coast. Club Med run a hotel here.

CESME – The pretty port of Cesme is a lively beach resort and a popular thermal centre. It is a sprawling resort made up of several small villages, most of which have their own harbour, their own beach and their own spas. Cesme's gently sloping sandy beaches are excellent for sunbathing and safe swimming.

THE MEDITERRANEAN COAST

MARMARIS – The fishing village of Marmaris, with its charming little marina, can boast some of Turkey's most beautiful beaches. You will not find vast expanses of beach, but secluded rocky coves with golden sand and clear blue water. Marmaris is a bustling resort and a busy yachting port. It also offers good watersport facilities for the more energetic sun-worshipper. In recent years Marmaris has become the 'in' place for the glitterati.

FETHIYE – The ancient town of Fethiye stands on a hillside overlooking a quiet bay strewn with tiny islands. The immediate coastline is particularly beautiful with pine forests stretching down to the sea shore and fine sandy beaches. One of the main attractions is the nearby Bay of Belcegiz where the famous lagoon called Olu Deniz is a paradise for sunbathers and swimmers.

KEMER – This pretty little resort is located on the Lycian Peninsula just west of Antalya, the principal resort of the Mediterranean. Kemer is known for its long, sweeping beach and small pine-clad coves with deserted sandy shores. Here a lively atmosphere is created by the new luxurious holiday village set in the pine woods which sweep down to the beach.

SIDE – This is a very attractive and very busy town – a typical sun, surf 'n' sand resort. Side is an ancient town flanked by two broad sandy beaches which are backed by sand dunes and fascinating ancient ruins. The immediate coastline is bordered with orange groves, cotton fields, banana plantations and flowering gardens. This is one of the Mediterranean's most lively resorts with plenty of cafés, restaurants and discos within walking distance of the beach. It would be ideally suited to a party of sun-worshippers and sightseers.

ALANYA – Like Side, Alanya is located on a rocky point between two vast sandy beaches. The town is dominated by an old Seljuk fortress which overlooks the beaches and provides one of the Mediterranean's most impressive sights. Alanya is fast becoming the most popular beach resort on the Turkish Mediterranean.

Apart from the Aegean and Mediterranean there is also the Black Sea coast. This is often ruled out by the serious sun-worshipper because air temperatures are slightly cooler, and water temperatures considerably cooler than those of the Aegean and Mediterranean; the sand is also noticeably coarser (more like fine shingle in some places). While the Black Sea resorts are popular among Turkish holidaymakers, this part of Turkey's coastline is less developed than the Aegean and Mediterranean and is not really geared towards international tourism. Nevertheless, the Black Sea coast does have some pretty resorts and very attractive beaches. If you find yourself in that area and fancy lazing on a beach for a few hours, KILYOS, SILE, INEBOLU and CAMLIK near Unye are names worth bearing in mind.

The Sightseer

Turkey is undoubtedly a sightseer's paradise. The entire country is steeped in history, mythology and tangible reminders of past civilizations. You don't have to look far for Turkey's magnificent sights – you cannot avoid them. The domes and minarets of countless mosques; the ancient castles and fortresses of past rulers, and numerous archaeological sites all add to the country's intrinsic beauty. Fortunately for the holidaymaker, many of Turkey's best sights are located fairly close to the coast, so whichever resort you choose you won't have far to travel for a sightseeing trip.

Many tour operators now offer two-centre holidays which allow you to combine a week's sightseeing in Istanbul with a week at one of the coastal resorts. If you book a holiday in any of the main beach resorts you will find plenty of reasonably priced excursions to the sightseeing centres in your region.

We have identified a few places which are worth visiting if you are particularly interested in sightseeing, but we can only scratch the surface here. A more detailed account of Turkey's great sights is given in the geographical breakdown of the regions.

ISTANBUL features in the itinerary of most serious sightseers visiting Turkey. Even from a distance, the fascinating skyline and ancient city walls make Istanbul a sight to behold. A boat trip along the Bosphorus and the Golden Horn will give you an overall impression of the city and whet your appetite for some real exploration. If you wish to see all the sights, a minimum of three days is recommended. Places of interest include: **Topkapi Palace**, the residence of the Sultan rulers for three centuries; **Aya Sofia**, one of the most beautiful churches in the Christian world; the **Blue Mosque**, the mosque of Sultan Ahmet; the **Grand Bazaar**, the world's largest covered market; the **Archeological Museum**; **Rustem pasha Mosque**; and the **Mosque of Suleiman the Magnificent**. Istanbul has many museums, including the **Mosaic Museum** and the **Museum of Turkish and Islamic Art**, which are well worth a visit.

If you are based in Istanbul and you are prepared to travel a little, other places worth visiting are TROY, with its famous Trojan Horse; CANAKKALE, with its fifteenth-century fortress; and IZNIK and IZMIT, both well known for their historic monuments from the Seljuk and Ottoman empires.

ANKARA, Turkey's capital, is a modern, orderly city which lacks some of the colour and historical charm of Istanbul. While it does not compare with cities like Rome or Paris as a sightseeing centre, it has an abundance of mosques, museums, mausoleums and monuments (most of which honour the beloved Mustafa Kemal Ataturk), and interspersed with its new Western appearance is plenty of evidence of the city's long history. Outside Ankara, central Anatolia's best sightseeing region is CAPPADOCIA which is rich in natural and historic sites and is becoming a popular base for tourists. The places to look out for are KAYSERI, the region's principal town, GOREME, NEVSEHIR, URGUP, BOGAZKALE and GORDION, to name only a few. In the heart of the Anatolian plateau, south of Ankara and also accessible from Antalya, is KONYA, famous for its magnificent Seljuk architecture and home of the Whirling Dervishes, a mystic sect of the Muslim religion.

IZMIR on the Aegean coast is an ideal base for the tourist interested in sightseeing. The city is dominated by the Velvet Castle high on Mount Pagos. From Izmir you will find regular excursions to the historic towns of PERGAMON and EPHESUS, and you are within easy travelling distance of CESME to the west, and PAMUKKALE and APHRODISIAS to the east.

ANTALYA, the major resort of the Mediterranean coast, also offers plenty of possibilities for sightseeing. You will have no difficulty travelling to the ancient LYCIAN PENINSULA or the historic sites of SIDE, PERGE and ASPENDOS. Many of the Mediterranean resorts, including ALANYA, MERSIN and SILIFKE, are historic sites in their own right or very close to sightseeing centres. A trip to the DAMLATAS CAVE near Alanya is a worthwhile excursion.

Eastern Anatolia and the Black Sea coast offer some of Turkey's best natural and historic treasures, but sightseeing in these regions is for the adventurous explorer rather than the tourist who likes to spend a few hours sightseeing and the rest of the day recuperating on the beach. To see these regions at their best you must be prepared to cover a fair bit of ground, and you cannot expect the comforts of the main resorts. Eastern Turkey's most famous site is probably **Nemrut Dagi**, with its colossal toppled statues of the gods. Excursions to Nemrut Dagi are sometimes available from Ankara and some of the Mediterranean resorts. Other places of historical interest are ERZURUM, the capital of eastern Anatolia, KARS, DOGUBAYAZIT, VAN and URFA.

On the Black Sea coast the **Monastery of Sumela**, near TRABZON, is one of the main attractions for sightseers. Other places of interest are KASTAMONU, GIRESUN, SAMSUN and GUMUSHANE.

The Socialite

If you are a serious socialite whose idea of a good holiday involves mixing with the world's beautiful and fashionable people, Turkey is increasingly becoming the place to go. Admittedly you won't find as many beautiful people as you would in the more exclusive resorts of the Côte d'Azur, but cruising off the Aegean coast or renting a villa in a place such as Bodrum is decidedly 'in' at the moment. Or if you want a really classy holiday in Turkey, charter a luxury yacht and sail along the coastline, stopping off at the more sophisticated resorts en route.

As this type of holiday requires a little more money than the average holidaymaker can afford, we recommend the main beach resorts as the best places to 'see and be seen'. All these resorts offer plenty of opportunities for socializing and meeting people – the beach, the pool-side, the hotel bar, the disco and the street cafés being the obvious ones. Some of the resorts in Turkey now have holiday villages which give you restaurants, discos and nightclubs all in the one area. You might be a little disappointed if you are a dedicated disco goer, as most of the clubs and discos are geared towards the young tourist who wants a quick bop, a few drinks and the opportunity to chat up the talent they met earlier on the beach. It won't cost you much for a good night out, but don't expect West End-style establishments.

MARMARIS on the Aegean coast is a bustling little resort which has become one of the 'in' places for the young, trendy set visiting Turkey. **BODRUM** and **KUSADASI** on the Aegean, and **ANTALYA**, **ALANYA** and **SIDE** on the Mediterranean, are all lively resorts which seem to attract a young and fun-loving crowd. See our 'Sun-worshipper' section for more details about the main beach resorts.

ISTANBUL and **ANKARA** are the places to go for nightlife if you prefer traditional shows, upmarket restaurants, cinemas, theatre, classical concerts and opera. Most of the nightclubs in the cities are cabaret-orientated rather than disco-orientated. For a reasonable all-in price you can see a show (which usually includes traditional belly-dancing) and enjoy a Turkish meal. The cities' larger hotels usually offer their own entertainment, but it can cost you more than a visit to a club. Istanbul and Ankara also have open-air nightclubs, known as Gazinos, which are popular meeting places for young people in the summer. Here you will find popular Turkish singers rather than belly-dancers.

Turkey has a very busy festival calendar, and if folklore, art and culture are high on your list of holiday priorities you might like to plan your trip around one of the main festivals. Some of the festivals to look out for are:

Camel Wrestling Festival	SELÇUK	January
Traditional 'Mesir' Fete	MANISA	March–April
Ephesus International Arts and Culture Festival	SELÇUK	April–May
Tulip Festival	ISTANBUL	April–May
Art and Culture Festival	SULTANHISAR	May
The Aksu Fete	GIRESUN	May
International Bergama Fete	BERGAMA	May–June
Traditional Kirkpinar Wrestling	EDIRNE	June–July
Music, Folklore and Watersports Festival	FOČA	June
Tea Festival	RIZE	June
Kafkasor Bullfighting Contest	ARTVIN	June
Javelin Contest	ERZURUM	June–August
Carpet and Rose Festival	ISPARTA	June
Cherry Festival	TEKIRDAĞ	June
Şarköy Wine Festival	TEKIRDAĞ	June
Art and Tourism Festival	MARMARIS	June
Samsun Industrial Fair	SAMSUN	July
Apricot Festival	MALATYA	July
Bursa Fair	BURSA	July
Ceramics Festival	KÜTAHYA	July
Kadirga Festival	TRABZON	July
Pop Music Festival	KUŞADASI	July
International Folk Dance Festival	SAMSUN	July

International Istanbul Arts and Culture Festival	**ISTANBUL**	July
Çeşme Sea Festival	**ÇEŞME**	July
Nasreddin Hoca Festival	**AKŞEHIR**	July
Arts and Culture Festival	**BURSA**	July
Handcraft Festival	**AVANOS**	August
Architectural Festival	**SAFRANBOLU**	August
Hacibektaş Commemoration Festival	**HACIBEKTAŞ**	August
Mengen Chef Festival	**BOLU**	August
Troy Festival	**ÇANAKKALE**	August
Izmir International Fair	**IZMIR**	August–Sept
Yağcibedir Carpet Festival	**BALIKESIR**	September
Grape Harvest Festival	**ÜRGÜP**	September
Grape Harvest Festival	**ALAŞEHIR**	September
Traditional Cuisine Contest	**KONYA**	September
Golden Hazelnut Award	**ORDU**	September
International Textile and Fashion Fair	**MERSIN**	Sept–Oct
Hittite Festival	**ÇORUM**	September
The Golden Orange Film and Arts Festival	**ANTALYA**	September
Demre Noel Baba Festival	**DEMRE**	October
Mevlana Commemoration Festival (ritual dances of the Whirling Dervishes)	**KONYA**	December

When you arrive at your resort the information desk at your hotel or the local tourist information office will give you full details of all the entertainment and festivals in the vicinity.

Healthy Holidays

THE GREAT OUTDOORS

With its vast regions of forested mountains, fertile valleys and areas of unspoilt beauty, Turkey is an ideal destination for the nature-lover or the great-outdoors type who likes to discover as much as possible about a country by foot. Turkey's potential for this type of holiday has only recently been recognized, and many tour operators now offer specialist package holidays for a range of outdoor pursuits including trekking, camping, birdwatching, botany and nature trails. You will find more details about this kind of holiday in the section 'Who Specializes in What'. In the meantime, here are some areas which will be of interest to the great-outdoors type.

LYCIA – This is the old name for the hill country in the extreme south-west of Turkey. It is a particularly beautiful area in which to discover the country's flora and fauna. Here nature-lovers can venture inland to the **XANTHOS VALLEY**, the heartland of ancient Lycia which has been accessible by road for only the past ten years, or pursue their interest in some of the pretty coastal resorts, such as **FETHIYE**, where the Taurus Mountains plunge down to the shore.

CAPPADOCIA – Situated in the heart of central Anatolia, this is a fascinating area for the tourist who enjoys wildlife, walking and exploring. Cappadocia is famous for its incredible carved cities beneath the earth's surface, where an ancient troglodyte civilization built homes and churches in the caves.

For the birdwatcher **ISTANBUL**, **BURSA**, **LAKE MANYAS**, **BANDIRMA**, **KULU GOLU** and the **ALADAGLAR MOUNTAINS** all offer the enthusiast the opportunity to study birds and, in some cases, migrations.

There are several national parks which are noted for their forests, rivers, springs, flora, fauna, birds and geological sites, and provide ideal bases for the tourist interested in walking, fishing, birdwatching, picnicking and camping. Some of the parks to bear in mind are ULUDAG near Bursa, KUSCENNETI (Bird Paradise) near Balikesir, SIPIL DAGI near Manisa, DUZLER CAMI near Antalya, MUNZUR VADISI near Tunceli, SOGUKSU near Ankara, YEDIGOLLER (Seven Lakes) near Zonguldak and ILGAZ DAGI near Kastamonu.

THE SPORTS ENTHUSIAST

Most hotels in the Aegean and Mediterranean resorts now offer their guests a wide range of sports facilities either free or for a minimal charge. The sports on offer include tennis, table tennis, volleyball, windsurfing, waterskiing, rowing, mini-golf, mini-football, riding and, of course, swimming.

Turkey is a popular destination for *watersports* enthusiasts, and a number of tour operators now specialize in these holidays. Ask your travel agent, or see our section 'Who Specializes in What', for further details. The clear, warm waters of the Aegean and Mediterranean seas are ideal for windsurfing and waterskiing, and facilities are available at all the main resorts, including BODRUM, MARMARIS, CESME, KUSADASI, ANTALYA, ALANYA and SIDE.

Yachting and *flotilla sailing* are also becoming increasingly popular and there are now around twenty British holiday companies offering sailing holidays or yacht charters in Turkey. Most of the sailing in Turkish waters is concentrated along the Aegean coast between KUSADASI and FETHIYE, where there are plenty of coves, inlets, sandy bays and safe mooring places.

Eastern Turkey offers plenty of possibilities for *mountaineering*, both for the amateur and the expert. Climbs recommended for amateurs are at HASANDAGI (3250m) south of Nigde, the MUNZUR MOUNTAINS (3300m–3500m) near Erzincan, and the KACKAR MOUNTAINS (4000m) which run parallel to the Black Sea between Rize and Hopa. The more experienced mountaineer can venture to SUPHAN DAG (4434m) starting from Adilcevaz near Bitlis, the CILO-SAT MOUN-

TAINS (2700–4100m) near Hakkari, and MOUNT AGRI (5165m), the highest mountain in Anatolia. Foreign tourists wishing to climb Mount Agri or the Cilo-Sat ranges require permission from the Turkish Mountaineering Club. For more information about mountaineering and permits contact the Turkish Tourism and Information Office, First Floor, 170/173 Piccadilly, London W1V 9DD (telephone 01-734 8681).

The *hunting* of wild boar is popular in Turkey, but foreigners can only hunt in parties organized by Turkish travel agents who have authorization from the Ministry of Agriculture, Forestry and Rural Affairs. The best areas for hunting are around MARMARIS and TARSUS. *Fishing* by tourists is also permitted, providing it is for sport and only amateur equipment is used. Foreigners caught fishing for commercial purposes face heavy penalties. The rivers and lakes of central Anatolia offer catches of pike, carp and trout, and for sea fishermen the main catches are grouper and tunny. Further information on the regulations and restrictions on hunting and fishing can be obtained through the Turkish Tourism and Information Office in London.

Turkey offers some fairly good facilities for *skiing*, the main centres being at ULUDAG south of Bursa, and SAKLIKENT south of Antalya. If you visit Saklikent in early spring it is possible to combine a skiing holiday with a beach holiday on the Mediterranean coast. See our section 'Winter Turkey' for more details about skiing.

The tourist keen on *walking* might like to discover Turkey's beauty by foot. A number of tour operators now offer holidays which are specially designed for the walking enthusiast. For further information consult your travel agent or see our section 'Who Specializes in What'.

If you prefer to spectate rather than participate, the Turkish national sport of *wrestling* might be of interest to you. Wrestling championships are held in KIRKPINAR near Edirne every July. It will certainly be different from any wrestling you have seen in the past, as the Turks cover themselves in oil to make it more fun. The other traditional sports are *camel wrestling*, which can be seen in many villages along the Aegean coast, and *Cirit Oyunu*, a game of dare-devil horsemanship which is played in eastern Turkey. The Turks are also great fans of *soccer* and *horse racing*, and you will find a football stadium and/or a race course in most of the cities.

SPA HOLIDAYS

Turkey has a surprising number of thermal spas. For many centuries the Turks have enjoyed warm mineral springs for their therapeutic and healing powers, but only recently have they been discovered by the foreign tourist. Due to the increase in tourists wishing to 'take the waters', the main thermal centres have now been developed to cater for large numbers of visitors. The major thermal resorts are:

BURSA – This city has been recognized as a thermal centre since the early centuries of Christianity when thermal baths were developed on a large scale at CEKIRGE, a suburb to the west of Bursa. As well as the public bathing facilities at Cekirge, many of the hotels offer their guests private facilities, allowing you to soak up the benefits of the mineral waters in the comfort of your own bathroom. The waters are said to help rheumatic and metabolic problems.

PAMUKKALE – This town, built on a plateau, is probably the most famous thermal resort as it can boast one of Turkey's most fascinating and beautiful natural sites. Thermal spring water, laden with calcareous minerals, has cascaded over the plateau's edge for centuries and has formed shallow basins overflowing with clear blue water and dazzling white stalactites. On the plateau itself you will find the contrast of the modern thermal centre, with its hotels and bathing facilities, and the ruins of the ancient city of HIERAPOLIS. One of the monuments on this site is the old thermal bath house, dating back to Roman times, which is now a museum. The waters at Pamukkale are suitable for drinking and bathing and are said to help heart and circulatory complaints.

YALOVA – This town is well equipped to cater for tourists as it is one of the main resorts on the Marmara coast. It is a popular destination for the holidaymaker seeking fine sandy beaches and warm thermal springs. The waters of Yalova are claimed to benefit those who suffer from rheumatic, urinary and nervous complaints.

CESME – For many years Turks have flocked to this small port to take advantage of its thermal springs. Modern hotels and attractive tourist facilities have now been developed so holidaymakers can enjoy them too. The nearby village of ILICA is a favourite with tourists as it has the double attraction of thermal baths and vast beaches. The waters of Cesme are said to cure a wide range of ailments including dermatological, gynaecological and urinary complaints.

DAMLATAS CAVE near Alanya will also be of interest to the health enthusiast. Inside the cave the level of humidity is exceptionally high, and is claimed to be of great benefit to sufferers of asthma and other respiratory problems. The cave is worth a visit even if you are not looking for a health cure, as it is said to be around fifteen thousand years old and has beautiful multi-coloured stalagmites and stalactites. There is a similar cave at NARLIKUYU near Silifke.

The Recluse

If you like to leave behind the crowds and the hustle and bustle of everyday life, Turkey offers several possibilities. Away from the coastal resorts and the main towns and cities, Turkey is a land of rolling plains and plateaux, forested mountains and lush valleys. You will have no difficulty finding areas which are unexplored and unexploited. If you're prepared to spend a little time looking, you can even find secluded coves and bays along the Aegean and Mediterranean coastline where you can enjoy a quiet beach holiday away from the masses.

One of the best and most relaxing ways to get away from it all in Turkey is to charter a yacht and sail along the Aegean and Mediterranean coastline. The only time you will have to leave the solitude and tranquillity of your boat is to stock up with provisions, or to stop off at a deserted beach along the way. The beautiful stretch of coastline between KUSADASI on the Aegean and ANTALYA on the Mediterranean is perfect for this type of holiday. Places to look out for along the way are YAVANSU, GUZELCAMLI, GUMBET, GUNNUCEK, OLU DENIZ, LARA BEACH and FINIKE. These are just a handful of the tiny resorts which offer quiet, unspoilt beaches which are ideal for sunbathing and swimming.

There is now a wide range of walking and camping holidays on offer which are a good choice for the more adventurous recluse. Destinations include ancient **LYCIA** in the extreme south-west of the country, **CAPPADOCIA** in central Anatolia, **VAN** and **ERZURUM** in eastern Anatolia and **TRABZON** on the Black Sea coast. You won't escape people and civilization altogether, but you will avoid the crowded hotels, the discos, the clubs and the hordes of sun-lovers.

If you want a complete break from the twentieth century, independent travel to eastern Turkey is the answer. Independent travel in Turkey is reasonably cheap, but you may find bus and train services slow and accommodation spartan, especially in eastern Anatolia. If it's a complete break you're after, this should not bother you. **HAKKARI**, **BITLIS**, **DOGUBAYAZIT**, **MUS** and **DIYARBAKIR** are some of the small towns in eastern Turkey which offer basic accommodation and provide easy access to the country's most remote regions, where you can easily find you are the only tourist for miles.

The independent traveller who wants to avoid package tourists at all costs should scan the brochures before leaving, take a note of the major resorts and holiday destinations and then steer well clear of them. For further information on independent travel in Turkey see our section 'Package v. Independent' and refer to the geographical account of the area you are interested in.

If sailing, walking, camping and independent travel all sound too much like hard work, simply choose one of the smaller resorts and book your holiday off-season.

The Family Holiday

If you are planning a family holiday you will probably be looking for a pleasant coastal resort with safe sandy beaches and plenty of things to keep your children amused – preferably without you dipping into your purse every five minutes. If these are your main criteria, most of the larger resorts on the Aegean and Mediterranean coasts will be suitable. Entertainment, eating places and tourist facilities tend to be geared towards the family holiday and the family budget. Many of the hotels offer a wide range of sports and leisure facilities for little or no cost, and there is plenty to do in the evenings for both children and parents.

MARMARIS on the Aegean and **SIDE** on the Mediterranean are particularly noted as good family resorts, as both have extensive sandy beaches, ideal for children, and clear, calm waters for safe swimming. Other resorts to consider for a family holiday include **KUSADASI**, **BODRUM**, **CESME** and **ALANYA**.

It is a good idea to ask your travel agent's advice before booking a family holiday, particularly if you have young children. Some of the larger tour operators now cater specially for the family holiday and offer facilities such as a babysitting service or reductions for very young children. Before booking your hotel and paying your deposit check the facilities – does it have a swimming pool suitable for young children or a children's play area, etc?

Unless you particularly want to take your family for a get-away-from-it-all type holiday in Turkey, most of the inland regions are unsuitable for young children. The majority of holidays in central and eastern Anatolia are geared towards walking and sightseeing, and temperatures can be extreme during the summer months.

Practicalities

Red Tape

British citizens who hold a full passport or a British visitor's passport may enter Turkey and stay for up to three months without a visa. If you wish to stay for longer, you can apply to the local Police Authority for an extension for up to three more months.

Embassy and Consulate Addresses

Visas can be obtained from the Turkish Consulate General, Rutland Lodge, Rutland Gardens, London SW7 (telephone 01-589 0360). If you run into trouble while on holiday and you wish to contact the British Embassy or the British Consulate, the addresses are: British Embassy, Sehit Ersan Caddesi 46/A, Cankaya, Ankara (tel: 12 74 310); and British Consulate, Mesrutiyet Caddesi 34, Tepebasi, Istanbul (tel: 14 47 540). There is another British Consulate at Necatibey Bulvari 19/4, Izmir (tel: 14 54 709).

Health Formalities

British citizens do not require a health certificate or vaccination certificates to enter Turkey, but it is a good idea to ask your doctor which, if any, vaccination you should have for your own protection. For further information see our 'Health' section.

Customs

In the main, Turkish customs present no problems for the foreign tourist, but there are certain rules which must be observed if you want to avoid trouble. The import of marijuana or any other narcotic is strictly forbidden and subject to heavy punishment. The export of antiques is also forbidden and violation of this regulation could land you in big trouble. The Turkish authorities take a dim view of currency violations, and might ask you to produce exchange slips and receipts on leaving the country to prove that you have purchased your souvenirs with legally exchanged currency.

When You Arrive – Foreign tourists entering Turkey are normally the subject of spot-checks, but nine times out of ten you will not even be asked to open your baggage. Personal effects, clothing, personal sporting equipment, medical items and one camera with up to ten rolls of film may be taken into the country duty free. If you like to stock up with goodies before your holiday, you may also import 400 cigarettes, 50 cigars, 200g tobacco, 1kg coffee, 1.5kg instant coffee (handy to know if you don't like the Turkish variety), 1kg tea and 5 litres of spirits. Weapons and sharp instruments (including camping knives) cannot be taken into the country without special permission, and antiques or valuable items should be registered on your passport to avoid any trouble when leaving the country.

When You Leave – You are more likely to have your bags checked and questions asked when you leave the country. If you remembered to register your valuables on entry and have exchange slips to cover the cost of your purchases, you have nothing to worry about. You are allowed to export souvenirs up to the value of 30,000TL, though this depends on the rate of inflation.

Money

The monetary unit of Turkey is the Turkish lira (TL). Turkish lira are available in the following denominations:

Notes – 500, 1000, 5000 and 10,000
Coins – 10, 50, 100 and 200.

Inflation in Turkey has come down, but is still very high – it now stands at around 30 per cent, compared to an incredible 130 per cent in the late 1970s – and this means a favourable rate of exchange for European currencies and the US dollar. Always keep the exchange slips you are given when changing foreign currency for Turkish lira, as you will be required to produce them if you wish to reconvert at the end of your holiday.

There is no limit on the amount of sterling or other foreign currency you can take to Turkey, but it is illegal to export more than the equivalent of $1000 worth of Turkish lira and $3000 worth of foreign currency.

HOW TO TAKE YOUR MONEY

You will receive a far better rate of exchange once you arrive in Turkey than you will at a British bank. It makes sense, therefore, to purchase only a little Turkish lira before you go. Calculate how much Turkish lira you need before you can get to a bank in Turkey, taking care not to underestimate and bearing in mind that the banks are closed at weekends. The bank just beyond customs at Istanbul airport is fast and efficient. The bank at Izmir airport opens at 04.30.

Travellers' cheques in sterling or other foreign currencies can be cashed at all Turkish banks. Some of the larger shops and restaurants also accept travellers' cheques, but it is essential to ask first and spend later. It is advisable to take travellers' cheques issued by a well-known bank to avoid any problems, and always have your passport with you for identification, when wishing to cash cheques. If you are concerned about getting the best possible rate of exchange for your cheques, the banks are always your best bet.

Credit cards are becoming more widely accepted in Turkey's larger resorts, but they might still be refused in the more remote areas. Even in the main resorts some establishments will not accept credit cards. Most large hotels and shops and restaurants will accept a range of cards, including Visa, American Express, Access, Eurocard and Diners Club, but don't take it for granted. Some smaller shops may try to charge commission of between 5 and 7 per cent but do not pay it. If you have no alternative, keep the receipt and contact your credit card company on your return to the UK.

Personal cheques for up to £50 can be cashed at Turkish banks if you have Eurocheques and a British Eurocheque encashment card. The Eurocheque scheme, however, is *not* one of the cheapest as the money is converted back to sterling at the low rate offered by your British bank. If you don't have a Eurocheque card and would like one, apply to your bank at least two weeks before leaving.

WHERE TO CHANGE MONEY

Traveller's cheques, foreign currency and personal cheques can be changed at the official rate of exchange at all banks. There are also currency exchange desks at the main airports and stations, and some shops, restaurants, hotels and travel agencies have a licence to exchange currency. Outside the banks, the rate of exchange might be marginally lower. If you are tempted to go for a higher rate of exchange on the black market, remember, it is illegal to exchange money in Turkey without a licence, and the authorities take a dim view of currency violations.

To Summarize:

Before leaving home, buy a little Turkish lira to see you through until you can get to a bank in Turkey. To safeguard your holiday money, but not make any great savings, take Eurocheques and a Eurocheque encashment card or traveller's cheques – preferably issued by a well-known bank. Turkey has a relatively low crime rate, but there is no point in taking chances, particularly as most banks now offer an instant refund for traveller's cheques which are lost or stolen. If you have a widely known credit card, take it for back-up. This way you can combine security with flexibility and convenience. Always remember to retain exchange slips.

Banking

Banks in Turkey are open from 9 a.m. to 1 p.m. and from 2 p.m. to 7 p.m. from Monday to Friday. On Saturdays and Sundays and official holidays they are closed all day. Bear this in mind and think ahead when planning your visits to the bank. Some banks will take up to fifteen minutes to exchange currency.

Insurance

It is definitely a false economy to cut back on holiday insurance, but many people do, and later regret it. Quite often these days, when you book a package holiday you find insurance has been included and the premium added to your final bill, whether you asked for it or not. Most tour operators arrange special holiday insurance schemes which offer you basic cover for baggage, accidents, medical treatment and cancellation, for a premium of about £15. While this saves you the trouble of finding a policy, it also means a healthy insurance commission for the person who arranged it. Remember, you are under no obligation to accept the policy offered by the tour operator or the travel agent. In some cases these policies are not as detailed as policies bought from a large reputable company, and there can be a delay in the settlement of claims at the peak of the holiday season. On the other hand, if you do have to make a claim while on holiday, there is often a representative at the resort who will handle the formalities and take some of the strain off you.

If you are not happy with the inclusive package insurance, you should go to an insurance broker and tell him where you are going, what you are taking, what you envisage doing and how long you will be away. He should be able to find a policy tailor-made for your needs – even if it does cost a little more than the policy offered by the tour operator. It is particularly advisable to find a more comprehensive policy if you are planning to participate in any high-risk sports, such as skiing. If it is imperative that you arrive home on the day stipulated you should also make sure you are covered for flight delays.

For the majority of people a basic £15-package insurance is sufficient, but most tour operators will not insure you if you suffer from a serious illness or disability, or if you have a history of bad health. You must remember that the onus is on you to tell the travel agent or insurance broker if you are not an average holidaymaker – whether it be for health or any other reason.

Hospital treatment is available to holidaymakers in all the Turkish government-run hospitals, but there is always a small charge for treatment. It is, therefore, essential to have some form of medical insurance in case you have an accident or serious illness while on holiday. Europ Assistance Limited of 252 High Street, Croydon, Surrey CR0 11NF, offer the cheapest and one of the best medical insurance policies Britons can buy. For a premium of about £15 per person, you are given access to a 24-hour telephone advice link in the UK, and a guarantee of on-the-spot cash for any service you require in an emergency, when you might have no ready cash. It also covers you for medical expenses which may arise from a car accident.

Independent travellers are strongly advised to take out good insurance cover before leaving. Unlike the tourist on a package holiday, who is at least guaranteed accommodation and transport home, you could find yourself out on a limb if your money and tickets were lost or stolen. Take every precaution to safeguard your trip before you go. Lloyds of London are particularly good for holiday insurance.

Health

Turkey poses no major health threats to the average holidaymaker, providing you are prepared to take a few necessary precautions and keep your eyes open.

The DHSS recommends Britons travelling to Turkey to vaccinate themselves against cholera, typhoid, tetanus and polio – but none of these are essential. If you do wish to be vaccinated you should always check with your doctor beforehand in case there is any reason against it. It is advisable to consult your doctor at least six weeks before departure to allow plenty of time for immunization. As malaria is still prevalent in some parts of Turkey, you should also ask your doctor about anti-malarial pills. These are taken before, during and after your holiday to prevent any risk of infection from mosquito bites.

In general, standards of hygiene and sanitation are very good in Turkey, but there are always exceptions – particularly in the remoter regions of central and eastern Anatolia. The best precaution is to keep your eyes open and avoid eating or drinking in places which you consider to be at all suspect. In many restaurants, especially the smaller ones, you will be invited into the kitchen to see what's cooking, which gives you an ideal opportunity to see what is going on behind the scenes.

Tap water is safe throughout Turkey, but most visitors prefer to drink mineral water. Apart from being cheap and abundant, the mineral waters taste far nicer than the tap water, which is heavily chlorinated; it is advisable to drink lots of water. You should also bear in mind that the Turkish diet is quite different from the British diet, and this could result in 'holiday tummy' while your system adapts to the change. If you have a delicate constitution, your local chemist should be able to advise you on what to take in the way of diarrhoea tablets, etc. If you have to visit a chemist during your holiday you will find that Turkish chemists stock most of the things you need for minor problems.

Hospital treatment is available to holidaymakers in all Turkish government-run hospitals, but there is always a small charge. Standards of care in these hospitals are generally good but may fall a little short of what you are used to at home. In the larger towns and cities there are private hospitals, clinics and dental surgeries, but these are quite expensive, so it is essential to take out some form of medical insurance. For further details see p. 42.

Pre-planning and Free Info

You can get a lot more out of your holiday in Turkey if you know a little about the country before you go. Make maximum use of your time by identifying which places you would like to see, and plan your holiday accordingly. A little time gathering information before you go can save you a lot of time and energy when you arrive. Once you get there you will have far better things to do than stand in queues at tourist information offices.

Most countries have a tourist office in London, and Turkey is no exception. It is well worth your while writing to the office before your holiday and asking them to send you general tourist literature. If you would like to pursue a particular hobby while on holiday (e.g. archaeology, skiing or watersports), ask them for any specific information they may have on it. If you are planning to tour or travel independently you could also request maps – which are not easy to come by in Britain – and accommodation listings. The Turkish Ministry of Culture and Tourism produces masses of leaflets covering many different areas, so if you know what region or regions you will be visiting it is a good idea to tell them. If you are interested in authentic Turkish culture – rather than the entertainment laid on for the tourists – you should ask for the Turkey Festival Days Calendar which is a country-wide guide to all the traditional folklore, music, craft and arts festivals. The address to write to is: The Turkish Tourism and Information Office, First Floor, 170/173 Piccadilly, London W1V 9DD (telephone 01-734 8681).

The service is free and the staff is always happy to oblige, but try to write well in advance of your holiday if possible, to ensure you receive the information on time. All the leaflets and booklets produced by the

Ministry are helpful and informative, but they are trying to sell Turkey so don't expect them to be as objective as some of the travel guides.

Another source of free info is your local library. Admittedly, this could lead to some heavy reading, but if you have any specific interest such as the country's history or wildlife, you could find the search rewarding.

An extremely useful source of information (free and impartial) comes from the travel agent Hogg Robinson. Their 'Resort Reports' go into great detail on what to expect at the resorts, and give an unbiased report on all the hotels used by tour operators. These files can be consulted free of charge in any of their agencies.

There are a few other guide books on the market which are worth considering. Collins's *Companion Guide to Turkey* by John Freely gives a very detailed, fairly dry account of the country which is aimed at the serious-minded independent traveller who's intent on touring the country in depth. *Fodor's Turkey* (Hodder and Stoughton) is the typical middle-class, middle-aged American guide, it is comprehensive, informative and well-researched. For most young(ish) Britons it concentrates too much on history, archaeology and expensive recommendations. *Turkey – A Travel Survival Kit* (Lonely Planet Publications) is another well-researched, informative guide written with the independent traveller in mind. *Let's Go – Greece and the Turkish Coast* (Harvard Student Agencies) gives a lot of useful information on travelling in Turkey, but is aimed more at the American back-packing brigade than package tourists.

And you are, of course, reading the best guide on the market!

Budgeting

For the foreign tourist, the cost of living in Turkey is very cheap compared with many European holiday destinations – and that's one of the reasons it's becoming so popular. Prices for food, drink, entertainment and internal transport all seem incredibly cheap by Northern European standards, mainly due to the strength of hard currencies like the pound and dollar against the Turkish lira. Unless you're really trying to operate on a shoestring budget, there's certainly no need to mar your holiday by constantly counting the pennies.

Obviously, the amount of spending money you need to take will depend largely upon what basis, if any, you book your accommodation. These days most package holidays offer accommodation on a half-board basis, which means you'll have to pay for at least one meal a day. If you've booked a self-catering holiday you'll obviously need more for food, but considering you can eat really well for around £5, this shouldn't affect the overall cost of your holiday in any big way.

The independent traveller can exist on a very low budget or a reasonably low budget, depending on the standard of accommodation required. If you're hoping to compete with package tour prices you'll probably have to accept lower standards of comfort and cleanliness, as package prices are very difficult to beat if you want decent accommodation for fourteen nights. But you'll find no shortage of cheap hotels and pensions, and again, eating will put no great strain on your finances.

Whether you're a package tourist or an independent traveller, you'll be able to get around the country fairly cheaply by bus, train or *dolmus* (shared taxi). Unless money is no object, don't plan to hire a car as this will really knock your budget for six. A week's car hire in Turkey costs between £200 and £250. The prearranged excursions laid on by the tour operators are more expensive than independent bus travel, but they provide a comfortable and trouble-free way of seeing the country and they are generally good value. For more details on internal travel see 'Moving Around the Country' on p.124.

If you consider that a sandwich will cost the equivalent of about 50p, a coffee or fruit juice 35p and a full-scale meal with wine £5, you can calculate how much you are likely to spend on eating. Drinking is also very cheap, providing you are prepared to drink the local brews and don't insist on your favourite British tipple. (The local wine is perfectly acceptable so this should be no hardship.) Turkish spirits and beers cost about 70p and a bottle of wine costs about £1. You will pay at least twice as much for imported brands as for local brands.

Entertainment and leisure will not break the bank unless you insist on visiting the 'trendy' nightclubs in the major cities, where you will pay well over the odds for a fabricated Westernized disco. Discos in the holiday resorts are very reasonably priced and folk entertainment is cheap and plentiful, particularly if you visit a town where a festival is underway. Admission charges for museums and official sites vary, but are generally low, and you'll find the cost of watersports refreshingly low compared with other Mediterranean destinations.

Students qualify for various discounts on travel, museum entrance, etc. Holders of an International Student Identity Card are entitled to a 10 per cent reduction on Turkish Airlines domestic flights (and an incredible 60 per cent off international flights); 50 per cent reductions on admission to museums and sites; between 15 and 50 per cent reductions on services by Turkish Maritime Lines; and up to 50 per cent reductions on entrance to cinemas and concerts. If you would like more information on student discounts before you go, write to: The Turkish National Youth Organization, Tunel, Istiklal Caddesi 471/2, Istanbul.

There are certain items you can take from home which will save you unnecessary expense when you arrive. If you prefer instant coffee to strong, sweet Turkish coffee pop a small jar into your suitcase, as you'll find it very expensive in Turkey. It's also wise to take any favourite brands of sun oil, toiletries, cigarettes, camera film and basic medical items. Once you arrive you'll have to put up with the local brands or pay a lot extra for imported brands.

The average holidaymaker on a two-week half-board package deal at one of the coastal resorts should get by easily on £250 to £300 spending money. When you're working out your budget, remember you're far better to end up with too much money than too little, so try to take a little more than you expect to spend. If possible, it's advisable to take an extra £100 as something to fall back on in case of an emergency. If you run out of money and have to transfer cash from home you'll encounter a lot of infuriating red tape and incur hefty bank charges.

Getting Yourself Organized

What to Take with You

Package holidaymakers visiting the coastal resorts in the summer can get away with the minimum of light, casual clothing and accessories, plus a shower-proof coat, just in case. In inland Turkey, where you'll be staying at higher altitudes, you'll need warm pullovers, because the temperature falls considerably at night. The atmosphere in the main towns and holiday resorts is particularly relaxed, so there's no need to take formal clothing or evening dress unless you're heading for one of the five-star international hotels in the cities.

If you're planning a winter break to Istanbul or one of the coastal resorts, you'll need slightly warmer clothing, but again, keep it informal. Winter temperatures are generally mild but it can become cool in the evenings. If you visit central or eastern Turkey during the winter months you'll definitely have to wrap up well.

The secret is to keep your luggage to a minimum; that way you'll be able to bring home more souvenirs and duty free goods. Think back to previous years when you returned from holiday with half your clothes unused.

If you're travelling independently you can also keep things to a minimum, unless you intend camping, in which case you'll need to take all your camping gear as the range in Turkey is not very impressive. Independent travellers heading for the remoter regions should pack a good First Aid kit and a comprehensive phrase book. The following items are definitely worth packing:

(1) Any photographic equipment you're likely to need, including film for your camera. Films sold in Turkey are expensive and of poor quality.

(2) Any English-language books or magazines you're likely to want for beach reading. Some of the resorts stock British or American books but they are usually overpriced.

(3) A small jar of instant coffee, unless you're particularly keen on the strong Turkish variety. The hotels are used to people coming down to breakfast clutching jars of Nescafé and asking for hot water.

(4) Toiletries and medicines, including suntan preparations. There are few countries which offer cheaper toiletries than Britain, and even if you do find some, the quality is likely to be suspect. Any prescribed medicines should definitely be brought from home as the equivalent drug may not be available abroad.

(5) Loo paper and soap. Once you're away from the better hotels and larger resorts you can't be sure that every bar and restaurant will be equipped, and there's really no substitute for them when you need them.

(6) A light headscarf is an essential item for any woman wishing to visit a mosque as it is generally insisted upon that women cover their heads, arms and shoulders before entering.

Part Two

HOW TO GO

Package v. Independent

If you are looking for a reasonably priced and carefree holiday in Turkey, a package holiday is your best option. In the past few years, British tour operators have begun to recognize Turkey's great potential as a holiday destination, and package holidaymakers can choose now from a wide range of holidays for every type and every budget. The holidays on offer range from two weeks in a busy resort such as Antalya to an away-from-it-all break in an unspoilt spot in the Aladaglar Mountains. Tour operators are increasingly offering destinations in inland regions such as Cappadocia, so you mustn't assume that a package holiday automatically means a Majorca-type experience. And there is no reason why a package holiday should confine you to one resort, as many operators now offer two-centre packages, sailing holidays and touring holidays in Turkey.

The all-inclusive cost of a package holiday is hard to beat for an independent traveller, unless you are a student (under twenty-two), in which case you qualify for an incredible 60 per cent discount on international flights by Turkish Airlines (THY) on producing an International Student Identity Card. Even then, independent travel in Turkey requires a good deal of pre-planning to ensure that all runs smoothly, and you'll have to be prepared for certain discomforts and hassles when travelling in the more remote regions. While accommodation is reasonably cheap outside the main resorts, it is often basic (at best), and good campsites and hostels are fairly thin on the ground.

There are, however, advantages to travelling independently in Turkey, as in any country, particularly if you enjoy the challenge of going it alone. You will be your own boss and not one of a crowd of tourists, and you will have a far better chance of sampling Turkish life as it really is. Turkey has a comprehensive public transport system and you should have no problems getting around quickly and cheaply (except in some parts of eastern Anatolia). Eating is also very cheap and you can eat well even on the lowest budget.

Package Holidays

Tour Operators in Britain Offering Packages to Turkey

There are now more than a hundred British tour operators who offer holidays in Turkey; some specialize in Turkey, while others offer only one or two Turkish destinations as part of their overall package programme.

The following table lists the names and telephone numbers of the British tour operators who run holidays in Turkey. Some of the firms are relatively obscure and their brochures will not be widely available, but if they offer the type of holiday you are after, don't hesitate to give them a ring and request a brochure. Those firms not discussed in any of the specific listings on the following pages can be assumed to be offering general holidays in Turkey. Every effort has been made to ensure that this list of operators is comprehensive and accurate, but please remember that we can only publish the details of the tour operators who have their brochures ready in time for our publishing deadline. In the fluctuating world of the travel business, tour companies spring up and go bust with amazing regularity, however the Turkish Tourist Office at 170/173 Piccadilly, London W1V 9DD (tel. 01-734 8681) will send you out a free copy of the updated comprehensive list on request.

General

A & J TOURS
146 Kingsland High Street, London E8 2NS
(Tel: 01-254 8128 Telex: 269259)
ABTA 88346

7 and 14 night or longer holidays in Istanbul, Izmir, Bodrum Peninsula, Ölüdeniz, Kas, and Side. Self-catering accommodation in Side only.

Fly-drive and Tailor-made holidays.
Flight-only and Accommodation-only facility.

ADVENTURE HOLIDAYS
10 Linden Park, Bangor, Co. Down, N. Ireland
(Tel: 0247 473783)

Holidays from Northern Ireland only.
Tailor-made holidays in the Bodrum area, specializing in yachting holidays.

Flight-only arrangements.

AEGEAN TURKISH HOLIDAYS
53A Salusbury Road, London NW6 6NJ
(Tel: 01-372 6902 Telex: 265260)
ABTA 71773 ATOL 997

7/14/21 nights in Istanbul, Kusadasi, Davutlar, Torba, Gündogdu, Akyarlar, Bodrum, Gökova, Marmaris, Turunc, Kalkan, Kas Beldibi, Antalya, Colaki, Side, Sorgun, Alanya. A large selection of self-catering villas offered with free car hire. Large selection of two-centre holidays.

Coach Tours: Trojan Horse Tour 7 nights.
Cappadocian Tour 7 nights.
Special Interest: Whirling Dervishes Tour 12 nights.
Gulet Cruising: 7 and 14 nights.
Fly-drive, Tailor-made, Flight-only available.

AEGINA CLUB
25A Hills Road, Cambridge CB2 1NW
(Tel: 0223 63256 Telex: 81684 AEGINA)
ATOL 0262

One or two-centre holidays of 1 and 2 week duration in Istanbul, Kusadasi, Davutlar, Torba, Bodrum, Kas, Kalkan, Antalya, Side, Alanya.

Fly-drive holidays of 1 to 3 weeks duration.
14 and 21 day Coach Tours of Western, Southern, Central and Eastern Turkey.
Tailor-made and Flight-only arrangements.
Coastal cruises.

ALLEGRO HOLIDAYS
15A Church Street, Reigate, Surrey RH2 0AA
(Tel: 0737 221323 Telex: 919114 ALEGRO G)
ABTA 12173 ATOL 1835

7 and 14 day holidays in Antalya, Alanya, Side.
Tailor-made and two-centre on request.

Fly-drive, Flight-only arrangements.

AQUARIUS TRAVEL
Western House, 9 Glandovey Terrace, Aberdovey, Gwynedd LL35 0EB
(Tel: 0654 72646 Telex: 35746 AQRSTL G)

7/14/21 nights at new studio apartments in beachfront villa, at Bitez, near Bodrum.

Fly-drive, Tailor-made and Accommodation-only.

AQUASPORT TOURS LTD
181 Edward Street, Brighton BN2 2JB
(Tel: 0273 685824/0273 685187)

7, 14, 21 and 28 day Fly-drive (motor caravans, estate cars with camping pack, motor boats with camping pack), camping, village rooms at: Antalya, Bodrum, Fethiye, Göcek, Izmir, Marmaris.
14, 21, 28 Watersports Holidays (diving, sailboarding, waterskiing) at Göcek.
1 to 3 week Gulet Cruising from Bodrum, Marmaris and Göcek.

BALKAN TOURS LTD
10 Lombard Street, Belfast BT1 1RB
(Tel: 0232 246795 or 325902 Telex: 747988)
ABTA 1510X ATOL 1171

May-October. 7/14 nights in Ayvalik, Cesme, Kusadasi. 7 day coach tour. Bulgaria-Turkey two-centre 14 days.

Fly-drive, Tailor-made, Flight-only, Accommodation-only.

BEACH VILLAS (HOLIDAYS) LTD
8 Market Passage, Cambridge CB2 3QR
(Tel: 0223 311113 Telex: 817428 BCHVLA)
ABTA 1415X ATOL 381B

2 week beachside villa and apartment holidays in Bodrum and Gümüslük.

Fly-drive holidays.

BEST YACHTING AND TOURISM
Kargi Marine, Hillier House, 509 Upper Richmond Road,
London SW14 7EE
(Tel: 01-873 3227 Telex: 9413819 HILHOU G)

Self-catering villas, apartments, traditional cottages and houses available for 7-28 days, on the Bodrum peninsula, the Gulfs of Fethiye and Finike and in a mountain village in the South, and in Ünye and Trabzon on the Black Sea. Also small pensions.

7-14 day sail/cruise/stay, 7-21 day two-centre combining Istanbul or Bursa with a resort or sailing holiday.

Fly-drive, Tailor-made and Accommodation booking service.

THE BLUE EYE TOUR COMPANY
3 Albion Hill, Loughton, Essex IG10 4RA
(Tel: 01-508 1930)

2 week or longer apartment holidays in Datca.

Special Interest: 1 week in Istanbul for retired people, throughout the year.

BLUESPOT TRAVEL LTD
28 Maddox Street, London W1R 9PF
(Tel: 01-408 0094/01-409 3034 Telex: 297547 BLUSPT G)
ATOL 2113

7 and 14 nights and flexible arrangements in Kusadasi, Bodrum, Marmaris, Turunc, Ölüdeniz, Kalkan, Kas, Kemer, Antalya, Side, Izmir, Cesme and Istanbul. (Two-centre and multi-centre holidays can be arranged). 14 day Eastern Turkey Coach Tour.

Fly-drive, Tailor-made, Flight-only, Accommodation-only arrangements.

BOSPHORUS HOLIDAYS
Silver House, 31-35 Beak Street, London W1R 3LD
(Tel: 01-437 7316 Telex: 296398 BOSPOR)

3 nights to 3 months or longer, in Istanbul, Izmir, Cesme, Kusadasi, Bodrum, Marmaris, Antalya, Side, Alanya and Mersin.

Special interest tours of 3 nights to 3 months can be arranged for individuals and groups.

Fly-drive, Tailor-made and Flight-only arrangements.

CARRINGTON CLASSICS
7 Elms Avenue, Eastbourne, Sussex
(Tel: 0323 647302)
ATOL 31827

14 nights holiday in Dalyon.
Coach tours to Marmaris and Fethiye one day at each.
River trips to Caunus and Köycegiz.

CELEBRITY HOLIDAYS AND TRAVEL
18 Frith Street, London W1V 5TS
(Tel: 01-439 1961/01-734 4386 Telex: 269304)
ABTA 18659 ATOL 1469

3,5,7 and 14 day holidays in Istanbul. 14 day holidays in Kusadasi, Bodrum, Marmaris, Ölüdeniz, Kalkan, Antalya, Side. Two-centre holidays.

Fly-drive, Tailor-made, Flight-only arrangements.

CLUB MEDITERRANEE
106/110 Brompton Road, London SW3 1JJ
(Tel: 01-226 1066/01-581 4769)
ABTA 19685 ATOL 1020

1 week or more at Club Med's Holiday Villages in Foca, Kusadasi, Kemer, Palmiye.
Prices include all sports facilities and tuition.

CLUB SPORTIF
(Part of Grosvenor Hall Leisure), Grosvenor Hall, Bolnore Road, Haywards Heath, Sussex RH16 4BX
(Tel: 0444 441300 Telex: 877156)
ABTA 54369 ATOL 1068

1 or 2 week Sporting Holidays at Club Alba, Antalya (tennis, windsurfing, sailing, diving, riding, waterskiing, cycling, health and fitness, archery, etc.).

Tailor-made holidays available.

CLUB TURKEY
113 Upper Richmond Road, Putney, London SW15 2TL
(Tel: 01-785 6389 Telex: 926631 CLUBTY G)
ATOL 754

7/14/21 nights in Istanbul, Antalya, Side, Alanya, Kemer, Kas, Kalkan.

Tailor-made holidays.

CONTIKI HOLIDAYS
Wells House, 15 Elmfield Road, Bromley BR1 1LS
(Tel: 01-290 6777)
ABTA 20305 ATOL 1274

7 and 14 nights in Datca at a resort exclusive to 18-35 year olds. Free watersports, private beach.
7 night mini-bus tour of Central Turkey, round trip from Datca.

Tailor-made holidays.

COSMOSAIR PLC
Tourama House, 17 Homesdale Road, Bromley BR2 9LX
(Tel: 01-464 3444 Telex: 896458)
ABTA 23318 ATOL 2275

7 and 14 nights in Kusadasi, Bodrum, Marmaris and Alanya.
Coach Tours: Highlights of Western Turkey and Istanbul.
Highlights of Central Turkey and Istanbul.
Flight-only arrangements.

CRUSADER CRUISING
14 Lissel Road, Simpson, Milton Keynes MK6 3AX
(Tel: 0908 670346 Telex: 825264 SILBUS)

1/2/3 week self-catering, hotel and camping holidays in Bodrum and the surrounding area.

Tailor-made holidays: 1/2/3 week Istanbul, Ismir. Fly-drive Flight-only and Accommodation-only can be arranged.

C.T.A. HOLIDAYS LTD
28 Cockspur Street, London SW1Y 5BN
(Tel: 01-930 4853 Telex: 885614)
ABTA 19261 ATOL 1000B

Up to 4 weeks in Istanbul, or as part of a two-centre Istanbul-North Cyprus holiday throughout the year.

Fly-drive, Tailor-made, Flight-only, Accommodation-only arrangements.

CYGNUS WILDLIFE HOLIDAYS LTD
96 Fore Street, Kingsbridge, Devon TQ7 1PY
(Tel: 0548 6178 Telex: 45772 TACOMM G)

15 day Birdwatching Holidays, led by experienced ornithological leader.

DALYAN HOLIDAYS (Bon Voyage Ltd)
1 Buckingham Way, Frimley, Camberley, Surrey GU16 5XE
(Tel: 0276 65460)

1 to 4 week holidays in Dalyan. Good choice of local hotels. An area of wildlife and archaeological interest. Holidays arranged all year round.

Tailor-made holidays and Accommodation-only can be arranged. Gulet Cruising from Göcek for any duration.

DELTASUN HOLIDAYS
58 Paddington Street, London W1M 3RR
(Tel: 01-487 4503/01-935 9535 Telex: 265685 DSUN G)
ATOL 2167

1, 2 and 3 week holidays in Istanbul, Kusadasi, Bodrum, Marmaris, Datca, Fethiye, Ölüdeniz, Kalkan, Kas, Antalya, Side, Alanya.

Coach Tours: Western Anatolia (1 week), Central Anatolia (1 week), Anatolian Highlights (2 weeks). Fly-drive, Tailor-made, Flight-only and Accommodation-only arrangements.

E.C. BUREAU
Dunstown, Mintlaw AB4 7UJ, Scotland
(Tel: 077982 249)

Weekly or monthly villa rentals throughout the year at Kabakum near Dikili on the Aegean Coast. Car hire can be arranged.

ENTERPRISE – REDWING HOLIDAYS
Groundstar House, London Road, Crawley, W. Sussex RH10 2TB
(Tel: 0293-517866 Reserv. 0293 560777 Admin. Telex: 878791)
ABTA 95301 ATOL 2366

7 and 14 night hotel and apartment holidays in Kusadasi, Altinkum, Gümbet (Bodrum), Marmaris, Icmeler, Kemer and Side.

Flight-only arrangements.

EURO AMERICAN TRAVEL
18 Hertford Street, Coventry CV1 1LF
(Tel: 0203 630709 Telex: MBX 203630703)
ABTA 94262

7 and 14 day holidays in Istanbul, Bursa, Konya and other places which are of interest to Muslim visitors.

Flight and Accommodation service.

EXODUS EXPEDITIONS
All Saints Passage, 100 Wandsworth High Street, London SW18 4LE
(Tel: 01-870 0151 Telex: 8951700)
ATOL 355B

Various adventure tours of 15, 16 and 24 days' duration, using a combination of camping and pansiyon accommodation. Walking holidays of 15 and 23 days' duration, camping and village accommodation. 15 day "Winter in Turkey" tour.

EXPLORE WORLDWIDE LTD
7 High Street, Aldershot, Hants. GU11 1BH
(Tel: 0252 319448 Telex: 858954 EXPLOR G)

A variety of adventure trips of 16 and 23 days' duration, mostly small hotel and guesthouse accommodation. 16 day Seatrek from Antalya to Marmaris. 16 day winter walking tour.

FALCON HOLIDAYS
33 Notting Hill Gate, London W11 3JQ
(Tel: 01-221 6298 Telex: 922889)
ABTA 68342 ATOL 1337

1 and 2 week holidays in Kusadasi, Altinkum, Gölköy, Gündogan, Bodrum, Gümbet, Türlbükü, Marmaris, Icmeler, Kemer, Beldibi and Side.

Two-centre Turkey/Greece. 1 week 'Classical' coach tour. 1 week Gulet cruises. Flight-only arrangements.

FALCON SAILING
33 Notting Hill Gate, London W11 3JQ
(Tel: 01-727 0232 Telex: 922889 Attn. SAILING)
ABTA 68342 ATOL 1337

1 and 2 week windsurfing holidays in Yalikavak, and dinghy sailing/windsurfing holidays in Bitez, both with Royal Yachting Association tuition.

Tailor-made windsurfing/dinghy sailing/yachting packages.

FATOSH TRAVEL
54 Green Lanes, Palmers Green N13 4TD
(Tel: 01-888 0706 (6 lines) Telex: 918494)

7/14/21 nights in Kusadasi, Gümüldür, Bodrum, Marmaris, Fethiye, Side.

Special breaks in Istanbul and Izmir. Tailor-made holidays, Fly-drive, Flight-only, Accommodation-only arrangements.

FIRST RESORT HOLIDAYS
London House, Old Court Place, 26-40 Kensington High Street,
London W8 4PF
(Tel: 01-938 3492 Telex: 94017418 FRES G)
ABTA 29032 ATOL 2097

7 and 14 night holidays in Istanbul. 7,14,21 and 28 nights in Marmaris, Ölüdeniz and Side, in hotels, apartments and pansiyons. Waterskiing tuition for beginners at Ölüdeniz.

Tailor-made holidays, Flight-only, Accommodation-only arrangements. 7 and 14 night fully crewed Gulet Cruises from Fethiye.

GALAXY HOLIDAYS
Pillar and Lucy House, Merchants Road, Gloucester GL1 5RG
(Tel: 0452 308798)

June and September 1989. 1 week tours including Istanbul, Bursa, Canakkale, Izmir (visiting Pergamum, Ephesus and Troy).

GOLDEN HORN TRAVEL
Golden House, 29 Great Pulteney Street, London W1R 3DD
(Tel: 01-434 1962 Reserv. 01-439 3029 Admin. Telex: 298287 GLDTR G)
ABTA 31193 ATOL 1751

1 and 2 week holidays in Istanbul, Kusadasi, Bodrum, Marmaris, Kemer, Antalya, Side and Alanya. Two-centre: Istanbul with any of the above, Kusadasi with Bodrum.

Coach Tours: 14 day Cappadocia tours, Historic South West tours, Classical tours. Self-catering holidays, Tailor-made holidays. Fly-drive, Flight-only, Accommodation-only arrangements.

HAMILTON TRAVEL LTD.
3 Heddon Street, London W1R 7LE
(Tel: 01-439 3199 Telex: 299176)
ABTA 79281 ATOL 1489

Year round holidays in Istanbul of 2 nights to 1 month duration.

Fly-drive, Tailor-made holidays, Flight-only arrangements

HANN OVERLAND
(HIGHCREST TRAVEL LTD) Overland Tours
2nd Floor, 268-270 Vauxhall Bridge Road, London SW1V 1EJ
(Tel: 01-834 7337 Telex: 914846 HANN OV G)

Coach Tours: 22 days Eastern Turkey and Black Sea. 16 days Göreme and South Coast. Göreme Walking Tour – 7-10 days. Short Treks – Eastern Turkey. Flight-only arrangements.

HCI CLUB HOLIDAYS
4 Broadway, Edgbaston Five Ways, Birmingham B15 1BB
(Tel: 021-643 2727 Telex: 335641)
ABTA 35391 ATOL 169

7 and 14 nights at Club Santana, Alanya, with free sports and entertainment.

Flight-only arrangements.

HIGHWAY HOLIDAYS
63 Grays Inn Road, London WC1X 8TL
(Tel: 01-405 1368 Telex: 8952517)
ATOL 89

Coach Tours: "In the Steps of St. Paul" plus Istanbul, Izmir, Pamukkale, etc. 12 days. "The Seven Churches and Byzantium" plus Istanbul, Adana, Tarsus, Göreme Valley, Konya, etc. 13 days. Tailor-made holidays.

HOLIDAYRAMA
23/25 Procter Street, London WC1V 6NS
(Tel: 01-831 8440/01-405 4355 Telex: 267224 BEEHIV)
ABTA 83380 ATOL 2135

7 and 14 night holidays in Istanbul, Kusadasi, Güzelcamli, Altinkum, Bodrum, Ortakent, Marmaris, Calis, Ölüdeniz, Alanya. Two-centre: Istanbul/Resort.

Coach Tours: 7 days – from Izmir Cappadocia – from Izmir Classical – from Dalaman Wonders of Turkey. Fly-drive holidays, Flight-only arrangements. 3, 7, 14 day Cruises departing from Bodrum, Marmaris, Fethiye, Antalya.

HORIZON HOLIDAYS LTD
4 Broadway, Edgbaston Five Ways, Birmingham B15 1BB
(Tel: 021-643 2727 Telex: 335641 HORIZON G)
ABTA 35391 ATOL 169

7 and 14 night holidays in Alanya, Side, Marmaris, Bodrum. Hotels and apartments.

Flight-only arrangements.

DAVID HOUSELEY
(Travel Consultants)
152 Colneis Road, Felixstowe, Suffolk IP11 9LQ
(Tel: 0394 283525)

15 day "Seven Churches of Asia" Coach tour.
Special arrangements for Church groups.

ILIOS ISLAND HOLIDAYS
18 Market Square, Horsham, W. Sussex RH12 1EU
(Tel: 0403 59788 Telex: 878168 ILIOS G)
ABTA 76635 ATOL 1452

1-2 week Self-catering holidays in select villas and apartments in Akyaka.

Fly-drive and Tailor-made holidays, Flight-only arrangements.

INTASUN HOLIDAYS
Intasun House, Cromwell Avenue, Bromley, Kent BR2 9AQ
(Tel: 01-290 0511/01-290 1900 Res. Telex: 896089)
ABTA 3691X ATOL 1960

Summer 1989 Brochure. 7, 10, 11 and 14 days in Kusadasi, Altinkum, Bodrum/ Gümbet, Bitez, Torba, Marmaris, Datca and Fethiye. 7 and 14 days in Alanya and Side. A wide choice of quality accommodation. Summer 1989 – Turkey – Plain and Simple Brochure: 7, 10, 11, 14, 21 days in Ayvalik, Foca, Cesme, Kusadasi, Altinkum, Torba, Bodrum/Gümbet, Bitez, Ortakent, Akyarlar, Turgutreis, Marmaris/Icmeler, Datca, Fethiye, Patara, Kas. 7, 14, 21 days in Alanya and Side. Accommodation in pansiyons, motels, hotels and apartments. A wide range of two-centre holidays.
Coach Tours, Fly-drive Holidays, Flight-only arrangements.

INTER-CHURCH TRAVEL LTD
The Saga Building, Middelburg Square, Folkestone, Kent CT20 1AZ
(Tel: 0303 47535 Telex: 966331)
ABTA 36869 ATOL 308B

Coach Tours: "The Journey of St. Paul" 11 nights Turkey/Cyprus. "In the Steps of St. Paul" 12 nights Turkey/Greece. "Black Sea Coast and Eastern Turkey" 13 nights. "Istanbul, Cappadocia, Antakya" 10 nights. Tailor-made holidays.

INTRA TRAVEL LTD
121-122 Tottenham Court Road, London W1P 9NH
(Tel: 01-383 7701 Telex: 928652 INTRA G)
ATOL 2392

7 and 14 nights in Istanbul, Sile, Kusadasi, Bodrum, Marmaris, Fethiye, Kalkan, Kas, Kemer, Antalya, Side, Alanya. Also two-centre holidays.

Coach Tours: Biblical, Archaeological, Ottoman, Conference/Incentives, School Trips. Fly-drive and Tailor-made holiday, Flight-only and Accommodation-only arrangements.

JENNY MAY HOLIDAYS
35 St John's Hill, London SW11 1TT
(Tel: 01-228 0321 Telex: 915320 JMHOLS G)

1, 2, 3 week villa holidays (some luxury with pools) in Bodrum, Bodrum Peninsula and Marmaris, from March to November. 1, 2, 3 week crewed Gulet cruises.

Fly-drive, Tailor-made, Flight-only, Accommodation-only.

LANCASTER HOLIDAYS
26 Elmfield Road, Bromley, Kent BR1 1LR
(Tel: 01-697 8181 Telex: 8953010 LANAIR G)
ABTA 3691X ATOL 1960

Travel Turkey – North and South (two brochures) offering 7, 14, 21 night holidays in Erdek, Ayvalik, Foca, Cesme, Kusadasi, Altinkum, Bodrum, Gümbet, Ortakent, Turgutreis, Akyarlar, Güvercinlik, Marmaris, Icmeler, Gökova, Turunc, Datca, Fethiye, Calis, Patara, Kalkan, Kas, Antalya, Side, Alanya.

3 and 4 night Istanbul City Breaks. Two-centre holidays. Coach and Stay holidays. 7 night Coach Tours: Jeep Tours from Fethiye.

LOGOTOUR LTD
189 Regent Street, London W1R 7WE
(Tel: 01-437 0535/0587 Telex: 265114 LOGOTR)
ABTA 42817 ATOL 2280

7 and 14 night holidays in Istanbul, on the Aegean and Mediterranean Coasts, throughout the year.

Fly-drive, Tailor-made holidays. Flight-only, Accommodation-only service.

MARK WARNER
20 Kensington Church Street, London W8 4EP
(Tel: 01-938 1851 Telex: 24304 SKIMWT)
ABTA 20358

1 and 2 week holidays in Clubhotels in the Bodrum area, with free watersports tuition.

METAK HOLIDAYS
69/70 Welbeck Street, London W1M 7HA
(Tel: 01-935 6961 Telex: 263188)
ABTA 43858 ATOL 1116

3, 4, 5, 7, 10 and 14 day holidays in Istanbul, Izmir and Antalya. 7 and 14 days in Kusadasi, Bodrum, Kemer, Side, Alanya.
Two and three-centre holidays, Fly-drive and Tailor-made holidays.
10 and 14 day Coach Tours which can be combined with a beach holiday. 7 day Yacht Cruises from Bodrum, and combinations of Cruise and Stay holidays.

Flight-only and Accommodation-only service.

MOSAIC HOLIDAYS
Tri-Sun House, Station Approach, Broadway, Yaxley,
Peterborough PE7 3EE
(Tel: 0733 244994 Telex: 32134 NNISAS G)
ABTA 99567 ATOL 2470

7 and 14 day holidays in Istanbul, Cesme, Kusadasi, Kemer, Beldibi, Side and Alanya. Two-centre: Istanbul/North Cyprus

Fly-drive and Flight-only arrangements. Coach Tours: 15 days Western Turkey.

MOSAIC SELECT
73 South Audley Street, London W1Y 5FF
(Tel: 01-493 3380 Telex: 918090 NNISAS G)
ABTA 99567

10 and 14 night Coach tours of Eastern Turkey, Black Sea Coast, Cappadocia, Turkey/North Cyprus.

Tailor-made holidays.

ORIENTOURS (LONDON) LTD
Kent House, 87 Regent Street, London W1R 8LS
(Tel: 01-434 1551 Telex: 21337)
ABTA 46485 ATOL 781B

Coach Tours: "Seven Churches of Asia" including Istanbul – 11 days. Cappadocia and Antalya – 12 days. Eastern Turkey – 12/14 days.

Fly-drive and Tailor-made holidays, Flight-only and Accommodation-only arrangements.

OVERSEAS CAMPING TOURS LTD
181 Edward Street, Brighton BN2 2JB
(Tel: 0273 685824/0273 685187)

7, 14, 21 and 28 day Fly-drive (motor caravans, estate cars with camping pack, motor boats with camping pack), Camping and Village room holidays, in Antalya, Fethiye, Göcek, Marmaris, Bodrum, Izmir. Watersports holidays (diving, sailboarding, waterskiing) in Göcek.

Tailor-made holidays.

PAGE & MOY LTD
136-140 London Road, Leicester LE2 1EN
(Tel: 0533 542000 Telex: 34583)
ABTA 47026 ATOL 133

10 night "Ancient Turkey" tour.

THE PERSONAL TRAVEL COMPANY
16A Terrapin Road, London SW17 8QN
(Tel: 01-673 8390)

1 week or longer holidays in Bodrum, Gölköy, Akyarlar, in traditional villas, tailor-made for the individual, family or group. Winter Breaks in Bodrum (1 week or longer).

Fly-drive and Flight-only available.

PROSPECT MUSIC AND ART LTD
10 Barley Mow Passage, Chiswick, London W4 4PH
(Tel: 01-995 2163/01-995 2151 Telex: 918705)
ATOL 2147

Art/Archaeological Tours: 5 days – Istanbul. 8 days – Istanbul, Bursa, Edirne. 13 days – South West Coast, from Izmir to Antalya. 16 days – Central and Eastern Turkey. 4 night Winter Breaks in Istanbul.

RAINBOW SAILING
Cardinal House, Church Row, Wernffrwd, Swansea SE4 3TT
(Tel: 0792 467813 Telex: 94015991 RAIN G)

Villa accommodation or villa/sail combination holidays in the Marmaris area. Any duration.

Tailor-made holidays, Accommodation-only.

RAMBLERS HOLIDAYS LTD
Box 43, Welwyn Garden City, Herts. AL8 6PQ
(Tel: 0707 331133 Telex: 24642 RTOUR G)
ABTA 50940 ATOL 990

Highlights of Eastern Turkey, 2 week multi-centre tour. Kusadasi and Fethiye, 2 week sightseeing/walking tour. Trabzon and Erzurum, 2 week walking tour. Istanbul – 1 week sightseeing/easy walking tour throughout the year.

Accommodation booking.

REGENT HOLIDAYS (UK) LTD
Regent House, 31A High Street, Shanklin, Isle of Wight PO37 6JW
(Tel: 0983 864212/0983 864225 Telex: 86197)
ABTA 51587 ATOL 856

Holidays in Istanbul, Kilyos, Ankara, Erdek, Izmir, Bodrum, Gümbet, Turgutreis, Beldibi, Antalya, Side.

Horse riding holidays, Gulet cruises ex Bodrum and Marmaris. Coach Tours: 7 and 12 nights. Fly-drive, Tailor-made holidays, Flight-only and Accommodation-only arrangements.

SAMSON TRAVEL LTD
127 Kingsland High Street, London E8 2PB
(Tel: 01-240 2687/01-240 5111 Telex: 927666 SAMSON G)
ABTA 90755

1 to 4 week holidays in Istanbul. 1 to 3 week self-catering and hotel holidays in Ören, Kusadasi, Bodrum, Yalikavak, Datca, Side and Alanya. 1 and 2 week Hunting holidays. 1 and 2 week Yacht Cruises from Bodrum and Marmaris.

Car-hire, Fly-drive, Flight-only, Accommodation-only arrangements.

SAVILE TRAVEL AND TOURS
32 Maddox Street, London W1 1PF
(Tel: 01-499 5101 Telex: 269529)
ATOL 2042

7, 10 and 14 day holidays in Istanbul (Ottoman Palaces, Mansions and Pensions), Bursa, Kusadasi, Bodrum, Türkbükü, Kalkan, Antalya.

Special fully guided tour to the war graves of Gallipoli and to Troy, including 3 nights in Istanbul. Cappadocia tour, combined with Ankara and Istanbul, using sleeper trains as part of the transport. Fly-drive and Tailor-made holidays, Flight-only, Accommodation-only arrangements.

SCHOOL TRAVEL SERVICE
24 Culloden Road, Enfield, Middlesex EN2 8QD
(Tel: 01-363 8202 Telex: 267444)
ABTA 54265 ATOL 103

9 day school party tour by air at Easter. Istanbul. Istanbul-Bursa-Izmir.

SERENISSIMA TRAVEL
21 Dorset Square, London NW1 6QG
(Tel: 01-730 9841/01-723 6556 Telex: 914032/28441)
ABTA 54693 ATOL 883B

4 days in Istanbul. 19 days in Eastern Turkey (Istanbul, Trabzon, Erzurum, Sarikamis, Dogubeyazit, Van). 9 days in Istanbul, Iznik, Bursa, Edirne.

SHERPA EXPEDITIONS
131A Heston Road, Hounslow TW5 0RD
(Tel: 01-557 2717 Telex: 892512)
ATOL 1185B

16 day Mountain Walking/Trekking holidays – Eastern and Southern Turkey.

SILVERSAND HOLIDAYS LTD
17B Riding House Street, London W1P 7PB
(Tel: 01-637 8728 Telex: 262598 SILVER G)

7, 14 and 21 night holidays in Istanbul, Kusadasi, Bodrum, Marmaris, Kemer, Antalya, Side, Alanya. Two-centre holidays.

7 and 14 day Western and Central Coach Tours. Fly-drive and Tailor-made holidays, Flight-only and Accommodation arrangements.

SIMPLY TURKEY
486 Chiswick High Road, London W4 5TT
(Tel: 01-747 1011 Telex: 8955503 SIMPLY G)
ATOL 2302

1, 2 or 3 week holidays Akyarlar, Ortakent, Gümüslük, Akyaka, Ölüdeniz. Mainly self-catering but also some pansiyon accommodation. 1, 2 or 3 week Special Interest (wild flowers, painting, archaeological, wild boar hunting, scuba diving) holidays which can be combined with a Blue Cruise. 1/2/3 week Gulet cruises.

Fly-drive and Tailor-made holidays, Flight-only.

SMALL WORLD SUN
2 Mount Sion, Tunbridge Wells, Kent TN1 1UE
(Tel: 0892 511733 Telex: 94070357 SSUN)
ABTA 9421X ATOL 2318

7 and 14 night House Parties at Güllük and Torba which can be combined with Gulet cruising. 14 night Turkey/Greece two-centre House Party (Torba and Kalymnos). 7 day Gulet cruises (can be combined with House Party holidays – 2 weeks).

SOVEREIGN HOLIDAYS – REDWING HOLIDAYS
Groundstar House, London Road, Crawley RH10 2TB
(Tel: 0293 560777 Telex: 878847 REDPRO G)
ABTA 95301 ATOL 2366

7 or 14 night holidays in Kusadasi, Bodrum, Antalya and Side.

STALLARD HOLIDAYS
29 Stoke Newington Road, London N16 8BL
(Tel: 01-254 6444 Telex: 265010 STAG G)
ABTA 56472

1–14 night holidays in Istanbul. Year round Short Break programmes – very flexible, will tailor itineraries to clients' needs.

Fly-drive holidays.

STEEPWEST HOLIDAYS LTD
449 Oxford Street, London W1R 1DA
(Tel: 01-629 2879 Telex: 297979)
ABTA 55395 ATOL 1898

7 and 14 night holidays in Istanbul, Sile, Izmir, Kusadasi, Bodrum, Marmaris, Datca, Göcek, Fethiye, Patara, Kalkan, Kas, Antalya, Side and Alanya. Two-centre holidays. Diving holidays. 7 night Central Turkey, 14 night Eastern Turkey Coach Tours. 7 and 14 night Blue Cruise.

Fly-drive and Tailor-made holidays, Flight-only, Accommodation-only arrangements.

SUNFARE HOLIDAYS
35 Virginia Street, Glasgow G1 3TX
(Tel: 041-552 5382/041-552 2711 Telex: 779480)
ABTA 1337 ATOL 230

1, 2 and 3 week self-catering and bed and breakfast holidays, direct from Glasgow, in Marmaris and Kusadasi.

Flight-only arrangements.

SUNMED HOLIDAYS
Groundstar House, London Road, Crawley, W. Sussex RH10 2TB
(Tel: 0293 560777 Telex: 878791)
ABTA 95301 ATOL 2366

1, 2 and 3 week holidays in Istanbul, Sile, Kilyos, Ören, Ayvalik, Kusadasi, Altinkum, Bodrum, Gümbet, Turgutreis, Ortakent, Marmaris, Icmeler, Ölüdeniz, Patara, Cavus, Kemer, Side. 1 week Walking Holidays.

Tailor-made holidays, Car Hire, Flight-only, Accommodation-only.

1, 2 or 3 week Gulet Cruising from Bodrum, Marmaris and Kemer, can be combined with a resort holiday.

SUNQUEST HOLIDAYS LTD
Aldine House, Aldine Place, 141/142 Uxbridge Road, London W12 8AW
(Tel: 01-749 9933 Res. 01-749 9911 Admin. Telex: 22319)
ABTA 57352 ATOL 754

1 week or longer in Istanbul and Istanbul resorts, Kusadasi, Bodrum, Fethiye, Calis, Kalkan, Antalya, Side, Alanya.

2 week two-centre holidays, Fly-drive holidays, Tailor-made holidays, Flight-only, Accommodation-only.

14 night Coach Tours: Istanbul/Alanya/Cappadocia. Alanya/Cappadocia. Kusadasi/Cappadocia

SUNSAIL CLUBS
The Port House, Port Solent, Portsmouth, Hants. PO6 4TH
(Tel: 0705 219827 Telex: 86734 ISLAND G)
ABTA 36996 ATOL 987

Watersports and Sailing Club Holidays in the Marmaris and Bodrum areas.

Flight-only and Accommodation-only arrangements.

SWAN HELLENIC ART TREASURES TOURS
77 New Oxford Street, London WC1A 1PP
(Tel: 01-831 1234 Admin. 01-831 1616 Reserv. Telex: 885551)
ABTA 27427 ATOL 0307

19 day Art Treasures Tour of Anatolia (Central Turkey, Mediterranean, Aegean and Istanbul). 17 day Art Treasures Tour of Istanbul, Western and Southern Turkey. 20 day Arts Treasures Tour of Eastern Turkey. Tours accompanied by Tour Manager and Guest Lecturer.

THOMAS COOK FARAWAY HOLIDAYS
PO Box 36, Thorpe Wood, Peterborough PE9 3SN
(Tel: 0733 503203)
ABTA 20606 ATOL 265

Russia and Beyond Brochure: 10 days out of a 20 day Tour spent in Turkey, visiting Istanbul, Ankara, Kayseri, Erzurum.

THOMSON HOLIDAYS
Greater London House, Hampstead Road, London NW1 7SD
(Tel: 01-387 9321 Telex: 261123)
ABTA 58213 ATOL 152

7 and 14 night holidays from May to October, in Bodrum, Gümbet, Bitez, Gümüslük, Fethiye, Calis Beach, Ölüdeniz, Kalkan, Kas, Kemer, Beldibi, Side, Alanya. 3 and 4 night breaks in Istanbul from March to October.

7 night Coach Tour of Western Turkey, plus option of 7 nights' stay in Kemer or Alanya. 7 night Gulet cruising. Fly-drive holidays, Flight-only service.

TIMSWAY HOLIDAYS
Nightingales Corner, Little Chalfont, Bucks. HP7 9QS
(Tel: 02404 5541 Telex: 837179)
ABTA 6808X ATOL 1107

7, 14 and 21 night holidays in Kusadasi, Güzelcamli, Gümüslük, Akyarlar and Side. 7 nights "South Anatolia", "Istanbul", Wooden Horse and Minarets" Coach Tours.

Fly-drive holidays, Flight-only arrangements.

7 night "Gulf of Gökova" and "Gulf of Datca" Cruises.

TJAEREBORG LTD
194 Campden Hill Road, London W8 7TH
(Tel: 01-727 2680 Telex: 298910)
ATOL 1071

7, 14, 21 and 28 night hotel holidays in Bodrum and Marmaris.

Fly-drive holidays, Flight-only and Accommodation-only service.

TOPAZ TRAVEL
7 Hartismere Road, London SW6 7TS
(Tel: 01-381 5189 (3 lines) Telex: 927526 TOPAZ G)
ATOL Agents for 754B

7 and 14 night "stay-put" and 4/10 night two-centre holidays (three-centre also available), in Istanbul Kusadasi, Bodrum, Bitez Türkbükü, Torba, Kalkan, Kas, Kekova, Silifke, Kizkalesi.

Educational, Flora and Fauna, Archaeological tours and tailor-made itineraries organized with/without lecturers.

7 and 14 night Coach Tours, with 7 night resort or Blue Cruise option. 7 and 14 night Blue Cruises. Fly-drive, Tailor-made holidays, Flight-only and Accommodation-only service.

TOP DECK TRAVEL
131/133 Earls Court Road, London SW5 9RH
(Tel: 01-244 8641 Telex: 8955339)
ABTA 59767 ATOL 2057

Overland tours, spending between 3 and 17 days in Turkey and visiting Istanbul, Gallipoli, Troy, Bursa, Ephesus, Pamukkale, Fethiye, Manavgat, Silifke, Göreme, Erzurum, Reyhanli and Dogubeyazit.

TOPSUN HOLIDAY AND TRAVEL
Groat House, Collingwood Street, Newcastle-upon-Tyne NE1 1XU
(Tel: 091-2221362 Telex: 934999 TXLINK G)
Ref. MBX066133098

Tailor-made holidays, Flight-only and Accommodation-only arrangements.

TOURKEY TRAVEL
49 Pembridge Road, London W11 3HG
(Tel: 01-243 0383 Telex: 8953686)
ATOL Agent for 2167

1 or 2 weeks self-catering apartment and villa and hotel holidays in Istanbul, Kusadasi, Didim, Bodrum, Marmaris, Fethiye, Kalkan, Kemer, Antalya, Side and Alanya.

Special Interest: Birdwatching, Istanbul Festival, Hunting tours. Blue Cruises and Coach Tours. Fly-drive and Tailor-made holidays, Flight-only and Accommodation-only service.

TRANSGLOBAL LTD
64 Kenway Road, London SW5 0RD
(Tel: 01-244 8571 Telex: 938358 GLOBAL)

8 fully-escorted 15/22 day tours for active travellers and young people. Hotel and camping options available: "Aegean Sailtrek", "Turkey Land and Sea", "Turkey Adventurer", "Turkey Discoverer", "Turkey Explorer", "Black Sea and Beyond". 4/5 day Gulet Cruising from Bodrum and Datca.

Tailor-made itineraries.

THE TRAVEL ALTERNATIVE
27 Park End Street, Oxford OX1 4HU
(Tel: 0865 791636 Telex: 83201 BISCOM Attn: T/A)

Three 16 to 19 day tours for small groups, with good standard hotel accommodation: "Cappadocian Experience", "Eastern Turkey Wildlife Adventure", "Nomadic Village Exploration".

Flight-only arrangements.

THE TRAVEL CLUB OF UPMINSTER
54 Station Road, Upminster, Essex RM14 2TT
(Tel: 04022 25000 Telex: 897124 TRAVEL G)
ABTA 59165 ATOL 172

1 and 2 week hotel and apartment holidays in Side.

TRAVELSCENE LTD
11/15 St Ann's Road, Harrow HA1 1AS
(Tel: 01-427 4445 Telex: 265647)
ABTA 5956X ATOL 034

Year round 3 and 7 night holidays in Istanbul.
Late bookings welcome.

TRESELDA LTD
7 Granville House, 49 The Mall, Faversham, Kent
(Tel: 0795 539603/0795 533763 Telex: 96446 SOLID G)

Istanbul (3-28 days) and two-centre with any resort. 7 to 28 day holidays in Amasra, Inebolu, Bulancak (Black Sea), Princes Islands (Sea of Marmara), Erdek, Bursa, Ayvalik, Datca (Aegean), and Bogsak, Tasucu, Kizkalesi, Arsuz (Eastern Mediterranean). Trekking Holidays (Black Sea Coast and Mountains). Rover Holidays (all areas).

Tailor-made, Fly-drive holidays, Flight-only and Accommodation-only arrangements.

15 day Cruise from Istanbul to Alanya.

TURKEY TODAY
44 High Street, Avening, Tetbury, Glos. GL8 8NF
(Tel: 0453 834028)

7, 14, 21 and 28 day one and two-centre holidays in hotels, pansiyons or self-catering, at Alanya, Anamur and Tasucu, which can be combined with North Cyprus.

Fly-drive, Tailor-made, Flight-only, Accommodation-only arrangements.

TURKISH CONNECTIONS
Golden House, 29 Great Pulteney Street, London W1R 3DD
(Tel: 01-439 7406 Reserv. 01-439 3020 Admin. Telex: 298287 GLD TR G)
ABTA 31193 ATOL 1751

3-28 day holidays in Istanbul. 1-4 week holidays in Kusadasi, Bodrum, Marmaris, Kas, Kemer, Antalya, Side, Alanya. Also two-centre holidays. Blue Cruises (4 to 7 days).

Student Travel: Hostels, cheap pansiyons (7 to 30 days). Coach Tours, Tailor-made holidays, Self-catering holidays, Flight-only, Accommodation-only service.

TURKISH DELIGHT HOLIDAYS
164B Heath Road, Twickenham, Middx TW1 4BN
(Tel: 01-891 5901 Telex: 925368 TDHOLS)
ABTA 69608 ATOL 2047

1, 2, 3 week one/two/three-Centre holidays in Bodrum, Türkbükü, Gümüslük, Ortakent, Gündogan, Turunc, Dalyan, Ölüdeniz, Patara, Kalkan, Kas.

1 and 2 week luxury Gulet Cruises. 4 day Coach Trips to Cappadocia from Kalkan, Kas, Patara or Ölüdeniz. Fly-drive holidays, Flight-only arrangements.

TURKISH VILLAS
35 Hanover Gardens, London SE11 5TN
(Tel: 01-735 6037)
ATOL 2042

A good selection of privately owned holiday homes to rent for one week and longer, from April to October in Türkbükü and Geris on the Bodrum Peninsula; on the south-west coast of Antalya and between Dikili and Ayvalik on the Northern Aegean Coast.

Tailor-made or Accommodation-only service and Fly-drive available, if preferred.

TURKISH WILDLIFE HOLIDAYS
The Grange, 8 Elmdon Park, Solihull, West Midlands B92 9EL
(Tel: 021-742 5420/021-705 5535 Telex: 337000 JBESOL)

14, 16 and 19 day adventure tours at good standard hotels for small groups. 11, 16, 19 day Birdwatching tours – May, August and September (escorted small groups).

Sail treks. Underwater adventures. Fly-drive holidays. Tailor-made Winter holidays in Istanbul and Antalya (duration to suit clients). Private small group tours arranged. Flight-only and Accommodation-only available.

TURQUOISE HOLIDAYS
35 D'Arblay Street, London W1V 3FE
(Tel: 01-629 5908/01-491 2448 Telex: 269923 TURLON G)
North London Office: 114 Green Lanes, London N16 9HE
(Tel: 01-249 7792)
ATOL 2158

1, 2, 3 week one or two-Centre holidays in Istanbul, Sile, Kusadasi, Altinkum, Bodrum, Akyarlar, Güvercinlik, Marmaris, Dalyan, Kalkan, Kas, Antalya, Side, Incekum.

Tailor-made Winter holidays in Istanbul (any length). Blue Cruises from Bodrum, Marmaris and Kas. Fly-drive and Tailor-made holidays, Flight-only arrangements.

UK EXPRESS TRAVEL SERVICES LTD
Whitehall House, 41 Whitehall, London SW1A 2BY
(Tel: 01-839 3303 Telex: 8956029)
ABTA 60497 ATOL 1362

1 week holidays in Istanbul, 1 and 2 week holidays in Kusadasi, Bodrum, Marmaris, Kemer, Alanya, or combining one of the resorts with Istanbul, if two-centre preferred.

Coach Tours: 2 week "Grand Scenic" can be combined with Alanya. 1 week "Best of Turkey", can be combined with Marmaris. 1 week "Central Turkey", can be combined with Alanya. 1 week "Eastern Turkey", can be combined with Alanya.

USIT CHARTERS LTD
52 Grosvenor Gardens, London SW1W 0AG
(Tel: 01-730 7285 Telex: 23472 USITUK)
ATOL STAC LTD 822

Special Student Charter Flights to Istanbul from June to September inclusive.

WALLACE ARNOLD/GLOBAL TOURS
Gelderd Road, Leeds LS12 6DM
(Tel: 0532 636456 Telex: 55482)
ABTA 62242 ATOL 0316

8 and 15 day Coach Tours: Izmir, Canakkale, Bursa, Istanbul. Optional extension to Cesme (8 days).

WAYMARK HOLIDAYS LTD
295 Lillie Road, London SW6 7LL
(Tel: 01-385 5015/01-358 3502)
ATOL 624

14, 15 and 16 night trekking holidays in Eastern, Central and Southern Turkey.

WINGS
Broadway, Edgbaston Fiveways, Birmingham B15 1BB
(Tel: 021-643 2727 Telex: 335641)
ABTA 35391 ATOL 169

7 and 14 night holidays in Kusadasi, Bodrum, Gümbet, Side. Hotels and self-catering holidays.

Flight-only arrangements.

WORLD STEAM LTD
3 Shadwell Grove, Radcliffe-on-Trent, Nottingham NG12 2ET
(Tel: 06073 4714/0533 714815 Telex: 377494 MKLEIN)

Self-catering and hotel holidays in Kalkan and Kusadasi, from May to October. Also Fly-drive.

Special Interest: 100% steam hauled special trains with sleeping and restaurant cars. Tours for steam enthusiasts. 1 week coach tours which can be linked with rail tour or beach holiday. "The Anatolia-Tigris Express". Special diesel-hauled train journey. Central, Eastern and Southern Turkey. Christmas tour for railway enthusiasts. Izmir/Burdur/Usak/Afyon by road and rail.

WORLDWIDE CHRISTIAN TRAVEL
50 Coldharbour Road, Redland, Bristol BS6 7NA
(Tel: 0272 731840 Telex: 449017)
ABTA 93522

10-15 day Religious and Historical Tours, mainly of Western Turkey.

Fly-drive and Tailor-made holidays, Flight-only and Accommodation-only arrangements.

Winter Holidays

AEGEAN TURKISH HOLIDAYS
53A Salusbury Road, London NW6 6NJ
(Tel: 01-372 6902 Telex: 265260)
ABTA 71773 ATOL 997

Holidays in Istanbul and Antalya.

AEGINA CLUB
25A Hills Road, Cambridge CB2 1NW
(Tel: 0223 63256 Telex: 61684 AEGINA)
ATOL 0262

3, 4 and 7 day breaks in Istanbul. 7 day holidays in Antalya and Side. 4 day tour of Bursa, Canakkale, Troy.

ALLEGRO HOLIDAYS
15A Church Street, Reigate RH2 0AA
(Tel: 0737 221323 Telex: 919114 ALLEGRO G)
ABTA 12173 ATOL 1835

7, 10, 14 day holidays in Antalya, and Antalya/Istanbul two-centre.

AQUASPORT TOURS LTD
181 Edward Street, Brighton BN2 2JB
(Tel: 0273 685824)

7 and 14 day Individual Hunting Holidays based at Edremit, Marmaris, Antalya.

BEST YACHTING AND TOURISM
Kargi Marine, Hillier House, 509 Upper Richmond Road,
London SW14 7EE
(Tel: 01-873 3227 Telex: 9413819 HILHOU G)

7-28 days and long-stay lets in villas on the South Coast. 7-21 days Winter Sailing from Göcek.

BLUESPOT TRAVEL LTD
28 Maddox Street, London W1R 9PF
(Tel: 01-408 0094 Telex: 297547 BLUSPT G)
ATOL 2113

3, 4, 7, 10 days and flexible arrangements in Istanbul, Izmir and Antalya.

Two and multi-centre holidays can be arranged.

BOSPHORUS HOLIDAYS
Silver House, 31-35 Beak Street, London W1R 3LD
(Tel: 01-437 7316 Telex: 296398 BOSPOR)

3 nights to 3 months or longer. Istanbul, Izmir, Ankara, Bursa, Kayseri, Bolu, Erzurum, Kars and Mersin. Skiing, City Breaks, Thermal resorts, all Tailor-made.

CELEBRITY HOLIDAYS AND TRAVEL
18 Frith Street, London W1V 5TS
(Tel: 01-439 1961 Telex: 269304)
ABTA 18659 ATOL 1469

3, 5, 7 and 14 days in Istanbul. 7 and 14 days in Side. Also two-centre Istanbul/Side and Istanbul/North Cyprus.

CLUB TURKEY
113 Upper Richmond Road, London SW15 2TL
(Tel: 01-785 6389 Telex: 926631 CLUB TY G)
ATOL Agent for 754

7 and 14 night Skiing Holidays in Uludag and Bolu. A la carte Skiing Holidays in Erzurum. Two-centre holidays combining skiing and Istanbul or Antalya.

Tailor-made holidays. School Parties: Skiing and Educational 1/2 week tours.

CRUSADER CRUISING
14 Lissel Road, Simpson, Milton Keynes MK6 3AX
(Tel: 0908 670346 Telex: 825264 SILBUS G)

1/2/3 week self-catering and hotel holidays in Bodrum and the surrounding area.

DELTASUN HOLIDAYS
58 Paddington Street, London W1M 3RR
(Tel: 01-487 4503/01-935 9535 Telex: 265685 DSUN G)
ATOL 2157

1/2/3 week holidays in delightful hotels in Istanbul, and 5-star hotel in Antalya.

Winter charter flights.

GOLDEN HORN TRAVEL
Golden House, 29 Great Pulteney Street, London W1R 3DD
(Tel: 01-434 1962 Telex: 298287 GLDTR G)
ABTA 31193 ATOL 1751

7/10/14 day holidays in Antalya, Izmir and Side. 3/7/14 day holidays in Istanbul.

Two-centre holidays: Istanbul with Antalya, Izmir or Side.

INTRA TRAVEL LTD
121-122 Tottenham Court Road, London W1P 9NH
(Tel: 01-383 7701 Telex: 928652 INTRA G)
ATOL: 2392

Long weekends in Istanbul and Izmir. 7 and 14 day holidays in Antalya.

Two-centre and Tailor-made holidays available.

METAK HOLIDAYS
69/70 Welbeck Street, London W1M 7HA
(Tel: 01-935 6961 Telex: 263188)
ABTA 43858 ATOL 1116

3, 4, 5, 7, 10 and 14 day holidays in Istanbul and Antalya.

Two-centre holidays combining the two, or North Cyprus.

PAGE AND MOY LTD
136-140 London Road, Leicester LE2 1EN
(Tel: 0533 542000 Telex: 34583)
ABTA 47026 ATOL 133

3 night holidays in Istanbul. 7 night Istanbul/Bursa.

Two-centre holiday.

REGENT HOLIDAYS UK LTD
Regent House, 31a High Street, Shanklin, Isle of Wight PO37 6JW
(Tel: 0983 864212 Telex: 86197)

3 to 28 night holidays in Istanbul, Izmir, Ankara and Antalya.

SAGA HOLIDAYS PLC
Saga Building, Middelburg Square, Folkestone CT20 1AZ
(Tel: 0800 300 456 Telex: 966331)
ABTA 36888 ATOL 308

14, 21 and 28 night Winter Holidays in Alanya.

SAMSON TRAVEL LTD
127 Kingsland High Street, London E8 2BP
(Tel: 01-240 2687/01-240 5111 Telex: 927666 SAMSON G)
ABTA 90755

3/4/7/14 day holidays in Istanbul, Izmir and Antalya.

Car hire, hotel arrangements, winter charter flights Christmas/Easter.

SAVILE TRAVEL
32 Maddox Street, London W1 1PF
(Tel: 01-499 5101 Telex: 269529)
ATOL 2042

Winter holidays in Istanbul, Bursa, Troy-Canakkale-Gelibolu, Antalya, Cappadocia.

STEEPWEST HOLIDAYS LTD
449 Oxford Street, London W1R 1DA
(Tel: 01-629 2879 Telex: 297979)
ABTA 55395 ATOL 1898

3, 7, 14 night holidays in Istanbul, Antalya, Fethiye and Izmir.

Two-centre holidays

SUNQUEST HOLIDAYS
Aldine House, Aldine Place, 141/142 Uxbridge Road, London W12
(Tel: 01-749 9933/01-749 9911 Telex: 22319)
ABTA 57352 ATOL 754

3, 4 and 7 nights in Istanbul. 3, 4 and 7 night Fly-drive and Business Travel. Long-stay holidays Antalya, Side, Kalkan, Kas. Two-centre holidays. Short breaks.

THOMAS COOK FARAWAY HOLIDAYS
PO Box 36, Thorpe Wood, Peterborough PE9 3SN
(Tel: 0733 503203)
ABTA 20606 ATOL 265

Great Little Journey Brochure: 5 days Istanbul/Bursa. 4 days Istanbul.

TOPAZ TRAVEL
7 Hartismere Road, London SW6 7TS
(Tel: 01-381 5189 Telex: 927526)
ATOL Agents for 754B

3, 7 and 14 night holidays in Istanbul, Antalya and Kas. Also two-centre holidays.

TOURKEY TRAVEL
49 Pembridge Road, London W11 3HG
(Tel: 01-243 0383 Telex: 8953686)
ATOL Agents for 2167

3, 4, 7 and 14 night holidays in Istanbul, Bursa/Uludag, Yalova/Termal. Whirling Dervishes Tour – December. 5 nights Istanbul/2 nights Konya. Winter Wooden Horse Tours – 7 days. Flight-only arrangements.

TRANSGLOBAL LTD
64 Kenway Road, London SW5 0RD
(Tel: 01-244 8571 Telex: 938358 GLOBAL)

"Turkey Panorama" 2 weeks winter coach tour of South-West and Central Turkey.

VENTURA HOLIDAYS
125 Aldersgate Street, London EC1A 4JQ
(Tel: 01-250 1355 Telex: 295921 VENHOL G)
ATOL 2034

3, 4, 7 and 14 day holidays in Istanbul, Bursa and Antalya.

Two-centres available.

Sailing and Yachting

ADVENTURE HOLIDAYS
10 Linden Park, Bangor, Co. Down
(Tel: 0247 473783)

Specialize in Yachting Holidays in the Bodrum area.

Arrangements from Northern Ireland only.

ANCASTA YACHT CHARTER
Port Hamble Marina, Satchell Lane, Hamble, Southampton, Hants. SO3 5QD
(Tel: 0703 454565 Telex: 477879 ANCA G)

From 1 week onwards, skippered and bareboat yacht charters from Marmaris and Göcek. 60 yachts from 60′.

Gulet cruising from Bodrum and Marmaris, 1 week or longer. Tailor-made holidays. Accommodation-only arrangements.

AQUARIUS CRUISING
Western House, 9 Glandovey Terrace, Aberdovey, Gwynedd LL35 0EB
(Tel: 0654 72646 Telex: 35746 AQRSTL G)

7, 14, 21 night, skippered and bareboat charters of yachts, catamarans, from Bitez.

Boats from 25′ to 50′, sleeping 2-10.

ARGOSY CRUISING
Harwood Bar, Great Harwood, Lancs. BB6 7TE
(Tel: 0254 887692 Telex: 63422 ARGOSY G)

1 week and longer charters (Marmaris-Fethiye – Kalkan – Kas).

"Trinidad" 48′ luxury cruising ketch.

BEST YACHTING AND TOURISM
Kargi Marine, Hillier House, 509 Upper Richmond Road,
London SW14 7EE
(Tel: 01-873 3227 Telex: 9413819 HILHOU G)

7 to 21 day skippered and bareboat charters from Göcek. 9-14m., 6-10 berth yachts. 7 to 21 day fully crewed Gulet charters, 6-14 berths, from Bodrum, Marmaris, Göcek, Kas and Antalya.

Flight and transfer arrangements available.

BLUE MOON CHARTERS
Blue Moon House, 92 Kingston Road, Portsmouth PO2 7PA
(Tel: 0705 662992 Telex: 86736 SOTEX G Attn BLMN)

1/2 weeks or more, crewed yacht or self-sail bareboats, all with 6 berths, from Marmaris.

Daily rate also available.

BLUESPOT TRAVEL LTD
28 Maddox Street, London W1R 9PF
(Tel: 01-408 0094/01-409 3034 Telex: 297547 BLUSPT G)
ATOL 2113

1 and 2 week crewed gulets and bareboat charters from Bodrum and Marmaris. Guaranteed departures Blue Voyages.

MV "Orient Express" Cruise Venice/Istanbul/Kusadasi and vice versa.

BOSPHORUS HOLIDAYS
Silver Street, 31-35 Beak Street, London W1R 3LD
(Tel: 01-437 7316 Telex: 296398)

Turkish Maritime Lines cruises (Marmara, Aegean, Black Sea): One way, day return, or up to 10 days.

CANBERRA CRUISES
P and O Cruises Ltd, 77 New Oxford Street, London WC1A 1PP
(Tel: 01-831 1234 Telex: 885551)

Cruise 013 (16 Sept–4 Oct) calling at Istanbul, with optional coach tours.

CRESTAR YACHT CHARTERS
Colette Court, 125/6 Sloane Street, London SW1X 9AU
(Tel: 01-730 9962 Telex: 918951 or 295054)

Cruise Aegean and Mediterranean Turkey with the experts in luxury, crewed yachts. The vessels include more than 80 motor and sail yachts from 47′.

Tailor-made cruises.

CRUSADER CRUISING
14 Lissel Road, Simpson, Milton Keynes MK6 3AX
(Tel: 0908 670346 Telex: 825264 SILBUS)

1/2/3 week bareboat and skippered sail boats based at Bodrum (34′ up), can be combined with accommodation for "Stay-and-Sail" holidays. 1/2 week Gulet Cruising from Bodrum or Marmaris, can be combined with "Stay-and-Sail" holidays.

DIVE AND SAIL
Commons Corner, Burleigh, Nr. Stroud, Glos. GL5 2SN
(Tel: 045 388 2267 Telex: 437269 SHARET G)

1 to 2 week, weekly "Live Aboard" dive charters on fully crewed and fully equipped yachts. Unlimited diving, qualified instructors. Non-divers welcome.

"Learn to Dive" packages. Flight-only arrangements.

FAIRWAYS AND SWINFORD TRAVEL
20 Upper Ground, London SE1 9PF
(Tel: 01-928 5044/01-261 1744 Telex: 8955803 SCN LDN)
ABTA 28608 ATOL 491

Cruising: in Turkish Waters on MV "Orient Express", in conjunction with 1 week stay in Istanbul or Kusadasi.

FALCON SAILING
33 Notting Hill Gate, London W11 3JQ
(Tel: 01-727 0232 Telex: 922889 (Attn Sailing)
ABTA 68342 ATOL 1337

2 week Flotilla holidays or independent charter. "Beneteau Oceanis 320" and "Mirage 28" boats.

HALSEY MARINE LTD
22 Boston Place, Dorset Square, London NW1 6HZ
(Tel: 01-724 1303 Telex: 265131 HALSEY G)

Private Yacht Charter on fully crewed yachts from 45′ to 120′ plus, along the South West Turkish Coast, from Izmir to Kekova.

ISLAND SAILING LTD
The Port House, Port Solent, Portsmouth, Hampshire PO6 4TH
(Tel: 0705 210345 Telex: 86734 ISLAND G)
ABTA 36996 ATOL 987

14 day Flotilla and Bareboat Sailing from Marmaris, Datca and Fethiye.

Flight-only and Accommodation-only service.

LANCASTER HOLIDAYS
26 Elmfield Road, Bromley, Kent BR1 1LR
(Tel: 01-697 8181 Telex: 8953010 LANAIR G)
ABTA 3691X ATOL 1960

14 night "Turkey/Greece" cruising from Bodrum. Choice of Blue Cruises (7 and 14 days) from Bodrum, Marmaris, Fethiye, Kas and Antalya. 3 night Mini-cruises from Fethiye and Kas.

14 night "Cruise and Stay" holidays.

LIZ FENNER WORLDWIDE YACHTING HOLIDAYS
35 Fairfax Place, London NW6 4EJ
(Tel: 01-328 1033 Telex: 262284 MONREF Attn 2641 Liz Fenner)

From 1 week to 2 months or longer holidays aboard crewed luxury sailing and motor yachts from 50′ to 250′, from Bodrum, Marmaris, Göcek, Fethiye, Kas and Antalya.

Tailor-made packages. 35′-55′ bareboat charters.

McCULLOCH MARINE CHARTER
60 Fordwych Road, London NW2 3TH
(Tel: 01-452 7509 Telex: 923753 Ref. 327)

Agent for Gulet specialists offering a large variety of fully crewed gulets and motor schooners. 6-12 berths for made-to-measure cruises around the South West Coast of Turkey. Flights and transfers arranged.

MV ORIENT EXPRESS
Suite 200, Hudsons Place, Victoria Station, London SW1V 1JL
(Tel: 01-834 8122 Telex: 914840 OELDN G)

Venice–Piraeus–Istanbul–Kusadasi–Patmos–Katakolon–Venice (7 nights). Weekly Saturday departures from Venice March–October 1990.

Stopover journeys available. Vehicle space available.

RAINBOW SAILING LTD
Cardinal House, Church Row, Wernffrwd, Swansea SA1 1PQ
(Tel: 0792 467813 Telex: 94015991 RAIN G)

Any number of weeks bareboat and skippered charter on 29′ to 40′ Beneteau yachts, from Marmaris.

SAGA HOLIDAYS PLC
The Saga Building, Middelburg Square, Folkestone, Kent CT20 1AZ
(Tel: 0800 300 456 Telex: 966331)
ABTA 36888 ATOL 308

3 Cruises: "Golden Fleece", "Homeric Cruise" and "Grand Cruise", visiting Kusadasi.

SERENISSIMA TRAVEL LTD
21 Dorset Square, London NW1 6QG
(Tel: 01-730 9841/01-723 6556 Telex: 914032/28441)
ABTA 54693 ATOL 883B

Cruising in the Aegean on board M/V "Serenissima Tura".

SUNDOWN MARINE YACHT CHARTERS
Sundown House, Rectory Lane, Woodmansterne, Surrey SM7 3PP
(Tel: 0737 551271/2 Telex: 8956867 SUNGRP G)

A full range of yacht charter holidays (any duration) in bareboat, skippered and crewed yachts from 28′ to 155′, Marmaris, Bodrum, Fethiye and along the coast. Specialists in Gulet cruises.

Tailor-made packages. All travel arrangements made.

SUNQUEST HOLIDAYS
Aldine House, Aldine Place, 141/142 Uxbridge Road, London W12 8AW
(Tel: 01-749 9933 Telex: 22319)
ABTA 57352 ATOL 754

7 or 14 night Yachting Holidays from Bodrum. Agents for Turkish Maritime Lines – all destinations. MV "Orient Express" Venice/Istanbul/Kusadasi. 14 night "Turquoise Cruise".

SWAN HELLENIC CRUISES
77 New Oxford Street, London WC1A 1PP
(Tel: 01-831 1234 Res. 01-831 1515 Adm. Telex: 88851)
ABTA 27427 ATOL 0307

A large number of Mediterranean cruises on the "Orpheus", many of which call at various Turkish ports, from Sinop to Mersin.

TEMPLECRAFT YACHT CHARTERS LTD
33 Grand Parade, Brighton BN2 2QA
(Tel: 0273 695094 Telex: 94013292 TYCL)
ATOL 2149

1 to 4 week skippered and bareboat charters (31′ to 51′ yachts) available from Marmaris, Göcek, Antalya and Fethiye.

Tailor-made arrangements.

TFC CRUISE LINES
49 Whitcomb Street, London WC2H 7DH
(Tel: 01-930 7541 Telex: 946102)
ABTA 72719

Cruises on "Achille Lauro" calling at Istanbul, Izmir, Kusadasi.

TOP YACHT CHARTER LTD
Andrew Hill Lane, Hedgerley, Bucks SL2 2UW
(Tel: 02814 6636 Telex: 23152 MONREF G)
ATOL 1761

2 weeks or more from Bodrum and Göcek: 26 yachts from 30′–49′ for bareboat charter from Bodrum to Göcek. 46′ to 60′ sailing yachts with skipper and hostess. Fully crewed Gulets, to take 6–12 guests. Flights on Wednesdays from Gatwick and Manchester to Dalaman.

Coach transfers, Flight-only arrangements.

VIAMARE TRAVEL
33 Mapesbury Road, London NW2 4HT
(Tel: 01-452 8231/2 / 01-452 0692/3 Telex: 9413206 MARE G)

Summer Ferry Services Italy to Turkey: Ancona–Patras–Heraklion–Kusadasi. Year round ferry crossing Rhodes–Marmaris.

YACHTCLUB CHARTER COMPANY LTD
307 New Kings Road, London SW6 4RF
(Tel: 01-731 0826 Telex: 268867 YACHTC G)
ATOL 2272

1–4 week bareboat charters of 28′ to 42′ yachts. Skipper also available. Large variety of Turkish Gulets complete with crew. Sailings from Bodrum and Fethiye. April to October. Daytime flights with coach transfers.

Tailor-made holidays, Flight-only and Accommodation-only arrangements.

YACHT CRUISING ASSOCIATION
The Port House, Port Solent, Porstmouth, Hampshire PO6 4TH
(Tel: 0705 219844 Telex: 869110 YCA G)
ABTA 36996 ATOL 987

14-day Flotilla Sailing holidays along the South Coast (Kas, Kekova), and Bodrum area.

Thanks to the Turkish Tourist Board for allowing us to reproduce their tour operator list. Correct at time of going to press.

Who Specializes in What

GENERAL TOUR OPERATORS

Every year, as tourism to Turkey increases, more general tour operators enter the market. Some of the big names are now established in Turkey, such as **Club Med, Sun Med, Horizon, Sovereign, Tjaereborg** and **Wings**. The following companies also offer a good selection to Turkey: **Aegean Turkish Holidays, Blue Spot Travel, Celebrity, Golden Horn Travel, Lancaster Travel, Intra Travel, Metak** and **Sunquest**. The cost of a two-week package ranges from £300 for a simple pension, to £750 for an A-category hotel.

SELF-CATERING

Most tour operators who offer self-catering holidays in Turkey, including **Beach Villas Limited** and **Aegean Turkish Holidays**, offer very good packages which include your flight, villa accommodation and a free car for the duration of your holiday. They also offer reductions for children (who travel free in some cases), which the majority of operators don't do. **Celebrity Holidays, CTA Holidays** and **The Personal Travel Company** offer to arrange any kind of package to any part of Turkey, and self-catering is one of the options you can choose from.

Other tour operators offering self-catering and tailor-made holidays include **Bosphorus Holidays, Golden Horn Travel, Regent Holidays, Saville Travel, Simply Turkey, Sunquest Holidays** and **Treselda.**

Self-catering accommodation in Turkey is good but more limited than hotel accommodation, therefore your choice of resorts may be restricted. The highest concentration of self-catering accommodation is in the south Aegean region, but you can also find villas and apartments in some Mediterranean resorts. The self-catering holidays offered by most firms tend to be more suitable for families or parties than for couples, as the price per person is lower the more people you have sharing a villa.

TWO-CENTRE HOLIDAYS

Turkey is an ideal destination for a two-centre holiday as it has two major attractions: the fascinating city of Istanbul, and miles of beautiful coastline. Most two-centre holidays in Turkey comprise four days in Istanbul followed by ten days at one of the coastal resorts such as Bodrum, Kusadasi, Cesme, Antalya or Alanya. This combination makes for a varied holiday and gives you a great opportunity to experience the diversity of the country.

British tour operators offering this type of holiday include **Aegean Turkish Holidays, Aegina Club, Blue Spot Travel, Bosphorus Holidays, Celebrity Holidays, Golden Horn Travel, Metak Holidays, Saville Travel, Steepwest Holidays, Sunquest Holidays, Treselda, Turkish Delight Holidays** and **UK Express.**

As well as their range of Istanbul/beach resort holidays, **Aegean Turkish Holidays** also offer an 'off the beaten track' two-centre holiday which takes you to Istanbul and Lake Van, one of eastern Anatolia's best sightseeing regions, and **Sunquest** have a package which combines hotel accommodation in Istanbul with self-catering accommodation on the coast.

Two-centre holidays are a good compromise for the tourist who enjoys one active week (i.e. walking and sightseeing) followed by a week lazing on a beach. While this type of holiday invariably costs more than a static one-centre holiday, the higher cost is usually justified by the extra travel and administration involved.

CAMPING HOLIDAYS

Very few tour operators offer camping holidays in Turkey, probably because good campsites are still relatively thin on the ground. Camping has not yet taken off in Turkey the way it has in other European countries, and most of the camping holidays available are touring holidays rather than the static camping holidays which are popular on the Continent.

Hann Overland offer camping, but only as part of a 10-day coach/camping tour of Göreme and the south coast; **Overseas Camping Tours** offer holidays in central and eastern Anatolia, giving you the option of flying to Turkey or of travelling overland; **Transglobal** do a 16-day 'Turkey Adventure' which is a camping tour of Istanbul, Gallipoli, Pamukkale, Ankara and numerous other places; **Top Deck Travel** operate European coach/camping tours which spend between 3 and 17 days in Turkey, and include Istanbul, Gallipoli, Ephesus, Pamukkale and Göreme.

While campsites in Turkey are few in number, those registered with the Ministry of Culture and Tourism, especially those owned by the Mocamp Kervansaray chain, are usually clean, well maintained and well located near tourist centres and principal roads. There are no guarantees of comfort or cleanliness if you choose sites which are not registered.

COST-CONSCIOUS HOLIDAYS

If the cost of your holiday is your main consideration, the best advice is to shop around and get hold of as many brochures as possible. It is also advisable to avoid peak season – and peak prices – by planning your holiday for late spring or early autumn. But remember, at the end of the day you'll get what you pay for, and if you decide to go off-season you can't expect to enjoy all the facilities of the high season.

Some companies who operate holidays in Turkey now offer a facility whereby they provide a choice of dates, destinations, flights and accommodation and allow you to plan your own individual package to suit your budget. Other companies give you a completely free hand in planning a tailor-made package. Operators who offer this type of flexibility include **Blue Spot Travel, Celebrity Holidays, The Personal Travel Company, Regent Holidays, Steepwest Holidays, Sunquest Holidays** and **Tourkey**. Your travel agent will be able to give you up-to-the-minute advice on the latest special offers.

Another way to reduce costs is to book at the last minute, taking pot luck on where you land. The Air Travel Advisory Bureau on 01-636 5000 or 061-832 2000 provides information on the best last-minute flight deals plus villas, hotels and apartments, and their service is free.

CRUISES

Cruising in Turkey's beautiful waters is definitely 'in', and every year there is a wider range of cruises to choose from. If you have money to spend on a luxury cruise **P&O** is the name to look out for. **Canberra** and **Sea Princess** are divisions of P&O and between them they offer a good choice of cruises in Turkish waters including 16–20-night cruises which call at Istanbul and Izmir, and 12–13-night cruises which call at several Turkish ports on the Mediterranean and Black Sea coasts. **K-Lines** and **Hellenic** cruises also operate Mediterranean and Aegean cruises which include stops in Turkey.

British Ferries offer a one-week Venice–Istanbul–Kusadasi–Venice cruise which includes a half-day excursion to Ephesus, and **Connection Holidays** offer Turkey–Greece and Turkey–Greece–Italy cruises.

If you want to confine your holiday solely to Turkish waters (with a few Greek islands thrown in for good measure), you can choose from a wide range of competitively priced cruises. Tour operators who offer Turkish cruises, which usually start with a flight from London, include **Aegean Turkish Holidays, Simply Turkey, Small World Holidays, Sunquest Holidays, Timsway Holidays** and **Treselda**.

Some operators, including **Sunquest Holidays** and **Treselda**, offer cruise/resort holidays which allow you to spend a few days in Istanbul or one of the coastal resorts followed by a cruise.

Individual cruising arrangements can be made through **Walford Lines** who are UK agents for Turkish Maritime Lines, the company used by many of the tour operators who offer Turkish cruise packages.

SAILING HOLIDAYS

Sailing along the Turkish coastline is definitely *the* thing to do at the moment – and there are a large number of yacht charter companies who can vouch for that fact. Yacht charter in Turkey has really taken off in the past three years and sailing packages now take a large share of the holiday market. The sailing holidays on offer can be divided into three main categories: skippered yacht charters, independent yacht charters and holidays which combine a week's sailing with a week at one of the coastal resorts.

Skippered yachts, which often sail as part of a flotilla, are the most popular of the three. This type of holiday allows you to enjoy the sun, surf and scenery while the skipper and his crew do all the work (including the cooking). Most of these holidays are centred around Bodrum and the south-west coast and they involve groups of between four and twelve people sharing a yacht on a full-board basis. The cost of the holiday usually includes a flight from Britain.

Skippered yacht charters in Turkey are offered by the following companies: **Aegina Club, Aquarius Cruising, Argosy Cruising, Blue Spot, Yacht Charter Ltd, Bosphorus Holidays, Crestar Yacht Charter, Crusader Cruising, Halsey Marine, McCulloch Marine Charter, Rainbow Sailing, Sundown Yacht Charters, Templecraft Yacht Charters, Top Yacht Charter, The Yacht Cruising Association** and **Liz Fenner Worldwide Yachting**. Some skippered charters, including those offered by **Falcon Sailing**, include free watersports.

If you prefer to go it alone, independent charter packages are available through **Blue Spot Travel, Crusader Cruising, Falcon Sailing, Rainbow Sailing, Sundown Yacht Charters, Templecraft Yacht Charters, Top Yacht Charter** and **The Yacht Cruising Association.**

The majority of combination sailing packages are villa/sailing holidays in the Bodrum area. This type of holiday is offered by **Aegean Turkish Holidays, Falcon Sailing** and **Small World. Rainbow Sailing** offer sail-and-stay holidays in the Bodrum area.

Sailing holidays have enjoyed increasing popularity in the last couple of years. Of the many companies, **YCA** provide a service we can testify as being of good value for money and well organized. Their flotilla holidays take you to some of the most spectacular locations in Turkey and although the initial fee looks a lot, the quality of instruction is good, and the food, drink and accommodation are of a very high standard. Early booking is important for YCA as their 171 boats tend to be taken up by many who return year after year, and their sailing school in Greece is heavily in demand throughout the season. In Turkey, the more experienced sailor will enjoy the route between Datca and Fethiye, and between Kas and Kekova.

VILLA PARTY HOLIDAYS

Villa party holidays, as opposed to self-catering villa holidays, bring together a small crowd of people (usually a group of between ten and twenty) to share a villa which is staffed with a cook and a housekeeper. This way you can relax in a friendly, informal atmosphere while somebody else does the work. The social aspect of a villa party holiday is one of its main attractions, so the tour operator tries to make each group compatible and provides a host of social activities such as drinks parties, barbecues and picnics to help the holiday along. The majority of these holidays combine a week ashore with a week's sailing.

Small World specialize in this type of holiday. Their villa parties are roughly divided into two age groups: twenties to thirties, and thirties to forties (if you're thirty you can decide which group you want to join). Most of the villas are equipped with windsurfers which can be used by guests free of charge. Small World also offer two-centre villa parties and a villa/cruise holiday which combines a week ashore with a week's sailing. All the reports we have on these holidays are very favourable.

CLUB HOLIDAYS

Club holidays have infiltrated the travel market in a big way during the past few years and Turkey is now being featured as a club destination by a number of holiday companies. The idea behind holiday clubs is that all the facilities, entertainment and services you are likely to need are provided by the operator, and everyone staying 'in the club' can enjoy free use of all facilities as part of the deal. As a result many people never leave the confines of the club – which normally takes the form of a large hotel complex or a holiday village. Everything is laid on for you, making this the ultimate 'packaged' holiday. If you're after a quiet time away from the crowds, this type of holiday is definitely not for you, as club holidays are notoriously sociable occasions. If, however, you're travelling alone or as a family with young children, it could be ideal.

While the choice of holiday clubs in Turkey is fairly limited as yet, the companies who have established clubs are among the best. **Club Mediterranée**, who are the world leaders in up-market club holidays, have four international villages: at Foča, Kemer, Kusadasi and Palmiye. Their holidays are geared towards the *bon viveurs* of this world, and encompass all the good points of a package holiday without the bad. From the moment you take off at Gatwick everything is taken care of, and none of the hassles that often accompany travelling to and in Turkey present themselves. The clubs themselves are set in beautiful surroundings: olive groves, white sandy beaches and spectacular scenery, and the facilities in the villages, particularly on the sporting front, are hard to equal. With a choice of swimming, sailing, windsurfing, waterskiing, snorkelling, kayak, archery, tennis, table tennis, aerobics, gymnastics and yoga between the two clubs, there is bound to be something for everyone; and if you're not the sporty type, there's a computer workshop at Foča and an arts and crafts centre at both villages. Excursions to local places of interest run from both sites, and to round off your day there are evening shows, performed by the ever ebullient *gentils organisateurs*, who are there to look after you, entertain you, and teach you whatever their particular skill is, be it sporting or arty. Unlike many club holidays, at Club Med you won't feel like the oldest swinger in town if you're over 25; there are just as many people over this age as under, and children are not regarded as a sub-species to be avoided at all costs, so a family holiday is a definite possibility.

The food and wine (which comes in unlimited supplies) is excellent, and though on first glance at the brochure prices you may feel Club Med are a bit over the top, once you have seen the quantity and quality of the product on offer you will most likely come away feeling it is really exceptionally good value. The edge that Club Med has over their competitors is the 'Frenchness' that inevitably emanates from this terribly Gallic organization: the style and panache with which everything is done, and the accent on the body beautiful, which attracts a fair share of the lotus-eating type clientèle, makes the man-watching by the poolside every bit as interesting as sitting on the promenade des Anglais in Nice!

The nearest British equivalent, **Mark Warner**, who also offers up-market, fun-filled club holidays (their Turkish location to consider is just outside Bodrum) cannot compete with this international feeling as it is a British-run club for up-market Brits. The facilities are good, though not as varied, but if you cannot face the prospect of trying out your Franglais over breakfast, and your O-level German over lunch, perhaps this is more for you.

COACH TOURS

These can be split into two main categories: coach tours in Turkey which commence with a flight from Britain; and coach tours which take you overland to Turkey via several other countries.

A large number of operators offer tours in the first category, but the widest range is offered by **Sunquest Holidays**. Sunquest operate a Crusader Tour which includes Istanbul, the Aegean and Mediterranean provinces and ends with a four-day stay in Alanya; a Cappadocia Tour which is the basic Crusader Tour with additional visits to Konya and Cappadocia; a tour of Lycia and the Turquoise Coast, and a 22-day Grand Tour of central and eastern Turkey. **UK Express** also offers a good range, including tours of eastern Turkey and the Grand Scenic tour.

Hann Overland offer a 16-day tour of Göreme and the south coast and a 22-day steamer/coach tour of eastern Turkey; **Overseas Camping Tours** offer minicoach tours in central and eastern Turkey; **Ramblers Holidays** operate tours to western Anatolia, eastern Anatolia and Cappadocia, and **Golden Horn Travel** offer tours to central and western Anatolia.

While coach tours are an effective way to see the country, they are relatively expensive. Bear in mind that Turkey has an efficient and elaborate network of internal coach services providing cheap local travel, and if you're young and adventurous you can get around without difficulty. Internal coach tours tend to attract the older traveller who prefers to do it the easy way, so check this point with your travel agent before booking. The tours offered by **Hann Overland** and **Overseas Camping Tours** combine coach travel with camping and therefore attract a younger crowd.

The overland coach tours in the second category are generally aimed at the younger market (18–35), but these can last for up to 70 days and may only spend a few days in Turkey.

Top Deck Travel operate 28- to 70-day tours which include visits to Istanbul, Pamukkale and Göreme and **Overseas Camping Tours** also offer overland tours to Turkey.

FLY/DRIVE HOLIDAYS

This type of holiday is becoming increasingly popular in Turkey and is now offered by a large number of tour operators. The fly/drive holiday gives you the chance to see the parts of the country you most want to see, and at your own pace. It is a good compromise for the tourist who dislikes the rigidity of flight/accommodation package deals, but doesn't want the hassle of travelling completely independently.

The cost of a fly/drive holiday usually includes a flight from Heathrow to either Istanbul, Izmir or Antalya, where you collect your car, and car rental for the duration of your holiday (including insurance). Accommodation is not included but most operators offer accommodation in a choice of resorts for an extra charge or will supply a list of reasonably priced hotels, pensions, campsites, etc.

Tour operators who offer fly/drive holidays in Turkey include: **Aegean Turkish Holidays, Aegina Club, Blue Spot Travel, Celebrity Holidays, Golden Horn Travel, Metak Holidays, Regent Holidays, Samson Travel, Simply Turkey, Steepwest Holidays, Sunquest Holidays, Timsway Holidays** and **Treselda**.

The overall cost of a fly/drive holiday is usually more than a straightforward package deal because you have to pay for accommodation, but in Turkey, where accommodation is cheap and independent car hire is incredibly expensive, this type of holiday generally represents good value for money. Fly/drive packages are suitable for groups of up to four people, and they are cheaper per head the larger the group.

ACTIVITY AND SPECIAL INTEREST HOLIDAYS

Watersports, including windsurfing, waterskiing, diving and dinghy sailing, are among the most popular tourist activities in Turkey. A number of tour operators now offer watersport packages which include your flight from Britain, accommodation, specialist instruction and use of equipment. **Falcon Sailing** offer windsurfing and dinghy sailing in Yalikavak and Bitez; **The Yacht Cruising Association** operate windsurfing and dinghy sailing holidays from their clubhouse hotel in Marmaris; **Mark Warner** offer the full range of watersports at their holiday village in Bodrum, as do **Club Mediterranée** at their villages in Kusadasi, Kemer and Foča (though the latter is decidedly up-market and fairly expensive). Holidays specifically designed for the diving enthusiast are offered by **Steepwest Holidays**.

Walking and trekking enthusiasts should check out **Exodus Expeditions** who offer 15- to 24-day walking tours; **Ramblers Holidays** who offer a two-centre walking holiday in Kemer and Side, and **Hann Overland** who offer a 7- to 10-day walking tour of Göreme and short trekking programmes in eastern Turkey. All of these provide exceptional value and are recommended.

Nature-lovers can discover Turkey's nature and wildlife through a number of specialist tours. **Cygnus Wildlife Holidays** operate a birdwatching tour which includes visits to Cappadocia, the Aladaglar

Mountains, the Mediterranean coast and Istanbul and **Simply Turkey** run a wild flowers tour.

Historians and archaeologists can choose from a vast range of cultural tours to Turkey's classical sites. The tours available are many and varied, and most of them have very detailed itineraries. The best thing to do, therefore, is have a good look at the brochures and find the tour which most appeals to you. Some of the tours, like those offered by **Orientours, Serenissima Travel** and **Simply Turkey,** are aimed at the serious historian and archaeologist and often include fairly detailed lectures. Other cultural tours, like those offered by **Aegina Club, Allegro Holidays, Blue Spot Travel, Metak Holidays, Overseas Camping Tours, Sunquest Holidays, Thomson Holidays** and **UK Express**, have a wider and more general appeal. **Swan Hellenic Art Treasure Tours** operate specialist holidays for lovers of art and architecture.

WINTER HOLIDAYS

An increasing number of tour operators are offering city breaks, sightseeing tours and fly/drive touring holidays in Turkey during the winter months. Between October and March the climate in the coastal regions is mild and reasonably dry, but Turkey doesn't really rank as a winter sun destination – even if some tour operators would have you believe otherwise.

Skiing is offered by several operators, including **Bosphorus Holidays** and **Club Turkey**. While Turkey has eight ski resorts, they are somewhat under-developed compared with those in Europe.

If you are prepared to shop around and scan the brochures carefully, you should be able to find a bargain city break. If you're looking for a full sightseeing trip or specialist holiday, you'll probably find winter prices are very similar to summer prices.

SUMMING UP THE PACKAGE SCENE

To sum up, package holidays in Turkey are, in general, very good value for money. At present, because Turkey has not yet broken into the mass tourism market, a basic two-week holiday will usually cost you a little more than the same holiday in Spain or Greece or in other East European countries such as Romania or Bulgaria. The main advantage of this is that you'll be spending your holiday in a beautiful country which is still relatively unspoilt.

With the decline of Spain and the tailing-off of Greece as holiday destinations, it is likely that Turkey's popularity will continue to increase and result in more tour operators entering the Turkish holiday market. The extra competition could result in better prices over the next few years. The choice of holidays available in Turkey is virtually unbeatable, and most activity holidays, whether they involve sailing, watersports, hunting or mountaineering, are reasonably priced compared with other Mediterranean countries.

Turkey is an ideal destination for package holidays which involve touring, sightseeing, walking or trekking because, as yet, few people have discovered the historical and scenic beauty of inland Turkey. Beach holidays in Turkey will also be a refreshing change if you have been used to the crowded resorts of Spain or the South of France.

Camping and coach holidays should be chosen with care, as campsites often fall short of standards in Western Europe and coach tours can be hot and exhausting – particularly in the height of summer.

The diversity of Istanbul, the coastal resorts and the inland regions makes Turkey a popular choice for multi-centre or two-centre holidays, and prices compare favourably with those of other countries.

Checklist

Anyone planning a package holiday should check the following points before booking:

(1) Is your travel agent competent? Unfortunately, many are not, and all too often it's the large chains of high street agents who give the worst advice and service. Try to avoid the obvious trainees when you go into the shop, and have a list of questions prepared so that you don't end up having to make several trips when one would do.

(2) Is your travel agent a member of ABTA? If not, think seriously about finding one who is. It could make a big difference to you if things start to go wrong.

(3) Having chosen your country of destination, do you really know all the holiday options that are available? Many of the smaller tour operators don't get their brochures into the high street travel agents, but that doesn't mean their holidays aren't reliable or worth checking out. Check against the list of operators and phone any likely-looking company for a brochure. Then at least you will know you have chosen the most suitable holiday.

(4) If the travel agent can't book the holiday you finally select, don't necessarily accept his/her substitute recommendation. Have your own second and third options sorted out beforehand, or if there really is no substitute, abandon the whole idea and consider something completely different. Remember that travel agents are in the business of selling holidays on commission – they don't much care what they sell, but they do like to clinch a sale before you leave the shop.

(5) As for the holiday itself . . . check the following before paying your deposit:

(i) Does the holiday price include airport or port taxes and security charges (for both the UK and abroad)?

(ii) Does it include meals on the journey?

(iii) Does it cost extra for a weekend flight or a daytime departure?

(iv) Is transfer between the point of arrival and your hotel included?

(v) Make sure you know on what basis you are booked in at the hotel, i.e. full/half board, or b. & b.

(vi) Are you clear about Supplementary charges made for single rooms, balcony/sea view, private bathroom, etc?

(vii) Is the insurance sufficient for you? Should it cover pregnant women/disabled people/sports holidays? Is the limit of personal baggage insurance high enough to cover all you are taking? Does it include a clause on delayed departures for your return journey? What provisions does it make for cancellations? Finally, check that you're clear about the procedure in case of theft or loss – often these matters have to be reported to the police within a specified time limit and a police report procured.

(6) And finally, before handing over your money, be sure to ask:

(i) What the position is on cancellations (from both parties' point of view).

(ii) What happens if your holiday is altered significantly – under the ABTA code you must be told and given the choice of accepting the new hotel/resort/flight, etc., or opting for a full refund. (Alterations caused by bad weather or industrial disputes will only be covered by your insurance.)

(iii) What is the score on over-booking? Is there 'disturbance' compensation to be paid? (There should be under the ABTA code.) Will the alternative accommodation be of an equally high standard? (It must be under the ABTA code.)

Once you have gone through all these points you should have a clear understanding of the contract you are signing and your travel agent will undoubtedly be in such awe of your intimate knowledge of the travel industry that you will receive preferential treatment all the way!

If, despite all this groundwork, you still have cause for complaint, ABTA's address is 55 Newman Street, London W1N 4AH. Write to them with full details of your complaint and enclose copies of all your correspondence with the travel agent or tour operator.

The Options for Independent Travel

Accommodation

If you decide to go it alone to Turkey there are several options open to you, but finding good accommodation in Turkey isn't always easy, particularly as you move away from the major cities and resorts.

Good hotels are not evenly distributed around the country. The best hotels, not surprisingly, are located in the main cities of Istanbul, Ankara and Izmir and in the major resorts on the Aegean and Mediterranean coasts. Outside the tourist regions of Cappadocia and Konya, inland Turkey has little to offer in the way of good hotels, which can be disappointing for the holidaymaker who wishes to avoid the main tourist centres.

If you are prepared to accept basic accommodation, hotels in Turkey are generally very cheap. Many hotels are now registered with the Ministry of Culture and Tourism and classified according to set standards and the facilities offered. The ratings, however, are not totally reliable as the system of classification is somewhat arbitrary, and a reasonable hotel will often have a low rating simply because it does not have a restaurant. There are five classifications ranging from deluxe to very basic. A double room in a deluxe hotel (Class L), which you will only find in the cities, is likely to cost between £50 and £70 a night. A Class 1 hotel will cost about £25 a night, a Class 2 will cost about £15 a night and a Class 3 will cost from about £10 a night. You can find a double room in a very cheap hotel or pension (Class 4) for as little as £5 a night, but expect standards to be correspondingly low. Standards of comfort and cleanliness can't really be guaranteed in accommodation below Class 1. Unregistered hotels are often as good as registered hotels, but you should ask to see your room before booking. Note that even better hotels sometimes don't provide lavatory paper or second linen on beds, so always ask first.

If it's a low-budget holiday you want, you'll have no difficulty finding rock-bottom accommodation – particularly in the remoter regions, where you'll be lucky to find anything else. If you're not on a shoe-string budget and you want a reasonable degree of comfort it's advisable to book in advance where possible, especially if you're outside the main tourist areas.

For the independent traveller the main alternatives to hotels are pensions, which are usually very small, basic, family-run hotels, and village rooms which are small rooms within the home of a Turkish family. Because accommodation is so cheap in Turkey there is little demand for hostels. If you are a student, a teacher or the holder of an International Youth Hostelling Card it is possible to stay in youth hostels, but very few tourists do. The majority of hostels are located near the cities and are used by students attending nearby universities. The only other alternative for the cost-conscious traveller is camping, but good campsites are still relatively thin on the ground in Turkey. If you are looking for a comfortable campsite (with electricity and running water) the name to look out for is **Mocamp Kervansaray**. There are only about ten of these sites dotted around the country but they all offer high standards and reasonable rates. It's possible to find fairly good sites, registered with the Ministry of Culture and Tourism, on most of the principal tourist routes. Camping on unregistered sites is only for the hardy and the adventurous.

If you're planning to travel independently and you know your route, you can contact **Touropa Britain Ltd**, who specialize in booking accommodation for the independent traveller through a computerized reservation system. If you're planning a camping holiday write to the Turkish Tourism and Information Office in London and ask for their leaflet *Camping in Turkey*.

By Air

If you wish to fly to Turkey the first thing to do is go to a good travel agency and gather as much information as possible on the different flights available.

If you're a student, under twenty-two and the holder of an International Student Identity Card, Turkish Airlines (THY) will give you an incredible 60 per cent discount on their international flights from Britain. USIT, the student and youth travel specialists, offer a return for under £150 to Istanbul in summer. Any student under 32, holding an ISIC card is eligible. Otherwise, unless money is no object, you won't want to pay the full return fare for a scheduled flight from London to Istanbul which starts at just over £600. The PEX ticket (at about £250 return) is your cheapest option with a scheduled flight, but this gives you no flexibility with dates and has to be paid for at the time of booking (fourteen days minimum in advance).

The best way to fly to Turkey is on one of the cheap charter flights now offered by many package tour operators. A charter flight from London to one of the major Turkish airports will cost, on average, between £150 and £200, depending on when you fly and who you fly with. In most cases you will be asked to pay a token charge for accommodation (usually £1) so that the tour company can legally claim to be selling a package holiday with travel and accommodation. This move is necessary to get round the law on the sale of inclusive air holidays.

Tour operators who offer flight-only deals to Turkey include **Aegean Turkish Holidays**, **Allegro Holidays**, **Blue Spot Travel**, **Celebrity Holidays**, **Golden Horn Travel**, **Holidayrama**, **Island Sailing**, **Metak Holidays**, **Regent Holidays**, **Samson Travel**, **Saville Travel**, **Simply Turkey**, **Steepwest Holidays**, **Sunquest Holidays**, **Timsway Holidays**, **Top Yacht Charter**, **Treselda**, **Turkish Delight Holidays** and **Wings**.

The tour operators use a number of airlines, but the majority of flights are with Turkish Airlines, British Airways, British Airtours and Air Europe. Charter flights are generally from Heathrow and Gatwick but they are restricted to the Turkish airports used by the tour operators like Istanbul, Ankara, Izmir, Antalya and Dalaman.

Charter flights undoubtedly offer one of the cheapest and easiest ways to travel to Turkey, and their availability should increase during the next few years as more package tour operators expand their interests to this country.

Bucket shops and Sunday newspaper advertisements are alternative ways of finding cheap flights to Turkey, but you should always read the small print very carefully before booking. Wherever you look, you're unlikely to find anything cheaper than a charter flight with a package operator.

By Sea

There is no direct route from the UK to Turkey by sea. While arriving by sea is the most romantic way to catch your first glimpse of the Istanbul skyline, it's not an easy option unless you consider one of the cruises available (see p. 93).

If you don't wish to forgo your independence by booking a cruise, the alternative is to make your own way to either Italy or Greece and from there complete the journey to Turkey by boat. Turkish Maritime Lines operate regular services from Ancona and Venice in Italy and from the Greek islands of Rhodes, Samos, Khios and Kos. A Greek company called Libra Maritime operate a route between Brindisi in Italy and Izmir.

Unless you are determined to arrive in Turkey by boat, this type of travel must come low on the list of practical options as it is neither cheap nor convenient. The journey from Italy to Turkey can take between two and three days, schedules are unreliable and fares are relatively high. On Turkish Maritime Lines you can pay between £100 and £300 for cabin accommodation, about £80 for a reclining seat and a further £100 if you wish to take your car. The journey from Greece is a lot shorter, but you will find Greeks most uncooperative when it comes to arranging travel to Turkey, so try to make your booking in advance.

On international routes Turkish Maritime Lines offer student reductions of 15 per cent on a single ticket and 25 per cent on a return ticket. Reductions of 50 per cent are available on domestic services.

If your heart is set on that romantic view of the skyline, you'd do well to take a charter flight to Istanbul and then treat yourself to a cheap boat trip up the Bosphorus.

By Car or Campervan

The drive from the UK to Turkey can be long and arduous, particularly if tackled during the peak season when both sun and tourists are out in force. The journey from London to Istanbul is approximately 2000 miles and will involve at least four days of constant driving. Driving to Turkey is only an economical option if there are three or four of you sharing the car, the petrol costs and the ferry fares.

The journey to Istanbul starts at Dover with a ferry to Ostend and from there the quickest route is through Brussels, Cologne, Frankfurt, Nuremburg, Linz, Vienna, Budapest, Zagreb, Belgrade, Nis, Sofia and Edirne. Alternatively, you can break off at Frankfurt and head for Stuttgart, Munich, Salzburg and Ljubljana and rejoin the route at Zagreb. If you take this route it is possible to drive from Munich to Italy and take a car ferry from Ancona to one of the Aegean or Mediterranean ports.

To enter Turkey by car or campervan you'll need an international driving licence and a Green Card international insurance certificate endorsed for both Europe and Asia. For visits of up to three months no additional documentation is required, and your car will simply be registered on your passport as imported goods and the registration cancelled when you leave. For visits of more than three months you require a special permit called a 'triptique' which can be obtained from the Turkish Touring and Automobile Club, Halaskargazi Caddesi 364, Sisli, Istanbul. If you wish to leave your car in Turkey while you visit another country, it must be placed under customs seal until you return.

In order to enter Bulgaria en route to Istanbul, British citizens need a transit visa. This can usually be obtained at the Bulgarian border, but the position changes from time to time so it's advisable to check with your travel agent when planning your holiday. If you wish to apply for a visa in advance you should contact the Bulgarian Legation, 24 Queen's Gate Gardens, London SW7.

Driving in Turkey is on the right-hand side of the road and the Turkish highway code is similar to that of most European countries. Speed limits are 50 kph (about 32 mph) in town and 90 kph (58 mph) out of town. The major roads are asphalt and are generally well maintained, but you will also come across secondary roads which have a gravel surface. In general traffic is lighter than at home – outside of large towns, that is – and driving can be a scenic and rewarding experience. Check your insurance carefully before leaving.

Petrol is relatively cheap compared with Western European countries, but prices fluctuate from one town to another depending on how close the filling station is to the refinery. If you're travelling in the remoter regions, it's a good idea to fill up wherever and whenever you can, as filling stations are not always easy to find.

If you have an accident while on holiday you should report it to the police immediately, even if nobody is injured. If your car should break down you'll find plenty of garages in the main towns and on all the principal routes. Nevertheless, make sure you have your car thoroughly checked and serviced before leaving home and if there are any spare parts you're likely to need, take them along just in case. Unless you drive a Renault or a Fiat like most Turks, spare parts may be hard to come by.

Everyone has their own preference when it comes to a driving holiday, but speaking as someone who has driven round the Continent in everything from a Daimler limousine to a battered old Mini, I feel it's worth putting in a word here about what to look for when choosing a car to drive abroad in. Obviously luggage capacity is an important consideration. Fuel economy, spare parts and comfort are the other major considerations. Don't try to squeeze too many people into a car, and remember, you'll return with more than you set out with. When we were researching this section of the guide we used our Honda Legend Saloon, which over any other car we'd tried gave us the best in terms of comfort, room and efficiency. It's worth bearing in mind if you intend doing a lot of holiday motoring, or if you're in a position to hire out one. A car with a bit of extra power is well worth having on long journeys – and safer.

By Bus

The choice of bus services, other than coach tours, from the UK to Turkey is very limited. There are a few companies who offer an overland service through Europe with an overnight stop in Yugoslavia, but the fares are not particularly cheap and it's not a comfortable way to travel.

Supabus operate a service from London to Istanbul with fares starting at around £115 single and £140 return. **Overseas Camping Tours** offer singles to Istanbul from around £70 and singles to Izmir from £80. The journey by bus takes approximately three days, including your overnight stop, and the buses are usually very basic (don't expect a video and a bar). It is also necessary to obtain a transit visa if the route includes Bulgaria.

There is a better choice of service from France and Germany, but even then the discomfort and the length of the journey make this a trip only to be undertaken by the stalwart. When you consider the amount of travelling time involved and the cost of the trip, it may make more sense to book a cheap charter flight and travel in comfort.

By Rail

If the bus trip from the UK to Turkey is bad, the train journey is far worse. The gruelling five-day journey is likely to leave you exhausted and disillusioned for the rest of your holiday, and it can also work out expensive unless you're under twenty-six and eligible for an Inter Rail Card.

British Rail offer tickets from London to Istanbul for £117.30 single and £229.30 return. If you are under twenty-six you can purchase an Inter Rail Card for £155 which entitles you to free rail travel throughout Europe including Turkey and Morocco. Note that the card is not valid in Bulgaria so you are liable to have to pay an extra charge at the border. Transalpino also offer a special London–Istanbul rail fare of £185 return for travellers under twenty-six. Their full return fare is also £229.30. The route from London takes you through Dover, Ostend, Munich, Stuttgart, Zagreb, Belgrade and Sofia. Again, you will require a transit visa for entry to Bulgaria. Alternatively you can travel from Venice or Munich on the *Istanbul Express*, or from Vienna on either the *Istanbul Express* or the *Balkan Express*. In theory this should reduce your travelling time slightly, but in practice it seldom does as connections from London can be difficult, trains rarely run to schedule and long delays are not uncommon. If you are at all interested in Ottoman architecture, consider getting off the train before Istanbul at Edirne where the Sblimiye mosque is a magnificent example of this style.

Unless you can afford to travel first class, the train journey through Europe can, at best, be described as unpleasant. The trains are often packed with Turks returning from a few months' work in Europe who are happy to suffer the discomfort in order to save money. Second-class carriages are usually cramped and smoke-filled and you'll be lucky to find any kind of catering service.

Train travel to Turkey is not recommended unless you intend to break the journey by visiting several European countries en route.

Hitch-hiking

This option is only for the hardy. It's impossible to say exactly how long it will take to get from Britain to Turkey, but if you bargain on less than four days you're being optimistic. Hitch-hiking in Central Europe can be relatively straightforward, but in Eastern European countries like Yugoslavia and Bulgaria it's not so easy – particularly in Bulgaria, where you'll require a visa for entry.

Once you arrive in Turkey you shouldn't find much difficulty travelling from west to east, but you could have trouble getting to the coastal resorts. Because bus travel is so cheap in Turkey, relatively few people own a private car, and those who do are often reluctant to pick up strangers. As a result, hitch-hikers have to rely on truck drivers who are usually found on the cross-country routes to Syria and Iran.

Useful Information

TIME DIFFERENCES

Turkish time is Greenwich Mean Time plus two hours, with no seasonal change for daylight-saving. This means Turkish time is two hours ahead of British time during the winter, but only one hour ahead during the summer when British clocks go forward to British Summer Time (GMT + one hour).

ELECTRICITY

The voltage in Turkey is 220 volts, 50 cycles AC, as in Europe. A few buildings in Old Istanbul are still on 110 volts, but the voltage is usually marked on the sockets.

WATER

The water in Turkey is perfectly safe to drink, but it often has an after-taste because it is very heavily chlorinated. Most people prefer to drink mineral water which is cheap and plentiful throughout the country.

TURKISH HOLIDAYS

There are three 'moveable feasts' celebrated by the Turks which may affect your holiday. The main national holiday, Kutban Bayram, lasts for four days, and banks can be closed for eight days in a row. Following this feast roads back to Europe are jammed with Turks returning to their jobs and it can take up to six hours to get into Bulgaria at the frontier. The dates of this feast change each year.

Part Three

WHEN YOU'RE THERE

Tourist Information

The Turkish Ministry of Culture and Tourism has information offices (called Turizm Burosu) in all the cities, principal towns and resorts, and they usually have at least one member of staff who can speak English to a reasonable standard. If you need information and you can't find anything which looks like a tourist office, try to find the town hall (Belediye Sarayi). In some smaller towns the town hall has its own information bureau, and even if it hasn't, the staff will try their utmost to help you.

If you're planning to tour the country or you require information about a specific type of holiday (e.g. mountaineering, driving, hunting), you should contact the Turkish Tourism and Information Office in London before you go and ask them to send you information on the parts of the country you intend to visit, or the activity you are particularly interested in. While the main tourist offices in Istanbul, Ankara and Izmir will be able to supply information on the whole country, the smaller offices tend only to provide general information about their own region. Office opening hours fluctuate from town to town, but the larger offices are normally open from 8.30 a.m. to 12.30 p.m. and from 1.30 to 5.30 p.m. As an alternative to tourist offices you can use the larger travel agencies for information on accommodation and excursions, etc.

The Ministry of Culture and Tourism produces useful maps, accommodation lists and brochures which highlight the country's main sites and main cultural events. If you remember to write to them well in advance of your departure, you should have no difficulty obtaining information about any type of holiday in any part of the country.

Sightseeing

Any trip to Turkey is a sightseeing trip, whether you plan it that way or not. There are very few towns or resorts which don't offer something of historical interest for the tourist. Apart from its historic cities and attractive beaches, Turkey also has plenty to offer in the way of natural scenic beauty. The inland regions of LYCIA and CAPPADOCIA are becoming popular destinations for the tourist who enjoys sightseeing, and excursions to these centres are now available from most of the coastal resorts. Whichever resort you choose, you will find reasonably priced excursions on offer to historic and natural sites in the area.

The regions between CENTRAL TURKEY and the AEGEAN and MEDITERRANEAN COASTLINES are ideal for driving/sightseeing holidays because the landscape is very attractive and you can't drive for more than a few miles without stumbling upon a historic site of some description. EASTERN TURKEY is also rich in historic and natural sites, but this part of the country is not so suitable for driving holidays because of the distance between sites and the scarcity of good accommodation. If you really want to see eastern Turkey you'd do better to take an excursion to one of the main sites like NEMRUT DAGI or base yourself in VAN where you'll find reasonable accommodation, attractive scenery, and a concentration of sites in the vicinity. The best historic and natural sites of each region are highlighted in the geographical breakdown of the country later in the book.

Museums and **official sites** are open every day except Monday, with very few exceptions. Admission charges vary from place to place, but they are generally low and students qualify for 50 per cent reductions. If you wish to take photographs in museums or at official sites you will often be asked to pay a small fee which will be related to the admission charge.

The various **festivals** which are held in different parts of the country throughout the year provide an entertaining form of sightseeing if you are interested in Turkey's art, culture and traditional sports. The Ministry of Culture and Tourism produces a calendar of festival days which can be obtained by writing to the Turkish Tourism and Information Office in London. For more details about festivals see 'The Socialite' on p. 29.

Shopping

A holiday in Turkey offers numerous possibilities for shopping. You can choose from the modern shops and boutiques or the colourful bazaars and bustling markets. In general, the shops are open from 9 a.m. to 1 p.m. and from 2 p.m. to 7 p.m., but many of the smaller shops keep longer hours and don't close for lunch.

You can't visit Turkey without visiting one of the country's many bazaars; even if you don't buy anything you'll enjoy the experience. In the bazaars and markets haggling is acceptable, indeed expected, and it offers a novel way of purchasing food and souvenirs. Turkey's most impressive market is undoubtedly the Grand Bazaar in Istanbul. With almost 4000 shops built along several miles of streets, the Grand Bazaar is the world's largest covered market.

You won't find much in the way of up-market department stores in Turkey, but the major cities do offer some exclusive jewellers' shops and fashion shops. In most shops, particularly the larger ones, goods will have a marked price, and if that is the case the shopkeeper will not be prepared to haggle. Some of the larger shops in the cities and principal towns will accept credit cards, but they usually charge you commission of between 5 and 7 per cent.

At the coastal resorts you'll find countless boutiques selling good quality Turkish handicrafts. Some of the best buys are woven rugs and carpets, embroidered headscarves, beaten copper ornaments and jewellery and light cotton dresses and shirts. Many craft shops also sell suede and leather goods, including coats and jackets, which are inexpensive compared with European prices.

You should always have a healthy scepticism about 'bargains'. A number of visitors were ripped off in Marmaris last year buying rugs which subsequently turned out to be worth less than was paid for them – the rugs were delivered to the UK complete with a bill for freight, duty, VAT and handling.

Food and Drink

Eating is certainly one of the highlights of a holiday in Turkey – partly because the food is so good, and partly because it's so cheap. The Turks are expert at taking simple ingredients and turning them into wonderfully tasty and original dishes. As most Turks consider cooking to be a work of art, they will use only the freshest meat and vegetables and take great care over each stage of preparation. As a result, Turkish dishes are of a very high quality, and Turkish cuisine is now considered by many to be second only to French cuisine. Essentially it is derived from the recipes of the peasants of the eastern regions, who originated from Central Asia, but now a strong Mediterranean influence is also detectable. A typical Turkish meal is a strange but complementary combination of Asian and Mediterranean cuisines.

If you're the type of holidaymaker who hopes to find egg and bacon and fish and chips while you're abroad, you'll be sadly disappointed. Otherwise you should find meal times an exciting experience. The average tourist breakfast is nothing to rave about, but lunch and dinner should more than compensate. Eating out in Turkey is by no means an expensive pastime, so you can enjoy the food without worrying about the cost. Whichever part of the country you visit, you'll find good, cheap restaurants open from early in the morning until late at night.

Breakfast in Turkey varies, depending on whether you eat in a hotel or one of the pastry shops. A typical hotel breakfast consists of bread with honey, jam, sheep's cheese and black olives, with a choice of tea or sweetened milk to wash it down. The high points of this type of breakfast are the bread, which is usually fresh and crusty, and the refreshing Turkish tea. If you prefer coffee with your breakfast, it's a good idea to take instant coffee and ask your waiter for hot water. Turkish coffee is very thick and sweet and is usually taken after dinner rather than at breakfast time. Most hotel restaurants will boil an egg for you on request, but bacon is very hard to find as pork is a forbidden food in the Muslim religion. If you visit a pastry shop early in the morning it's not uncommon to find chicken soup and cheese pastries on the breakfast menu.

Lunch and dinner are the main meals of the day: you can eat a large meal at lunchtime or in the evening, whichever you prefer. If you're on a package holiday on a half-board basis, check whether you are given this kind of flexibility. It may be that you have to take your meal in the evening.

Most Turkish meals begin with a selection of hors d'oeuvres (*meze*) which include pickled vegetables, stuffed vine leaves, potato fritters, aubergine purée, tiny cheese pastries and a variety of exotic salads. The most famous *meze* is *dolma*, which is a pepper or aubergine stuffed with rice, pine nuts and currants.

When you are choosing a main course you'll always find lamb, fish, pilaf and aubergine featuring high on the menu. Kebabs are one of the favourite ways to eat lamb. You can choose either a 'sis kebap', which is pieces of meat and vegetables cooked on a skewer, or a 'doner kebap', which is thin slices of charcoaled meat eaten with bread and salad. Lamb casseroles and moussaka-type dishes which combine meat with aubergines, tomatoes and garlic are also very popular. Fish dishes are excellent, especially in Istanbul and the coastal resorts. The most popular fish are tunny (*palamut*), sea bass (*levrek*), sardines (*sardalya*), swordfish (*kilic baligi*) and turbot (*kalkan*). Fish is normally grilled or poached with vegetables and herbs. Pilaf (*pilav*) is a Turkish speciality. A basic pilaf is rice or cracked wheat boiled in either meat stock or tomato stock. This can be varied by adding either nuts, currants and onions or meat and vegetables. Another speciality is *borek* which is layers of flaky pastry stuffed with cheese or meat. If you visit a restaurant and you don't understand the menu, you'll probably be invited into the kitchen where you can inspect the pots and make your own selection.

A variety of snacks, including tasty grilled sandwiches and savoury pastries, are also available throughout the day. A favourite Turkish snack is *lahmacun*, which is a soft pizza topped with lamb, onion and tomato.

Turkish desserts are either milk-based like rice pudding (*sutlac*), or very sweet but delicious pastries which are soaked with syrup or honey and stuffed with fruit and nuts (*baklava*). If you want to avoid heavy desserts you can ask for 'krem karamel' or a selection of fruit, which will usually include delicious melon and peaches.

With the exception of yoghurt, Turkish dairy products are disappointing. Milk and butter are not up to European standards, and cheeses, which are made with goat's milk or sheep's milk, have a dry and bitter taste. Turkish natural yoghurt is very good, and when whisked with cold water it becomes drinking yoghurt (*ayran*). It is used as an ingredient in many dishes and is often used as a dressing for salad.

Some of the specialities to look out for are:

Kadin Budu – meatballs with fried rice
Kuzu Dolmasi – baked lamb stuffed with rice
Kilic Sis – charcoaled swordfish
Hunkar Begendi – stewed lamb with aubergines
Asure – a boiled pudding with nuts and figs
Kabak Tatlisi – pumpkin cooked with sugar and nuts

If you are eating out, there is a choice of several types of cafés and restaurants. A *restoran* or *lokanta* is the standard type of restaurant which usually has table service and a full lunch or dinner menu. A *hazir yemek* is a 'ready food' restaurant where various soups and stews are made early in the morning and heated up on demand. (These are basically working-class cafeterias with table service.) The food is generally good, but it usually tastes better at lunchtime than it does in the evening. A *kebapci* is a restaurant which specializes in roast meats. Here you can eat kebabs, rissoles, meatballs, cutlets, soup and salad. A *bufe* is a café/snack bar which sells sandwiches, pizzas, pastries and puddings, and a *kuru yemis* is a snack stand which sells dried fruit and nuts and a selection of confectionery. If you wish to eat European food (the kind you're used to at home), you'll have to visit a restaurant in one of the expensive international hotels.

For value for money you should choose a smallish family-run restaurant which sells authentic Turkish food. If you dine out in a hotel you're likely to pay a lot more for the same meal. An average lunch or dinner, with wine, will probably cost less than £5, though you can eat for less if you wish. If you pay more than this you'll probably be paying for better service, comfort or atmosphere rather than better food.

Drinking in Turkey is a varied and inexpensive pastime. The Turkish state-owned company Tekel produces much of the country's wine and beer and all its spirits. Spirits which are not produced by Tekel are imported by the government and are consequently expensive.

Turkish wines come as a most pleasant surprise to the British, who do not associate the country with quality wines. Tekel produces a variety of red and white wines, ranging from just-about-drinkable cheap table wine to moderately-good expensive wines. Most restaurants also stock wines produced by the two major private companies, Doluca and Kavaklidere, who produce a large range of quality wines (not quite up to the standards of French wine, but perfectly acceptable). If you're looking for a cheap but palatable table wine, try those produced by Doruk and Dimitrakopulo.

Among the best beers in Turkey are those produced under licence by Tuborg. The Turks are great drinkers of beer (*bira*), and most restaurants and bars sell light beer (*beyaz*), which is similar to our lager, and dark beer (*siyah*). The local brew produced by Tekel is a mild and slightly flat dark beer, but the private company Efes Pilsen brew good light and dark beers. It's considered 'good form' by the Turks to eat with your drink, so you may well be offered peanuts or hazelnuts when you order your beer. Beer prices are fairly reasonable.

Turkey's national drink is a strong spirit called raki, which means 'lion's milk' when translated. Raki is a clear, aniseed-flavoured drink which turns cloudy when mixed with water (similar to French Pernod). Turks usually drink raki with their meals, but if you're not used to strong spirits you're better off sticking to wine. Tekel also produces its own brands of gin, vodka, brandy and whisky which are easily recognizable by their Turkish names (*cin*, *votka*, *kanyak* and *viski*). While the gin, vodka and brandy are perfectly acceptable, the whisky is more an acquired taste.

In the soft drinks range you can choose from Turkish lemonade (*Yedigün*), Turkish orangeade (*Fruco*), Pepsi and Coke. If you want a healthy, refreshing drink, try the natural drinking yoghurt (*ayran*) or one of the sparkling mineral waters (*maden sodasi*).

Turkish coffee (*kahve*) is strong, sweet and gritty, but it's the only type of coffee to be found outside the expensive international hotels. Coffee tends to be an after-dinner drink, but Turkish tea (*cay*), which is full of flavour and very refreshing, is consumed at all times of day.

Nightlife

If your idea of a good night out is relaxing over a leisurely meal, you've picked the right country. If you select a good restaurant in any of the larger towns or resorts, you can enjoy a slap-up meal for two, with wine, for less than £10. For a little extra you can combine your meal with a cabaret-type show in one of the larger hotels. If you are staying in Istanbul, it's possible to dine while enjoying a romantic boat trip along the Bosphorus.

If raving into the small hours is more your scene, you'll probably have to content yourself with a poor imitation of a Western European nightclub. Discos and nightclubs in the major cities are generally over-priced and over-rated. You'll find the best discos are those laid on by the hotels in the larger coastal resorts, which give you the opportunity to meet your fellow holidaymakers. Some of the livelier resorts are KUSADASI, BODRUM, MARMARIS and ALANYA – if this type of nightlife is high on your list of priorities you should choose your resort carefully or you could be disappointed.

There is a lot of Turkish folk music, and each region has its own folk dance and traditional costume. The various festivals which are held in different parts of the country throughout the year also provide a good night out if it's authentic Turkish entertainment you're looking for. Some of the festivals to look out for are the International Istanbul Festival (20 June–15 July); Bodrum Art and Culture Week (1–9 September); the Marmaris Music and Art Festival (8–17 June); and the Mevlana Commemorative Festival (9–17 December).

If you go to Turkey hoping to see some authentic, traditional belly-dancing you could be sadly disappointed, as this ancient art seems to be dying out with increasing Westernization and the arrival of tourism. Visit one of the small, downtown clubs frequented by Turks and you're likely to witness a show which borders on the cheap and nasty and has little to do with art or culture. The alternative is to visit one of the larger hotels (though this is more expensive) to see the sort of show tourists want.

Classical concerts, theatrical shows and opera can normally be found in Istanbul, Ankara and Izmir. In the larger towns you may find a cinema showing a British film, but you'll have to ignore the sub-titles.

For more details about nightlife and festivals see also pp. 29 and 152.

Communications

It isn't particularly easy to keep in touch with home from Turkey. While it is possible to phone, telex and write to Britain, the speed and efficiency of services leave great scope for improvement.

POST OFFICES

Post offices are usually located in the main squares of towns and cities and can be recognized by a yellow sign bearing the black initials PTT (Posta, Telefon, Telgraf). Major post offices are open from 8 a.m. to midnight from Monday to Saturday, and from 9 a.m. to 7 p.m. on Sundays. Small offices are open from 8.30 a.m. to 12.30 p.m. and from 1.30 p.m. to 5.30 p.m. from Monday to Friday. You can use post offices to buy stamps and telephone tokens, to make telephone calls and to send letters and telegrams.

If you wish to send a parcel home from one of the cities you must go to a special parcel post office (Paket Postahane) where your package will undergo a customs inspection. This normally involves a lot of red tape, and the process is so slow you begin to wonder if it's worth the bother. In small towns you'll probably find that the PTT office also serves as a Paket Postahane and the formalities usually take a lot less time.

Poste restante is only available at the central post offices (Merkez Postahane) in the major cities. Poste restante mail should be addressed Poste Restante, Merkez Postahane, followed by the city of your choice (Istanbul, Ankara or Izmir).

TELEPHONES

PTT operate two telephone systems: one with operator service, and one automatic. Both systems are cheap but they tend to be slow and inefficient. For a long-distance call you can use either system, but don't promise to phone home unless you really have to. If you use an operator-type phone you place your call with the operator and then you wait . . . and you wait . . . and you wait. If you're lucky you may wait only five minutes, but don't be surprised if you're still there half an hour later. When you place your call you can tell the operator how urgent your call is. *Normal* means not urgent, *acele* means urgent and *yildirim* means very urgent. Unfortunately, this system seems to determine how much your call will cost rather than how long it will take to get through. Beware of making long-distance calls from your hotel, as you will be charged a hefty commission. To use the automatic system you must first buy tokens (*jetons*) from the post office and then find an international automatic call box (*milletlerarasi*). This system doesn't necessarily make the process any quicker, as you'll probably have to stand in a queue and when you eventually get to the phone it's quite possible that the international lines will be engaged . . . so back to the end of the queue. Local calls are easier. Simply buy your tokens, dial your number and place a token in the slot when your call is answered.

Moving Around the Country

Compared with Western European countries, relatively few people in Turkey own a car, and the Turks therefore rely heavily on public transport and private bus operators. As a result, Turkey has a most impressive network of internal transport which makes moving around the country easy and inexpensive.

BUSES

There are literally hundreds of private coach operators providing an elaborate network of bus services which covers the entire country, from the large cities to the smallest of towns. The bus trade is very competitive and, as a result, fares are cheap and services frequent. In the cities and principal towns you will find bus terminals, while in the smaller towns buses normally leave from the main square. Whichever the case, you'll always hear booking clerks trying to out-shout each other with fares and destinations. If possible, visit the terminal or town square the day before your trip to check departure times and the availability of seats. For busy routes it's advisable to buy a ticket in advance. Buses are the most popular mode of internal transport in Turkey, mainly because they are cheap and in many cases quicker and more comfortable than trains. Free mineral water is always available on buses, and longer journeys include stops for refreshments.

This type of bus travel is a lot cheaper than the organized coach excursions you will find on offer, but bear in mind that excursions are not only less hassle but usually involve a round trip which takes you to more than one town or place of interest.

THE *DOLMUS*

This is a cab or a minibus which has the destination and fare displayed in the front window, and the driver leaves when every seat is taken. Payment is made en route or when you reach your destination. This is a quick and cheap means of transport which is ideal for short journeys in and around town or between towns.

TRAINS

Turkish Railways (TCDD) are state-owned, and services in general tend to be slow but are improving each year. Train services connect most of the cities and principal towns, but large stretches of coastline are unserved. While fares are inexpensive, the trains can be busy and booking is essential. If you choose to travel by train it's better to travel at night and book a sleeping couchette; if you must travel by day it's advisable to go first class. The best train is the Blue Train (Mavi Tren) which provides the express service between Istanbul and Ankara – even then it takes seven and a half hours. Other than the Blue Train, don't consider taking any train which isn't called *Ekspresi* or *Mototren*, or you could be in for a long and tedious journey.

If you wish to travel on the Blue Train or on any of the better trains, you should book as far in advance as possible, particularly if you want to reserve a couchette or a first-class seat. To purchase a ticket or make a reservation you must go to the station you will be departing from. Students with an International Student Identity Card qualify for 20 per cent reductions on train fares.

CAR HIRE

Because private cars are still something of a luxury to most Turks, car rental is very expensive. In fact, a week's car hire in Turkey can cost almost as much as a complete two-week package holiday. Rates vary, but a week's rental with unlimited mileage and insurance can cost between £200 and £250. This is the price for a small or medium-sized car, usually a Renault or a Fiat which has seen better days.

Admittedly, Turkey is the ideal country for a driving holiday – but there are cheaper ways of doing it. Many tour operators now offer fly/drive holidays (see 'Who Specializes in What', p. 90) which include prearranged car hire and usually work out cheaper in the long run.

If you do decide to hire a car, you'll find international car rental companies in Istanbul, Ankara, Izmir, Bodrum, Marmaris, Kusadasi and Antalya. Most companies will allow you to collect your car in one city and leave it in another, and most will accept widely known credit cards for payment. You will need an international driving licence.

Avis, the largest car hire company in Europe, are among the best. They operate in ninety-three countries and their prices are among the most competitive. It's best to hire your car *in the UK* before you go. This way you get a guaranteed price in sterling which cannot be altered whatever happens to exchange rates, and you also have much more of a comeback if things go wrong. You can book either through your travel agent, or an Avis office. In Turkey Avis operate in many towns and cities, including all the major resorts, with more than one office in many towns.

Hertz operate their 'Europe on Wheels' programme in Turkey. Pre-booking in the UK will allow you to take advantage of their special rates.

Europcar's Super Drive service is also worth considering. Cars can be ordered before leaving the UK, with just a minimum 24 hours notice necessary. *Budget rent-a-car*, the world's number three, are well worth considering for a vehicle. Operated under licences, they have a comprehensive insurance and can be found in even the smallest locations. Today you can find Budget in every Western European country, including Yugoslavia, making them a serious contender for the package holiday market. The travel and leisure programmes they offer vary from year to year, but there will always be one aimed at the holiday market so enquire at any local Budget office.

FLIGHTS

Turkish Airlines (THY) operate domestic flights between all the major cities and to many of the principal towns. If you wish to travel from one side of the country to another, flying is probably the only practical option, as a train or bus trip from Istanbul to Van takes approximately two days. It is also the best way of travelling in eastern Turkey, if you want to cover a lot of ground, because of the vast distances involved.

Fares are a little cheaper than fares for domestic flights in most parts of Europe, but flight schedules can be somewhat erratic. Don't plan to fly anywhere without first checking availability, as internal flights are very busy. Where possible, buy tickets well in advance. THY offer 10 per cent reductions for students with an International Student Identity Card.

BOATS

Turkish Maritime Lines operate an Aegean/Mediterranean service (*Akdeniz*) which sails from Istanbul to Iskenderun in ten days, calling at several ports including Izmir, Kusadasi, Bodrum, Antalya and Alanya, and a Black Sea service (*Karadeniz*) which sails from Istanbul to Hopa in nine days, calling at all the principal ports en route. TML also offer a number of cruises in the Aegean and Mediterranean and run many local services and ferry boats in the Sea of Marmara and across the Bosphorus.

The Aegean/Mediterranean and Black Sea services are good for travelling from one port to another, but they are not really sightseeing trips as they make only a brief call at each port. Fares are very cheap, and the boats are old and colourful. Reductions of up to 50 per cent are available for students and teachers. Journalists and family groups also qualify for discounts on some services.

TAXIS

Taxis other than the shared taxis (*dolmus*) are expensive and not really worth considering unless you want to get to an airport or a station in a hurry. If you do use a taxi, always state your destination and check the fare before setting off. In the larger cities most taxis have a meter which should be switched on at the start of the journey. In other towns taxis will carry a tariff which you should ask to see. In Istanbul there is sometimes neither meter nor tariff, in which case you'll have to negotiate a fare before accepting the ride.

Problems/Emergencies

MEDICAL

For minor medical problems you'd do best to visit a chemist (*eczane*, *apotheke* or pharmacy), where you'll be able to obtain advice and general medical supplies. If the chemist is closed, or the problem is serious, go to any of the state hospitals. You will be charged a small fee for hospital treatment, but this will be covered by your holiday insurance. (Always keep receipts.)

POLICE

You'll come across three types of police in Turkey: the Jandarma are soldiers employed as policemen to enforce law and order and catch criminals; the Polis are the national force which controls traffic and carries out general policing duties in the towns and cities; and the Belediye Zabitasi are the market police who are more like weights and measures inspectors. In cases of theft or a road accident always inform the Polis, and remember to ask for a copy of your statement for insurance purposes. The Polis can be recognized by their green uniforms and white caps. (Turkey has a refreshingly low crime rate.) Martial law was lifted in all provinces in May 1987.

EMBASSIES AND CONSULATES

The address for the British Embassy is: Sehit Ersan Caddesi 46/A, Cankaya, Ankara (tel: 4-27 43 10). The British Consulates can be found at Mesrutiyet Caddesi 34, Tepebasi, Istanbul (tel: 14 47 540), and the Vice Consulate at Necatibey Bulvari 19/4, Izmir (tel: 51 211795). Contact any of these addresses if you lose your passport or other documents.

WORK

It is extremely difficult for foreigners to gain legal employment in Turkey except with foreign companies which have bases in Turkey.

WOMEN ALONE

Women travelling alone in Turkey may sometimes find the going tough, particularly in the more remote areas. The majority of Turks are Muslim, and Muslim men have an attitude towards women very different from that of Western men. Away from the main holiday centres they are not accustomed to seeing scantily clad unaccompanied women, and if you insist on walking through town in skimpy shorts and T-shirts you can expect cat-calls. If you're unsure about what is considered 'proper', take your lead from the local women. If things get nasty, make as much noise as possible and look for a police officer.

A Potted History

Turkey has had a long and turbulent history, and has witnessed the rise and fall of many great empires. Since earliest times, the country's geographical position between Europe and Asia has made it an inescapable battleground for clashing invaders from East and West. This concise history of the major events which have shaped Turkey's destiny will give you a better understanding of the country's culture, and help you appreciate more fully the art, architecture and historic sites you will inevitably come across.

Early Times

Stone Age artefacts and wall paintings found in the Mediterranean regions show evidence of human life as early as 7500 BC, though it wasn't until the Bronze Age (almost 6000 years later) that cities of any significant size emerged. The first known inhabitants of Turkey were the Proto-Hittites, a Middle Eastern people who eventually took control of central Anatolia and much of Syria. The Hittite Empire started to crumble around 1200 BC, following a mass invasion by the Phrygians (and other sea people) from the Greek islands. By this time, Achaean Greeks had already infiltrated the Aegean coast following their attack on Troy (the famous Trojan War). Western Anatolia was slowly taken over by invaders of Greek and European origin, and as the Hellenic influence grew stronger, it replaced the Hittite culture.

Around 500 BC, the armies of Persia penetrated Anatolia from the east and crept slowly westwards towards the Aegean. Anatolia came under Persian control for two centuries until Alexander the Great crossed the Dardanelles from Macedonia in 334 BC, and thereafter conquered the entire Middle East. When Alexander died at the age of thirty-three, his land was divided up by his generals, which weakened the empire and enabled several small kingdoms to flourish.

The Roman Empire

The Romans were the next major influence on Turkey. Tired of the various Anatolian rulers threatening their growing empire, the Romans decided that life would be easier if they conquered Anatolia, too. By AD 190 they had gained control of the Aegean coast. Sixty years later, on the death of the last king of Pergamon, the most powerful of the Anatolian rulers, his kingdom passed to the Romans. This allowed them to move further inland and establish a capital city at Ephesus.

The birth of Christ in Palestine had a dramatic impact on the Roman Empire. By AD 300, despite severe persecution of Christians, the new religion had spread throughout the empire. In AD 324, when Constantine succeeded Diocletian as Emperor, he declared equality for all religions and put an end to the persecution of the Christians. He built a city on the shores of the Bosphorus at Byzantium, a Greek colony founded 900 years earlier, and made this his new eastern capital in a bid to fend off the Persians who were threatening Ephesus from the south-east. The new capital was later to be named Constantinople.

The Byzantine Empire

As the western Roman Empire was weakened by attacks from the Persians and the European barbarians, the eastern Empire, which became known as Byzantium, gained in strength. It was Constantine's successor, Justinian, who took the Byzantine Empire to its zenith. Under his rule the Byzantine armies recaptured Anatolia and took control of the Balkans, Egypt and North Africa. The first real threat to the Byzantines came with the birth of Islam in the seventh century. Only 100 years after the birth of Mohammed in Mecca in AD 570, the armies of Islam, followers of the new Muslim faith, had conquered the Middle East and were trying to break the Byzantine stronghold in Constantinople.

The Seljuk Turks

The Muslim caliphs (Mohammed's deputies) ruled the Middle East for almost four centuries, constantly challenging Byzantium, until they found themselves confronted by a new force – the Turks themselves. The first Turks, the Seljuks, were descendants of the Mongols, a strong and ambitious people. The Seljuks had already gained strength in eastern Anatolia and could not resist challenging the great power of the Muslims. By the middle of the eleventh century the Turks had captured Persia and Anatolia, and the Seljuk Empire was threatening Byzantium.

The Ottoman Empire

By the late twelfth century, in the aftermath of the Crusades (the Holy Wars), Byzantium was beginning to disintegrate and the Mongol armies of Genghis Khan were threatening the Seljuks. This left Anatolia with several small Turkish/Mongolian emirates which were ruled independently until the Osmanli emirate took the initiative to bring them together. The Osmanli family were courageous fighters and their uniting of the tribes was the beginning of the great Ottoman (Osmanli) Empire.

The Ottomans rapidly gained power, advancing to the east and the west, and in 1453 the Turks captured Constantinople, ending more than nine centuries of Byzantine rule. From then on the Turks seemed invincible. Sultan Suleiman the Magnificent took the empire to its greatest strength, conquering Eastern Europe, the Balkans, the Middle East and North Africa. By the 1520s the Ottoman Empire was posing a real threat to Western Europe – Yugoslavia and Hungary had fallen and in 1529 the Turks were fighting at the gates of Vienna. Though they never managed to penetrate Central and Western Europe, the Turks consolidated their control of the Balkans, Eastern Europe and North Africa. It wasn't until the nineteenth century that decadence, political and social backwardness and internal power struggles seriously eroded the empire's strength and credibility. As the decline took hold, the subjugated areas began to reclaim their independence and Turkey became known as 'The Sick Man of Europe'.

It was then that a new and powerful political movement emerged. The young Turks began to push for the abolition of the Sultanate and the adoption of a Western-style constitution. But it was the First

World War which dealt the final blow to the great Ottoman Empire. Turks sided with Germany and the Axis, and were defeated by the Allies; the Allied forces moved into Istanbul to negotiate the Treaty of Sèvres which divided up the Ottoman Empire.

Kemal Ataturk

It was a young general named Mustafa Kemal who prevented Turkey from being wiped off the map completely. Unhappy with the way his country was being treated, he organized a resistance movement (the National Assembly) based in Angora (Ankara). When Greece in 1919 pre-empted the Treaty of Sèvres and invaded Izmir, this provided the spur the Turks needed to stand up and fight for their country. When the Turks, under the leadership of Kemal, won the War of Independence in 1922, the country's destiny was placed in his hands. Within weeks Kemal had organized elections, and in 1923 the Republic of Turkey was founded, ending 631 years of Ottoman rule. Shortly after this the treaties of the First World War were renegotiated.

Kemal's main aim was to modernize Turkey in line with Western standards, and to this end he introduced a number of swingeing reforms. Islamic law was replaced with Western-style civil law; the Arabic alphabet was replaced with a Latin-based alphabet; symbols of Ottoman backwardness such as polygamy and the fez were outlawed, and women were given the right to vote. Mustafa Kemal changed his name to Kemal Ataturk (Father of Turks), and Turks with only one name were forced to adopt a family name. In 1930 Constantinople was renamed Istanbul, Angora became Ankara, the capital of the new Republic, and the names of many other towns and cities were changed. In little more than ten years Kemal Ataturk bridged the gap of centuries.

Recent Years

Despite Ataturk's achievements, attempts to fully Westernize Turkey have been hindered by political extremism and the reluctance of some

Turks to give up ancient religious traditions. In the early days of the Republic, Ataturk's People's Party was the only recognized political party, but in the late 1940s a democratic constitution was adopted and an opposition party was formed. Since 1950, when the People's Party was first overthrown by the new Democratic Party, the country has struggled to maintain a multi-party system. The foundations of its democracy have been constantly threatened by the infiltration of Marxist extremists and right-wing religious fanatics, and on several occasions the military has stepped in to restore order and prevent political street killings. The last military intervention was in 1980, when cold-blooded political violence had taken the country to the brink of civil war. Since then, the enforcement of martial law and a concerted crackdown on political troublemakers has helped to restore stability. In 1982, a new democratic constitution was drawn up and approved by a 91 per cent referendum. This was followed by a win for the Motherland party in the November election of 1983. Democracy is now fairly established in all Turkey's institutions and full EEC membership was applied for in April 1987.

Part Four

THE COUNTRY

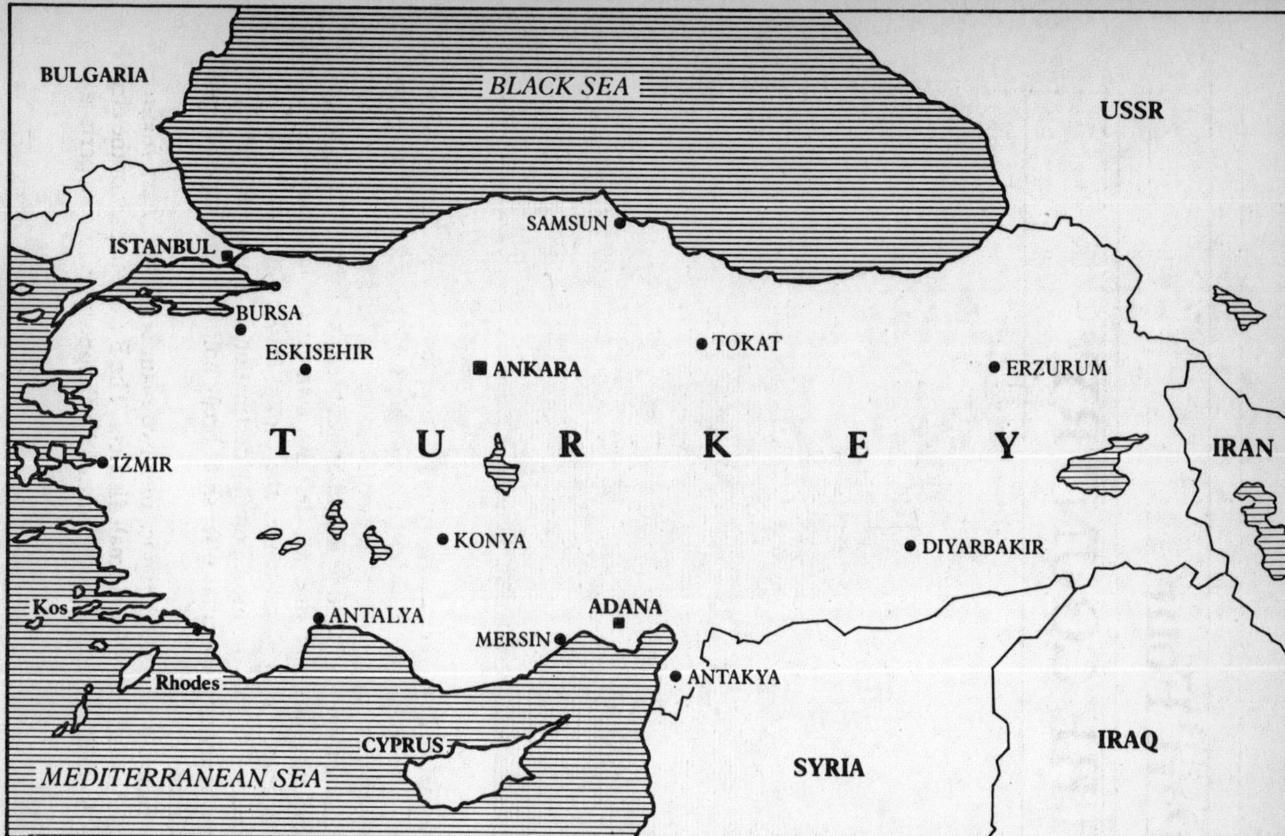
BULGARIA
BLACK SEA
USSR
ISTANBUL
SAMSUN
BURSA
ESKISEHIR
ANKARA
TOKAT
ERZURUM
TURKEY
IRAN
IŻMIR
KONYA
DIYARBAKIR
Kos
ANTALYA
ADANA
MERSIN
ANTAKYA
Rhodes
CYPRUS
MEDITERRANEAN SEA
SYRIA
IRAQ

Istanbul

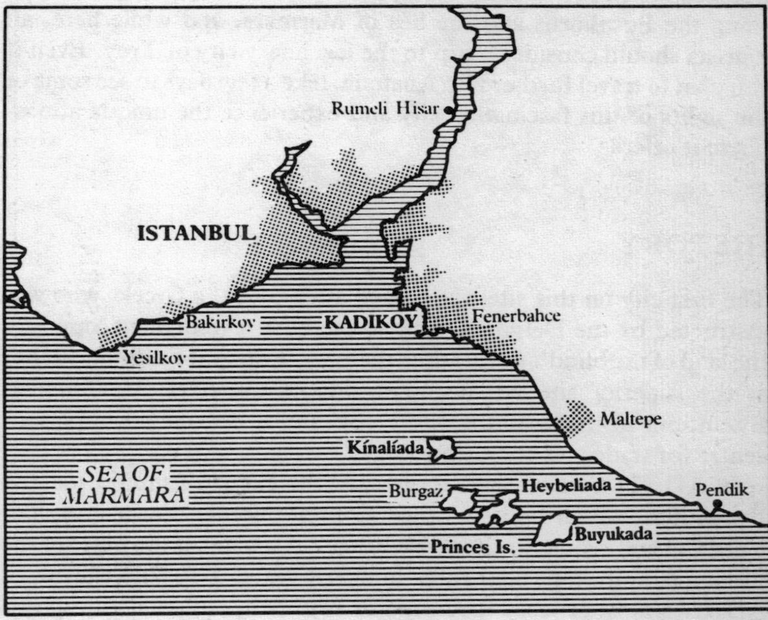

No matter how you travel to Istanbul, your first view of the city will be impressive. It rises beside the blue waters of the Golden Horn and Bosphorus rivers into a dramatic skyline of domes and minarets. Almost three thousand years old, it has been the heart of three world empires and each one has left its own particular mark on the landscape. Though no longer the capital of the Turkish Republic, Istanbul is still the most popular destination in Turkey for tourists and many tour operators offer short break holidays here, especially in winter.

Basically, Istanbul divides into two main areas which are further subdivided into several small districts. The European part of the city is divided by the Golden Horn and the European and Asian parts are separated by the Bosphorus Strait. The vast majority of the sights are on the southern bank of the Golden Horn.

Istanbul is a good centre for *sightseers*, as there is an infinite variety of places to visit – peaceful mosques, awe-inspiring palaces and frenzied bazaars. For *sun-worshippers* there are beaches and resorts along the Bosphorus and the Sea of Marmara, and while here, all tourists should consider a trip to the legendary city of Troy. Even if you plan to travel further into Anatolia, take a few days to see some of the sights of this fascinating city and experience the unique atmosphere it offers.

HISTORY

The first city on this site was named after Byzas, a Greek, who was instructed by the Delphic Oracle to establish a settlement 'opposite the land of the blind'. At this time there was a town at Kadikoy but not at the superior site on the other side of the river. He founded Byzantium in the seventh century BC and it became an important centre for trade and commerce.

In AD 324 Constantine reorganized the Roman Empire, making Byzantium, which he now called Constantinople, the new capital. Enlarged and rebuilt as the 'New Rome', it remained the heart of the Roman Empire for about three hundred years. The Nika Revolt of AD 527 almost deposed the Emperor Justinian, but after widespread devastation he set out to reconstruct the city on an even grander scale. The crowning glory of this period is Aya Sofya, at that time the greatest church in the Christian world.

During the last years of Byzantine rule, the Arabs began to move across Anatolia, and when Mehmet II came to power, he decided to capture Constantinople. The Ottomans besieged the city walls and in 1453 claimed it for Islam. Mehmet the Conqueror, as he was now called, made the new Moslem city of Istanbul the centre of his growing empire. The Golden Age of the Ottoman Empire was during the reign of Suleiman the Magnificent, and during this period Sinan, Turkey's most famous architect, designed many mosques, among them the Suleimaniye Mosque, one of the largest in Turkey.

Istanbul retained its importance into the nineteenth century when the *Orient Express*, the first luxury express train, connected the city with Paris. In 1922, however, when Ataturk founded the Turkish Republic, he moved the government to Ankara and Istanbul became officially a provincial city.

COMMUNICATIONS

Ataturk Airport is located about 23 km outside the city and flights operate from here to airports in Izmir, Ankara, and the other main Turkish cities. Buses run from the airport to the Turkish Airlines Building in Shishane; alternatively, tickets for taxis can be purchased for a standard fare in the Arrivals area.

The European coach terminal is at Topkapi, outside the city walls, and better quality bus companies will provide transport from here to hotel areas by *dolmus*. Asian buses arrive and depart from the bus station at Harem, with connections to all other Turkish destinations, night and day. It is usually quicker to travel long distances by coach than by train, since there are often direct links between cities.

The point of arrival for trains from Europe is Sirkeci Station, which is right in the centre of Istanbul. There is a service from here to the beaches at Florya and Atakoy, but if you want to travel further into Anatolia, you must transfer to Haydarpasa Station in the Asian part of the city. Ferries cross between the two stations every 15–20 minutes. Trains run from Haydarpasa to the beaches on the Asian shore of the Bosphorus and the Sea of Marmara, as well as to Ankara.

Karakoy Maritime Station is the passenger terminal for ships. The trip along the Black Sea coast operates out of here, as do many of the excursions up the Bosphorus.

Tourist information is available from the offices operated by the Ministry of Culture and Tourism and these are open between 8 a.m. and 7 p.m. As well as desks at the airport and at the terminal at Karakoy, there is an office at the Hippodrome near Sultanahmet Square, one near the Blue Mosque and Topkapi Palace and another in the entrance to the Hilton Hotel. These information offices will provide maps and brochures for sightseeing and will also give advice about accommodation.

TOURIST INFORMATION AND USEFUL ADDRESSES

Tourist Information Offices

Regional Directorate of Istanbul,
Mesrutiyet Cad. 57
Galatasaray, Istanbul
Tel: 1432928, 1456875, 1433472 Open 9 a.m.–5 p.m.

Karakoy Maritime Quay
Tel: 1495776 Open 9 a.m.–5 p.m.

At the entrance to the Hilton Hotel
Tel: 1330592 Open 9 a.m.–5 p.m.

Ataturk Airport
Tel: 5737399, 5734136 Open 8 a.m.–8 p.m.

Sultanahmet Square
Tel: 522 49 03 Open 9 a.m.–5 p.m.

Post Office

Merkez Postahane,
Eminonu,
Istanbul
Open 8.30 a.m.–12 midnight Mon.–Sat. Sundays 9 a.m.–7 p.m.

American Express

At the entrance to the Hilton Hotel

Student Travel Organization

Accommodation
Topkapi Ataturk Student Centre,
Londra Asfalti Cevizlibag Duragi,
Topkapi,
Istanbul
Tel: 525 02 80 (Girls)
525 50 32 (Boys)

Train Stations
European Lines: Sirkeci Railway Station
Tel: 527 00 51
Asian Lines: Haydarpasa Railway Station
Tel: 336 04 75

International Airport
Ataturk Airport Tel: 573 35 00
Domestic Routes Tel: 573 1331
International Routes Tel: 573 0433

International Bus Station
Topkapi Bus Station Tel: 5253146
Harem Bus Station Tel: 360080

Tourist Police
Turizm Polisi,
Alemdarkarakolu,
Sultanahmet
Tel: 527 4503

American Emergency Hospital
Amiral Bristol Amerikan Hastanesi,
Guzelbahce Sok,
Nisantasi,
Istanbul
Tel: 131 40 50

Consulates
UK: Mesrutiyet Cad. 26,
Galatasaray,
Istanbul
Tel: 1447540 Open 9 a.m.–5 p.m.

USA: Mesrutiyet Cad. 106,
Tepebasi,
Beyoglu,
Istanbul
Tel: 1513602 Open 8 a.m.–6 p.m.

GETTING AROUND

Getting around Istanbul can be difficult, since the narrow streets are not especially suited to modern methods of transport. The *bus service* in the city is good and fares are low. Tickets for buses can be bought from kiosks situated at transfer points or from bus stations. The biggest terminals are at Sirkeci Station, Eminonu (near the Galata Bridge), Beyazit, and Taksim Square. From Taksim, buses depart for the European shore of Marmara: a Number 96 for Yesilkoy and a 94 for Florya; or a Number 40 will take you along the European shore of the Bosphorus. On the Asian side, buses set out from Kadikoy for the Sea of Marmara, and from Uskudar for the shore of the Bosphorus.

Dolmuses are a very efficient way of travelling. These are minibuses, recognizable by their yellow band, which work on the system that each passenger pays his fare according to his destination. There are *dolmus* centres at Taksim Square, Sirkeci Station, Eminonu, Kadikoy, Karakoy and Uskudar, but to get to Sultanahmet, the area around Istanbul's most famous sights, you'll need to get off at Cagaloglu and walk a few blocks.

Ferries are an enjoyable way of travelling any distance and there are many of them, running short hops along the Bosphorus and Golden Horn as well as operating a linking route. Car ferries cross the Bosphorus and the Sea of Marmara from Kabatas to Uskudar; Sirkeci to Harem and Istinye; Pasabahce, on the Bosphorus, to Kartal; Yalova to Kartal; and Darica to Yalova, on the Sea of Marmara.

Since so many of the sights of Istanbul are so close to each other in the old part of the city, however, the best and probably the quickest way to get from one to another is to walk. This will also give you a chance to see some interesting street scenes.

THE SIGHTS

There are so many places for the sightseer to visit that it will take at least three days to view the major ones. A good starting point is **Topkapi Palace**, which is situated on the point of the Old City, overlooking the Bosphorus and Golden Horn, and was the seat of the Ottoman Emperors from the fifteenth to the nineteenth century. The palace is open from 10 a.m. until 7 p.m. in July and August, and from

10 a.m. until 5 p.m. during the rest of the year (closed Mondays). Admission does not include the guided tour of the harem, which costs extra, as does a permit to take photographs.

Mehmet the Conqueror built the first residence on this site in 1453 and the basic layout is still the same today. There are three courts: the first is the Court of the Janissaries; the second contains the family quarters and harem; and the third, the private audience chamber of the sultan. **The Church of St Irene** stands in the first court and is used as a concert hall during the International Festival, although for centuries it was an imperial arsenal. The Janissary Corps was composed mainly of Christians who had been taken from the Balkans as boys, taught to speak Turkish, and instructed in the ways of Islam.

Between the Court of the Janissaries and the second court stands the **Ortakapi Gate** constructed by Suleiman in 1524, through which no one but the sultan could pass on horseback. The second or **Divan court** is a park with trees and roses, though *divan* actually means 'place of hard work'. In fact the hard work was done in the **Assembly Rooms** where the Grand Vizier met with his council. Exhibits in this part of the palace include Turkish porcelain, weapons and an impressive collection of Chinese porcelain. It is well worth taking the tour of the restored harem, much of which was built during Sultan Suleiman's reign. Among the hundreds of halls, passages and apartments you will see the private family rooms, as well as those of the infamous concubines.

Few people were allowed to enter the third court, where the sultan had his private quarters. Now a fascinating garment exhibit gives an impression of the opulent lifestyle of the sultans, an impression borne out by the incredible display of jewels in the **Imperial Treasury**. There are so many jewels that the effect is breathtaking, and of particular interest are the famous Topkapi Sword, encrusted with emeralds, and the Spoonmaker's diamond.

Within the third court there are gardens with pools, fountains and kiosks, of which the two most attractive are the **Revan Kösk**, built after claiming Grevan back from Persia in 1635, and the **Baghdad Kösk**, constructed after the conquest of that city in 1638.

The **Museum of Archaeology** is just outside Topkapi Palace and contains one of the finest collections of Greek, Hellenic and Roman exhibits, some from the excavations at Troy, Ephesus, Miletus and

Sidon. There are fascinating statues, coins, mosaics and jewellery, but perhaps the most outstanding is the white marble sarcophagus of Alexander.

Next door is the **Museum of the Ancient Orient**, where artefacts from the Hatti, Hittite, Babylonian and Sumerian civilizations can be seen, and opposite this is **Cimlik Kösk** built by Mehmet the Conqueror in the fifteenth century, the oldest non-secular building in Istanbul. It is now the **Museum of Turkish Porcelain** and houses displays of Iznik, Seljuk and Ottoman tiles. The museums are open daily from 9 a.m. till 5 p.m. but are closed off-season on Mondays. There is half-price admission at weekends.

Aya Sofya, the Church of Holy Wisdom, was built between AD 537 and 582 under instruction from Emperor Justinian. It was considered the most important church in the Christian world until the conquest of Constantinople in 1452, when Mehmet the Conqueror rode through the door and claimed the city for Islam. The church was immediately converted into a mosque, and it remained a place of Moslem worship for five hundred years until Ataturk declared it a museum in 1935.

Aya Sofya opens from 9 a.m. until 5.30 p.m. every day but is closed on Mondays; in July and August it stays open until 7 p.m. It costs about 50p for an admission ticket to the main building and a little extra for access to the galleries. From the outside it doesn't look especially impressive, but on entering you will see why it was so admired for its beauty. The central dome is built over a square space, the characteristic feature of the Byzantine Church, and rises 150 feet above the floor with some of the old Christian mosaic still intact.

Since water has always been a problem in Istanbul, the Romans took it upon themselves to install a system of city plumbing, and the cisterns are an unusual sight. The **Yerebatan Cistern** to the west of Aya Sofya is an outstanding example excavated by Emperor Constantine, especially noteworthy for its vaults and 336 Corinthian columns. If you are interested in Roman architecture, head to Ataturk Boulevard where the double arches of the **Aqueduct of Valens** can be seen, built in AD 375 to supply water to the palaces.

To the south-west of Aya Sofya is the **Blue Mosque,** one of *the* sights of Europe. It is an imposing feature on the skyline of Istanbul, with its six minarets, domes and semi-domes, and it gets its name from the blue tiles of Iznik which form its interior decoration. Laid out in the standard Ottoman design, it has a fountain for ablutions in the middle of the forecourt and a portico on three sides. Parts of the Blue Mosque have been made into a **Textile Museum** where kilims and flat woven rugs are exhibited, some in a Bedouin tent. A **Carpet Museum** is located in another part of the building, exhibiting fine Turkish carpets of traditional design.

Directly behind the Blue Mosque is the **Mosaic Museum**, where you can see some fifth- and sixth-century pavements from the palace of the Great Emperor of Byzantium (open 9.30 a.m. to 5.30 p.m. daily; closed on Mondays). It was set up to preserve some of the beautiful mosaics found in the palaces originally on this site.

The street in front of the Blue Mosque follows the original course of the **Hippodrome**, the chariot-racing stadium built by Constantine the Great which was the hub of Byzantine social life. Unfortunately, very few of the decorative monuments which lined the centre of the course remain, but the **Obelisk of Theodosius**, carved in Egypt around 1500 BC, can still be seen. To the south of the obelisk is the **Bronze Serpentine Column** which Constantine brought back from the Temple of Apollo at Delphi, and the **Brick Obelisk** stands at the southern end of the Hippodrome.

On the western side of the Hippodrome you'll find the **Palace of Ibrahim Pasa**, the Grand Vizier and son-in-law of Suleiman the Magnificent. It is one of the most luxurious private residences ever built in the Ottoman Empire, and will give you an idea of the opulent lifestyle of the rich Ottomans.

Little **Aya Sofya** was constructed in AD 550 under Emperor Justinian and is situated not far from the Hippodrome. It's a typical Byzantine church and, like all other churches in the city, was converted into a mosque when the city was captured by the Ottomans in 1452.

The Mosque of Suleiman the Magnificent is perhaps *the* most beautiful sight of Istanbul. Suleiman was the fourth ruler of the Ottoman Empire and is considered by many Turks to have been the greatest (he was certainly the richest). He commanded that this mosque be built in 1550, with specific instructions that it be bigger and more impressive than Aya Sofya. The result is enormous, and with its hilltop position has become the landmark of Istanbul. The

Museum of Turkish and Islamic Art is in the Palace of Ibrahim Pasa and there are exhibits of antique carpets, korans, Seljuk tiles and miniatures.

Another mosque to visit is **Rustem Camii**, which was built in 1561 by Sinan on the orders of Rustem Pasa, the Grand Vizier of Suleiman the Magnificent. Constructed during the zenith of the Ottoman Empire, it contains the country's finest examples of Iznik tiles.

From here it's well worth going into the **covered bazaar** (Kapali Carsi), a whole town in itself. There are four thousand shops and you'll find it a good place to pick up Turkish crafts to take home as souvenirs. Look for flat woven rugs in traditional designs; copper and silverware; embroidered bags and shirts, leatherware and, of course, Turkish carpets, and be prepared to haggle over prices. The maze of streets is named after the crafts and trades sold there – the Goldsmiths, the Carpetsellers and the Jewellers – and in the centre of the market you'll find the old **Bedesten**, full of interesting antiques. Remember, however, that you cannot take antiques out of the country.

Further out towards the city walls is **Fatih Camii**, the mosque of the Conqueror. Built between 1463 and 1470, this was the first imperial mosque erected after the conquest of Istanbul, and it takes its name from Mehmet the Conqueror. A large complex of hospitals, theological schools, a library and a caravanserai surround it. This became the hub from which the city expanded. The present-day mosque isn't the original one; that was destroyed by an earthquake, and since then the buildings have been restored several times.

The **city walls** are most impressive fortifications. They were constructed by Emperor Theodosius in the fifth century and stretch for four miles from the Sea of Marmara to the Golden Horn. The inner rampart is almost 12 feet thick and once had forty watchtowers and seven great gates. It is no wonder they have been breached only twice throughout history – first by the Crusaders in 1204 and then in 1453 by the Ottomans.

Just inside the city walls is the **Kariye Museum**. Originally the 'Church of the Holy Saviour Outside the Walls', this is now a museum of Byzantine art and the most important Byzantine monument in Istanbul. The fourteenth-century mosaics and frescoes which decorate the interior have been extensively restored and tell the story of Christianity. Like other museums, it is open from 9 a.m. until 5 p.m. and is closed on Mondays.

In the suburb of Eyup you will find the **Pierre Loti Café** where the author wrote his novels about daily life under the last sultans. The city has changed since then but the view is still impressive, though drinks are expensive. From here head to **Eyup Camii**, the mosque built by Mehmet in 1458 at the place where Eyup, the standard bearer of the Prophet Mohammed, died during the assault on Constantinople in AD 669. Restored after an earthquake in 1798, it is still a very sacred place for Moslems, so ensure that you are suitably dressed.

At Eminonu, near the Galata Bridge, **Yeni Camii** or the New Mosque is one of Istanbul's best-known sights. It was commissioned in 1557 and is of typical Ottoman layout, though the tiles here are not as impressive as those at Rustem Camii. The **Spice Market** or Egyptian Bazaar is situated behind Yeni Camii and was constructed as part of the mosque complex in 1660. Its name comes from the spices that were once sold there, but it is not as interesting nowadays, since the spice vendors have been replaced by stalls of toys, clothes and other domestic goods.

At the entrance to the Bosphorus from Istanbul harbour you can see **Leander's Tower**. Although there has been a lighthouse on this site since the twelfth century, the present building dates from the eighteenth century. Another tower well worth a visit is the **Galata Tower**, built by the Genoese in 1216. It is 228 feet high and from the top there is a superb vista of the city, the Bosphorus and the Golden Horn. Open from 10 a.m. until 6 p.m. as an observatory, it becomes a nightclub and restaurant in the evening.

Also in the New City, just north of Taksim Square, you can see the **Military Museum** which opens from 9 a.m. until 5 p.m. and is closed on both Mondays and Tuesdays. You will find exhibits of Ottoman battle dress and other military paraphernalia, and occasionally you have the opportunity to hear a military band concert.

Dolmabahce Palace is on the European shore of the Bosphorus. Sultan Abdul Mecit moved the royal residence here in 1854 in an attempt to modernize his country. The white marble palace contains 365 rooms of which the most impressive are the throne room and the reception salon. It was here that Ataturk died in 1938 and all the palace clocks are stopped at 9.05, the time of his death, to commemorate this. The palace is open between 9 a.m. and 12 noon, and from 1.30 to 4.30 p.m. Once again, photography fees are extra and guided tours are compulsory.

For one of the best views of the Bosphorus, go to **Yildiz Park** which is open from 9 a.m. to 6 p.m. daily. Here you can see the **Yildiz Palace**, built over many centuries but finally finished at the end of the nineteenth, and the kiosks are well worth a visit. Two of these are restaurants, while the **Sale Kösk** houses an exhibition of nineteenth-century memorabilia, and **Yildiz Kösk** serves as a residence for visiting heads of state.

Another interesting palace, this time on the Asian shore of the Bosphorus, is **Beylerbeyi Palace**, constructed in 1865 under Sultan Abdul Aliz. This was a summer residence for the sultans and a guest-house for foreign dignitaries – Napoleon's Empress Eugenie stayed here, as did Tsar Nicholas II of Russia. You can visit from 9 a.m. until 5 p.m. every day but Monday, when it is closed.

Kucuksu Palace to the north of Beylerbeyi was the favourite picnic spot of Ottoman royalty, who often came here to get away from the hot city. The area is delightfully named after the streams which flow on either side of it, the 'Greater Heavenly Stream' and the 'Lesser Heavenly Stream'.

If you travel further north along the Bosphorus either by boat or by road, you will pass **Rumeli Hisar** and **Anadolu Hisar**. Rumeli Hisar, on the European shore, was constructed in only four months in 1452 during Mehmet's campaign to take Constantinople. It is now used for drama presentation during the International Festival and there are often displays of folk dancing. Anadolu Hisar, on the opposite shore, dates from 1391, although it was repaired and strengthened by Mehmet later. It was from these two watchtowers that Mehmet was able to control all the shipping and cut off vital supplies to the city. It's also worth catching the commuter ferry which zigzags its way up the Bosphorus – a fantastically scenic experience that comes *very* cheap.

ACCOMMODATION

Finding accommodation is not usually a problem in Istanbul, though if you have set ideas on where you want to stay it is advisable to book, especially between June and September. The most expensive hotels, which charge international rates, are situated around **Taksim Square** in Beyoglu, while more moderately priced rooms are to be found in **Laleli** – a pleasant residential area which is very convenient for the sights of the Old City. Many tour operators use hotels in this quarter. It is possible to find very cheap accommodation in **Sultanahmet**, but do be prepared for water shortages and basic standards. A list of those establishments licensed by the Ministry of Culture and Tourism is available from the tourist offices at Sultanahmet Square, the Hilton Hotel and the airport.

The **Etap Marmara** on Taksim Square (tel: 151 46 96) is the tallest and most expensive hotel in Turkey with 428 rooms, a nightclub, cafés, restaurants and a swimming pool, while Turkey's only casino is in the **Hilton** in Cumhuriyet Cad. (tel: 131 46 46) which has 411 rooms, 13 suites and offers a variety of restaurants and a swimming pool. In the **Sheraton** at Taksim Park (tel: 131 21 21), with 459 rooms the city's largest hotel, there is a swimming pool, a nightclub and restaurants. A smaller establishment still within the luxury category, and used by some tour operators, is the **Hotel Divan**, Cumhuriyet Cad. (tel: 131 41 00). It has only 98 rooms and is noted for the 'Divan' pub restaurant.

For slightly less expensive accommodation, you might try the **Dedaman** Hotel, Yildiz Posta Cad. 50, situated between Taksim Square and the Bosphorus Bridge (tel: 172 88 00). Services include a swimming pool and a sauna. On Mesrutiyet Cad. the **Etap Istanbul** and **Pera Palas** are recommended. The Etap Istanbul is a 200-room hotel with a pool and a disco (tel: 151 46 46), while the Pera Palas offers you the opportunity of a nostalgic trip back to the opulent days of the sultans (tel: 151 45 60). It is an enormous old building with spacious bedrooms and bathrooms. Tour operators also use the hotel **Macka** on Eytam Cad. 35 (tel. 140 10 53) which has 184 rooms.

On Siraselviler Cad. the **Dilson** (tel: 143 20 32) and **Keban** (tel: 143 33 10) offer more moderately priced accommodation as does the **T.M.T.** (tel: 167 33 34) at Gayrettepe, Buydere Cad. And for the economy-minded traveller, the **Yenehir Palas** (tel: 149 88 10) and the **Kavak** Hotel (tel: 144 58 44) offer comfortable accommodation at a modest price. You might also try the **Gezi** Hotel (tel: 145 21 67) at Mete Cad. near to Taksim Square, the **Konak** Hotel on Cumhuriyet Cad. (tel: 148 47 44) or the Hotel **Opera** at Inonu Cad., Taksim Square (tel: 143 55 27). A new hotel worth trying is the **Ottoman**, Kadi-galimani Cad. 85 in the Kadira district, close to Sultanahmet.

With 102 en-suite rooms and many international luxury services, it was opened in June 1989.

Most of the more reasonably priced hotels are situated in the Old City. The **Burc Keban** in Laleli (tel: 47 528 80) and the **Kalyon** (tel: 526 62 50) at Sahu Yolu in Sultanahmet are at the top end of the moderate price range. But it is worth viewing the **Toro** (tel: 528 02 73) and **Sahinler** Hotels at Koska Cad. in Laleli. The Toro has air-conditioning.

If you are really short of cash, you might consider the Hotel **Inka** on Mesruyret Cad. 222 (tel: 143 17 28) and **Italya** at Tomtom Kaptan Sok. 2/4 in Beyoglu (tel: 143 49 69). The Hotel **Terminal** at Iskendar Cad. 60 (tel: 149 99 46), Hotel **Oriental** at Cihangir Cad. 60 (tel: 149 82 71), Hotel **Ciddle** at Aksaray Cad. (tel: 522 42 11) and **Topkapi** Hotel (tel: 525 42 40) are smaller establishments which also offer cheap rooms.

Sultanahmet and Laleli are *the* places to look if you want real value for money. Try the **Side** Hotel at Koska Cad. 33 (tel: 526 71 78), the **Eyfel** on Kurultay Sok. 19 (tel: 520 97 98) or the Hotel **Florida** on Fevziye Cad. 38, all in Laleli. The **Kent** (tel: 527 78 50), the **Astor** (tel: 522 44 23), the **Bern** (tel: 523 24 62) and the **Kilim** (tel: 586 08 80) are all reasonable. The **Sultan Tourist Hotel** on Yerebatan Cad. (tel: 520 76 76) is good, with double rooms at around 2500TL, as are the **Gungor** on Divan Yoln Cad. (tel: 262 319), and the **Yoruk** at Incilicavus Sok. 35 (tel: 276476).

Student accommodation is available at the **Topkapi Ataturk Student Centre** in Topkapi (tel: 525 02 80 for women and 525 50 32 for men) and also at the **Yucelt Interyouth Hostel** (tel: 522 4790) which provides very cheap double rooms. **Istanbul Youth Hostel,** Cerrahpasa Cad. 63, Aksaray (tel: 212455) is passable, but hardly central. Some of the university dormitories are open in the summer and give very cheap but very basic accommodation. You can get information about these from the tourist offices.

There are also several campsites, of which **Yesilyurt** (tel: 738408) and **Atakoy** (tel: 720 802) are two of the nicest.

If you want to see the sights of Istanbul but don't wish to stay in the city, there are some pleasant hotels further out which may interest you. For luxury accommodation on the Bosphorus try the **Buyuk Tarabya** at Tarabaya (tel: 162 10 00), which has 262 rooms but no beach, or the **Bebek** Hotel (tel: 163 30 00) at Bebek which is a reasonable place to stay and not nearly as expensive. On the Asian shore at Uskudar the Hotel **Harem** (tel: 333 20 25) and the **Engin** Hotel at Kadikoy (tel: 336 03 79) serve the budget traveller.

At Yesilkoy, on the Sea of Marmara, the **Cinar** (tel: 573 29 10) is a luxury hotel with a nightclub and restaurant, while the **Yesilkoy** pension near the beach serves budget travellers. On the Asian shore of Marmara the **Dragos** at Cevizli (tel: 352 50 03) and **Suadiye** (tel: 358 11 20) provide luxurious accommodation but if you are driving to the shore for a few days you might try the **Erdim** Motel (tel: 353 36 09) for something cheaper.

EATING

In a city so close to the sea, fish is naturally a speciality. Blue fish, swordfish, turbot and red mullet are all delicious and worth trying. The Kebapci and Kofteci kebab stalls provide a convenient place to stop off for lunch, and for those with a sweeter tooth there are shops selling baklava with all sorts of fillings. To accompany your meals the Turkish white wines offer a reasonable alternative to the more familiar European wines, while raki, the national drink, is very similar to anisette.

There are many restaurants in Istanbul where you can eat well at a reasonable price. The cost of a meal can depend more on the surroundings than on the quality of the food itself, and the dishes in a modest little lokanta are often just as appetizing and far cheaper than those in a more elegant restaurant.

The hotels serve both European and local food. They certainly provide the most formal setting but they are not necessarily the best place to eat, although the **Divan** does have a very good restaurant. You'll find an international menu at the **Dortler Mevsim** at Istiklal Cad., and although the dining-room at the **Pera Palas** is superb, the food isn't as impressive as the decor. The **Liman Restaurant** at Karakoy is noted for its seafood and its marvellous view of the Bosphorus; it is only open at lunchtime, however.

For a more moderately priced menu try the **Sempati Pub** on Malaskargazi Cad. or alternatively the **Hallo Pub Café**, the **Deutsches Kaffee** or the **Pandorosa**, all of which are in Taksim. In

Yildiz Park the **Kadir Kosku** and the **Malta Kosku** offer a tremendous view of the Bosphorus as well as reasonable food.

The restaurants in the old part of the city are more traditional and in general provide better value for money. It is worthwhile eating in some of the lokantas and inexpensive restaurants in Laleli and Sultanahmet, especially if you want to experience the real atmosphere of Istanbul. Try the **Delfino**, opposite the Blue Mosque in Sultanahmet Square, or the **Murat** on Ordu Cad. in Aksaray. If you want lunch while sightseeing, you'll find that the **Topkapi Lokanta** at Topkapi Palace provides a good meal and an interesting view.

There are some wonderful seafood restaurants at some of the fishing villages along the Bosphorus which are certainly a pleasant place to spend an evening. In Emirgan the **Abdullah** is famed for its stuffed mussels, while at Tarabaya the **Balikcil** is situated right on the bay, and the **Garaj** and **Kosem Bistro** are also recommended.

NIGHTLIFE

Turkey is famous for its belly-dancers, but those in some of the clubs may not live up to expectations as they tend to be rather commercial. There are floorshows at the big hotels – the **Sheraton**, the **Hilton** and the **Etap Marmara** – but it is better to head for the shows at the **Kervansaray** or the **Pariziyen**, both on Cumhuriyet Cad., if you want this sort of entertainment. For a nightclub with a superb view of Istanbul go to the **Galata Tower** in Sishane, where the observatory becomes a club and a restaurant at night.

If you want to gamble, go to the **Hilton** which has Turkey's only casino. It is open from 8 p.m. until early morning.

An alternative to a nightclub is the *gazino*. These are open-air restaurants which serve dinner and have some sort of cabaret entertainment – usually a popular singer. The best of these are on the European shore of the Bosphorus. At Bebek try the **Bebek Asiyan** or the **Bebek Park**, while in the city the **Regine Gazinosu** and the **Yeni Hydromel** offer good food and a pleasant atmosphere. If Eastern entertainment does not appeal, there is a disco at the **Etap** Hotel at Mesrutiyet Cad.

The Turks love folk dancing, and during the summer displays are often put on for tourists. If you are interested, ask at the tourist offices for information as to where and when there are performances. If you prefer more classical dance, there are good ballet and opera productions in the Ataturk Cultural Palace on Taksim Square. Theatre is presented here from October till June, but if a straight play in Turkish seems rather heavy, check to see if there are any performances of Shakespeare at Rumeli Hisar on the Bosphorus which is used extensively during the festival.

The Istanbul International Festival takes place in June and July every year. It attracts performers from all over the world so be sure to get information about what is on if you are in the city during this time. The highlight is Mozart's *Abduction from the Seraglio*, staged at Topkapi Palace. In the summer, don't forget that there are Son et Lumière performances at Topkapi Palace and the Blue Mosque. Classical concerts are given by the Musical Academy of Istanbul in the Ataturk Cultural Palace.

There are many cinemas in Istanbul and if you look around, you'll probably be able to find one or two undubbed films.

PRINCES ISLANDS

The Princes Islands are situated in the Sea of Marmara, six miles south-east of Istanbul. In Byzantine times these islands served as a useful destination for shipping unwanted items – anything from monarchs to stray dogs. In the nineteenth century the European businessmen developed the islands as summer resorts and many hotels and villas sprang up at this time and remain there still. There are nine islands and a boat trip will take you to either BUYUKADA or HEYBELIADA, the two largest. The express ferry leaves from Kabatas and takes just under an hour to make the trip to the islands, though there is also a slower ferry from Sirkeci. As the boat heads out of the Golden Horn there is a great view of the Old City: Topkapi Palace, Aya Sofya and the Blue Mosque.

BUYUKADA is the largest of the islands, a pleasant wooded place where the pace of life is very slow. No cars are allowed on the island so transport is by bicycle or horse-drawn carriage. You can spend a very relaxing day wandering about the island looking at some of the lovely old houses and stopping off to eat in one of the open-air restaurants.

HEYBELIADA is smaller but is the site of the Turkish Naval Academy; you can take a tour of the island by horse and carriage. Life here is slow and relaxing and you can travel over to the beach on the far side of the island and watch the fishermen repair their nets.

SHORE RESORTS

Istanbul is surrounded by beaches, on the shores of the Sea of Marmara and on the Black Sea coast. Trains leave for the European shore of the Sea of Marmara from Sirkeci Station and for the Asian shore from Haydarpasa Station. You can also reach the beaches by car along the shore route.

The beaches at Florya, Yesilkoy and Atakoy have fine restaurants and are popular with the Istanbulis. On the Asian shore there are beaches at Moda, Fenerbahce, Caddebostan and Suadiye.

On the Bosphorus the resort of Tarabaya has little restaurants specializing in fish, and the beach at Mucha is particularly lovely.

TROY

Visitors to Istanbul with an interest in history will want to travel south along the Aegean to the ruins of the ancient city of Troy, where according to classical literature the Trojans and Greeks battled over Helen, reputedly the most beautiful woman in the world. Troy is located 13 km south of the town of Canakkale at the point of the Dardanelles Straits. A bus service runs from Istanbul to Canakkale.

Until 1871 it was thought that Homer's *Iliad* was based on legend not history, but Heinrich Schliemann's excavations suggest that the city of Troy did indeed exist on this site. The trenches show the position and layout of nine cities on different levels, the earliest dating as far back as 3000 BC. A guided tour is advisable. Also of interest is a large replica of the Trojan Horse and a museum containing some of the finds at the site.

Thrace and Marmara

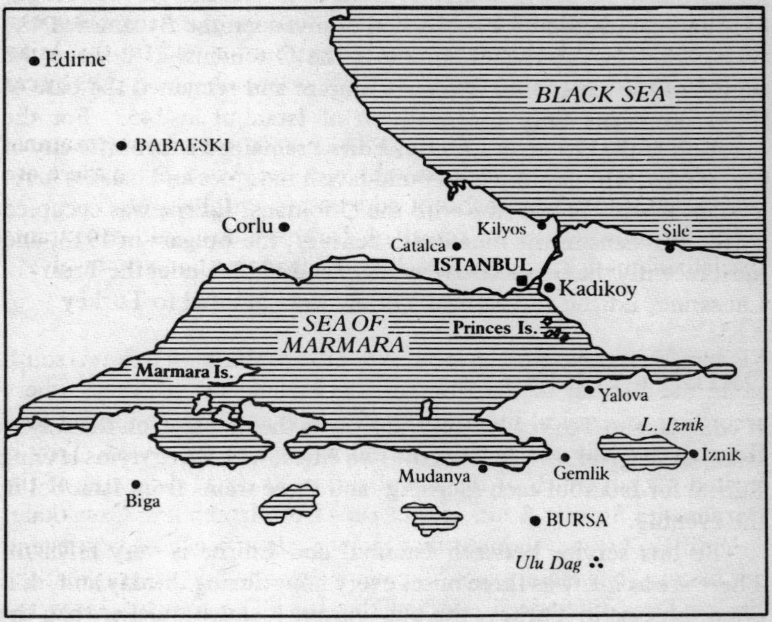

Thrace is situated in European Turkey to the north of the Aegean and the Sea of Marmara. Bordering on Greece and Bulgaria, it is the first region of Turkey that you'll come to if you travel to Turkey by rail or by bus. Edirne, the capital city of this small province, is well worth a visit.

Edirne

Edirne is situated just across the border from Greece and is notable for its many classic Ottoman buildings and numerous mosques: the skyline is dominated by domes and minarets. The old city has a charm of its own, with narrow cobbled streets, horse-drawn carriages, overhanging balconies on the Ottoman houses and craftsmen's stalls in the streets.

The city was founded in 125 BC by the Emperor Hadrian and takes its European name, Adrianople, from him. Adrianople was fought over and conquered by a succession of invaders: the Byzantines, the Avars, the Crusaders and, in 1361, the Ottomans. It became the capital of the expanding Ottoman Empire and remained the base of their campaigns until the conquest of Istanbul in 1453. For the duration of the Ottoman Empire, Edirne remained a favourite city of the sultans, who continued to build lavish mosques and palaces here. The invasions did not stop with the Ottomans: Edirne was occupied by the Russians in the nineteenth century, the Bulgars in 1913, and most recently the Greeks between 1919 and 1922. Under the Treaty of Lausanne, Edirne and eastern Turkey were granted to Turkey.

ORIENTATION

If you come to Turkey by train, Edirne is the first stop on the way to Istanbul. A good service links the two cities, with three trains leaving Edirne for Istanbul each morning, and three trains from Istanbul in the evening.

The bus service between Istanbul and Edirne is very efficient. There are as many as three buses every hour during the day and, as is often the case in Turkey, the bus journey is much quicker than the train journey. Buses operate out of the bus terminal on the outskirts of the city, and *dolmuses* and city buses connect the bus station with the city centre.

There are two tourist information offices in Edirne, one in the centre at Hurriyet Meydani (tel: 1518) and another on Londra Astalti. These offices are especially helpful if you are looking for good, cheap accommodation.

SIGHTS

Edirne is famed for its mosques, the most important of these being the **Sultan Selim Camii**, built between 1568 and 1574 during the reign of Sultan Selim. It was designed by

Mimar Sinan, Turkey's greatest architect, and is considered by many to be his most magnificent achievement. The central dome of the mosque is over 100 feet in diameter and has 999 windows. As a result the interior is bright and spacious. There is superb Iznik tiling around the prayer niche and a very ornate pulpit. The four minarets are over 200 feet high and each has three balconies, making the mosque quite a landmark for miles around. The courtyard is most impressive, with red and white marble arches surrounding a fountain. The **medrese**, which was part of the mosque complex, is now a **Museum of Islamic Art** exhibiting old photographs of Turkish wrestlers (see below); it is open from 9 a.m. to 5 p.m. and closed on Mondays.

Across the square, the modern **Archaeological and Ethnographical Museum** houses a collection of Turkish embroideries, costumes and jewellery. Like other museums in Turkey, it is open from 9 a.m. to 5 p.m. and is closed on Mondays.

In the centre of the square is a statue of two huge wrestlers, representatives of Turkey's national sport – grease wrestling. Edirne has been the centre of this sport for six centuries, and every July the national championships are held on **KIRKPINAR ISLAND**. At this time of year the city is packed out with spectators, and the championships are indeed well worth seeing.

Eski Camii, the oldest Ottoman building in the city, is situated behind the statue. Built in 1414 under Sultan Mehmet I, it closely resembles the Ulu in Bursa, with row upon row of pillars and arches supporting numerous domes. Behind the mosque there is a restored *bedesten* (or covered market) which dates from the fifteenth century and was constructed to raise income to finance the mosque. Behind it is another of Sinan's designs, the **Rustem Pasa Kervansaray**. It was built in the sixteenth century to house travellers, and is still used for this purpose as it has now been restored as the **Hotel Kervansaray**.

In the centre of town the **Üç Şerefeli Camii** is well worth a visit. It was constructed in the early fifteenth century and shows the transition in architectural style from Seljuk to Ottoman: whereas the Seljuks built mosques with many domes, the Ottomans preferred one huge dome giving an atmosphere of spaciousness. There are four minarets, and the mosque is named after the tallest one, which has three balconies and towers above the courtyard.

Opposite the mosque the **Sokullu Hamam** (bath house) – another of Sinan's works – is the most beautiful in Edirne. It is still in use today, so if you want to relax in a Turkish bath, this is the place to go.

North-east of the city centre the **Muradje Camii** was founded in the fifteenth century as a centre for the Whirling Dervishes and is notable for the fine Iznik tiles which decorate the prayer niche. The other great mosque in Edirne is the **Beyazit II Camii**. Situated on the far side of the river, it has an ornate marble prayer niche and is one of the most extensive mosque complexes in Turkey, with a soup kitchen, a theological school, a hospital, a hostel and an asylum for the mentally ill. The complex has been recently restored and is a good example of its type.

ACCOMMODATION

The most interesting place to stay in Edirne is without doubt the **Hotel Kervansaray** on Eski Istanbul Cad. The restored sixteenth-century building is inexpensive and full of character. It has been out of action for two years but may be ready in 1990. The **Sultan Hotel** (tel: 1372) on Talat Pasa Cad. provides moderately priced accommodation and on the same street the **Hotel Kervan** (tel: 1355) is less expensive and has a good restaurant. Edirne is full of cheap pensions and the tourist information office will be more than willing to help those on a tight budget to find a room for the night. If you are camping, try the **Kervansaray Mocamp** on the Istanbul road.

The shore of the Sea of Marmara offers something for everyone. Beaches and shore resorts stretch right along the coast, and the museums and mosques in Bursa and Iznik will be of great interest to the sightseer. There is a National Park at Uludag, an interesting excursion for those with outdoor interests, and Marmara is a particularly fascinating region for the historian and the archaeologist, with numerous excavations, the most famous of which is Troy. The typically Mediterranean climate of hot summers and mild winters and the easy access from Istanbul make this region a popular destination for tourists.

Bursa

Bursa is an attractive city situated at the foot of Mount Uludag. The sixth largest city in Turkey, it takes its name from its founder,

Prusias, who was king of the region of Bithynia in 200 BC. Later, when the region came under Byzantine control, the Emperor Justinian built a palace and bath house here. Bursa was captured in the early fourteenth century by Orhan I and became the first capital of the Ottoman Empire. Although Edirne soon succeeded it as capital in 1361, Bursa is still an important commercial centre.

ORIENTATION

There is a small airport at Bursa and regular flights are operated from Istanbul by Bursa Air, a private airline. For details about flights you can contact either a travel agent or the Ataturk airport in Istanbul (tel: 573 35 10).

There is no rail service to Bursa so if you don't fly, the best way to come is by bus or by ferry. Travelling by bus is especially convenient if you want to stop off at Izmit on the way, and buses run frequently from Harem Bus Station in Istanbul.

The most interesting way to get to Bursa is by ferry across the Sea of Marmara. Ferries leave Kabatas Dock in Istanbul at 9.45 a.m., 2.15, 6.10, 8.15 p.m. every day but Sunday, and carry passengers across to Yalova from where a bus service operates to the centre of Bursa, a journey of about half an hour.

A hydrofoil service departs in the morning from Istanbul to the port of Mudanya, which is half an hour's journey by bus from Bursa.

Getting around the sights is made easy by the extensive bus and *dolmus* service, and a book of tickets for the city buses should be purchased at the bus station. Maps of the area and brochures to aid sightseeing are available from the Tourist Information Office in the city centre on Ataturk Cad. 82 (tel: 12 359).

SIGHTS

Ulu Cami is a good starting place for sightseers. This Seljuk mosque was built between 1396 and 1399 and was restored in 1967 after an earthquake. With as many as twenty domes, its exterior is most impressive, and the interior is no less magnificent, with a walnut pulpit and walls decorated with exceptional calligraphy.

Further down Ataturk Caddesi, the **Orhan Gazi Cami** was

constructed in 1336 by Orhan I, the conqueror of Bursa. It has twice been destroyed and twice restored but still retains the original design. The market area is located behind the mosque and the **Bedesten**, or covered market, at the centre is an interesting place to look for souvenirs; copper and brass, carpets and kilims.

Bursa's most famous sight is the **Yesil Cami** (the Green Mosque) and the **Yesil Turbe** (the Green Tomb), both named because of the turquoise tiles which decorate the exterior. They were constructed in 1421 during the reign of Mehmet I the Celebi. Yesil Cami is considered by many to be the most superb of the Imperial mosques in Turkey and its architecture shows the emergence of a distinctly Turkish style. Across the street is Yesil Turbe, the tombs of Sultan Mehmet. It is open from 8.30 a.m.–12 noon, 1.30–5.30 p.m. and there is no charge for admission. The interior has exquisite tiling and the Sultan's sarcophagus is decorated in blue and gold. The medrese of the mosque complex is now a **Museum of Turkish and Islamic Antiquities** with a fine collection of jewellery, calligraphy and antique books. The museum is open from 8.30 a.m.–12 noon, 1.30–5.30 p.m. every day, but is closed on Monday.

Another mosque complex is the **Muradiye Cami** which is set in a park. It was built in 1426 and is surrounded by tombs, including the mausoleum of Murat II which has a dome and Corinthian columns.

In CEKIRGE, the **Eski Kaplica Baths** are worth a visit. They were originally built by Justinian, though the structure today dates from the fourteenth century. Also in Cekirge the **Kultur Park** is a pleasant place for a stroll and is the site of the **Archaeological Museum**. Open from 8.30 a.m.–12 noon, 1–5.30 p.m. Tuesday–Sunday, it has exhibits of coins and other artefacts from Hellenistic, Roman and Byzantine times. In July there is a fair in the park when the famous Sword and Shield Dance of Bursa is performed. The dance, performed without music, is a martial representation of the Ottoman conquest of the city.

ACCOMMODATION

The best hotel in Bursa is the **Celik Palas** (tel: 61900) on Cekirge Cad. It has a pool and charges moderate prices. On Murat Cad. the **Hotel Akdogan** (tel: 60610) is a more modern hotel which also has a swimming pool. The **Hotel Dikmen** (tel: 14995) and the **Hotel Gonluferah** (tel: 62700), like other hotels in Cekirge Cad., have facilities for bathing in local mineral waters. Inexpensive rooms are available at the **Hotel Diyar** (tel: 65130) on Cekirge Cad., and at the **Hotel Hunkar** on Acemler Cad. which has superb marble baths although its location is not central. Those on a really tight budget might try the **Ternizel Hotel** (tel: 11682) and the **Sifa Hotel** (tel: 11483) both on Birinci Murat Cad. in Cekirge.

EATING

Bursa is famed for its *bursa kebap*, a doner Kebab with a savoury sauce and browned butter. This speciality was created at the **Kebabci Iskendergolu** on Ataturk Cad. and is also served at the **Bursa Kebabci** on Ataturk Cad., as well as at the many kebaci stall. The other culinary speciality in Bursa is the *inegol koftesi*, a grilled rissole which is well worth trying and is served at the many koftesi in the city.

ULUDAG

Every visitor to Bursa should take an excursion to the forests and lakes in the National Park on Uludag, Mount Olympus, 21 miles south-west of the city. Uludag is seven and a half thousand feet high, and as you would expect, there is a superb panoramic view from the top. The most exciting way to make the trip is by cable car from the cable car terminal at the foot of the mountain, but for the faint of heart, there is also a *dolmus* service to take you to the top.

The National Park is open all year round; in summer it is an ideal place to walk and picnic, and in winter it is Turkey's main ski resort. The season runs from December until April with all the facilities for a skiing holiday; ski hire and instruction and many inns and hotels, which provide accommodation for skiers.

Sea of Marmara

The Sea of Marmara is one of the loveliest parts of Anatolia and it is well worth considering a trip to some of the smaller towns in this region. Many stretches of the coastline are secluded and quiet with beautiful beaches. *Sun-worshippers* should head for GEMLIK or MUDANYA, coastal resort towns which are easily accessible from Bursa or from Istanbul. One of the most attractive parts of the area is ERDEK, which has a particularly charming setting with beaches, vineyards and olive groves – a pleasant place to spend some time. Further inland there is a bird sanctuary in the **Kuşcenneti National Park** on Lake Manyas, inhabited by over two hundred different species of birds.

YALOVA SPA is 45 miles north of Bursa. The town of Yalova itself is one of Marmara's main resorts and its immediate coastline is dotted with small sandy beaches. The sulphurous thermal springs, which are said to benefit rheumatic and nervous complaints, are about seven miles south-west of the town. There are several cheap hotels and pensions built around the spas, many of which offer private bathing facilities. The **Termal Hotel** and the **Guney Hotel** are among the best. Yalova town centre also has a good selection of modest accommodation including the **Ferah Hotel** and the **Gokcedere Hotel**. There are frequent hovercraft services between Yalova and ISTANBUL, and regular bus services to BURSA and IZNIK.

The historic town of **IZNIK** is 45 miles south-east of Yalova and 60 miles north-east of Bursa. Built on the eastern shores of IZNIK LAKE, the town lies on a fertile plain surrounded by hills, vineyards and peach orchards. Known in ancient time as Nicaea, the town's history can be traced back to the fourth century BC when it was developed into one of the region's principal towns by Lysimachus, one of Alexander the Great's generals. Nicaea prospered as part of the Roman Empire in the first century AD and became an important ecumenical centre as part of the later Byzantine Empire. The town was conquered by the Seljuk Turks in the eleventh century and 300 years later it was added to the great Ottoman Empire. In the sixteenth century it became famous for its thriving tile industry. Craftsmen from the Ottomans' subjugated regions in Persia were drafted to Iznik to manufacture the tiny coloured tiles which now decorate many of Turkey's most beautiful mosques. Although Iznik has a wealth of historic monuments which make it a haven for sightseers, it does not have much in the way of tourist facilities. The majority of visitors to Iznik are based in Bursa or the resorts of the Marmara coast.

One of Iznik's most famous sights is **Santa Sophia**, the ancient church which was the meeting place of the Ecumenical Council in the eighth century. The church is not the town's most beautiful structure but it has a fascinating history. Inside there are splendid mosaics and murals which date back to early Byzantine times and you can see later construction which was carried out by the Ottomans in the sixteenth century after the church was converted into a mosque. In the centre of Iznik, not far from Santa Sophia, there are several interesting Islamic monuments including the fourteenth-century **Haci Ozbek Camii**, the town's oldest mosque; the **Seyh Kutbettin Camii**, a badly ruined fifteenth-century mosque which gives a good view of the town, and the fifteenth-century **Yesil Camii** (Green Mosque) which has a minaret decorated with the green tiles which eventually made Iznik famous. Opposite the Yesil Camii you will see the **Nilufer Hatun Imareti**, a fourteenth-century soup kitchen which now houses the town's main museum. The museum contains a varied collection of exhibits including marble statues, ceramic tiles and examples of local embroidery. Iznik has two sets of **city walls**: its inner walls built by the Romans in the second century, and its outer walls built by the Byzantines in the twelfth century. The well-preserved Roman walls feature four principal gates to the north, east, south and west of the town, and the Byzantine walls have 100 towers and a moat. The town's only other major tourist attraction is IZNIK LAKE where it's possible to swim and sunbathe on the small beaches near the town. When you're not sightseeing, swimming or sunbathing Iznik is a pleasant place to do some souvenir shopping. Along the town's main street you'll find numerous little shops which sell tiled and embroidered gifts.

Accommodation in Iznik is fairly modest, but perfectly adequate for an overnight stop, which is all most visitors require. The best hotels are the **Iznik Motel** and the **Hotel Burcum** on the lakeside, which are both simple and very cheap. The **Hotel Babacan** in the town centre is even more basic and offers rock-bottom rates.

The town's restaurants are also modest, but there are some pleasant little eating places beside the lake. The **Kirikcatal Restaurant** is recommended for its charming atmosphere and its excellent fish menu. There is a wider selection of restaurants in the town centre and prices are generally lower. The **Inegol Restaurant** is a good place for traditional Turkish fare.

An hourly bus service operates between Iznik and Bursa and there are frequent buses to Yalova.

The Aegean Coast

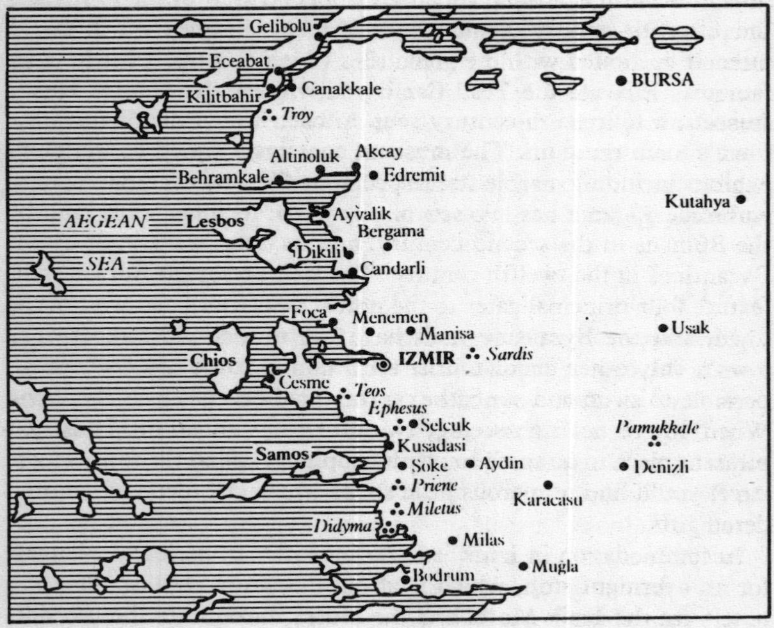

The Aegean is Turkey's most popular holiday destination – mainly due to its wide appeal to different types of holidaymakers. This is where you'll find the country's most spectacular beaches, between Izmir and Marmaris, though the entire coastline offers crystal blue water, sandy beaches and quiet coves. But there's a lot more to the Aegean than sand and surf. Travel only a few miles inland, almost anywhere along the coastline, and you'll find ancient towns and cities such as Troy, Bergama, Efes and Aphrodisias which reflect the history of the region, from the Greeks to the Romans and the Seljuk and Ottoman Turks. Travel further inland and you'll discover parts of the country where organized tourism is still unknown. Even the country's busiest beach resorts – Kusadasi and Bodrum – are relatively unspoilt and uncommercialized, and both have plenty of secluded bays and picturesque fishing villages in their immediate vicinity. This combination of beautiful beaches, interesting historic sites and guaranteed sunshine from April to October makes the Aegean a good base for the sun-worshipper and the sightseer alike. There's even something for the health-conscious in the form of thermal spas at Cesme and Pamukkale. A large number of British tour operators now offer competitively priced holidays to all the main coastal towns, and excursions to the major historic sites are available from the resorts. Turkish Maritime Lines operate cruises along the Aegean coast and regular ferries to the Greek Islands from Cesme, Kusadasi, Bodrum and Marmaris.

HISTORY

The influence of past cultures can still be clearly seen in almost every town of the Aegean region. Since earliest times Izmir and the Aegean ports have been the target for invaders trying to penetrate Anatolia from the west and, consequently, this stretch of land has changed hands numerous times. The early Hittite and Hellenistic civilizations, the Roman Empire, the Byzantine Empire and the great Seljuk and Ottoman Empires have all left their mark on the Aegean provinces.

In 1922, after the First World War, it was at Izmir that Mustafa Kemal's armies defeated the Greeks in the War of Independence to secure their claim to Turkey as we know it today. Shortly after this victory Kemal founded the Republic of Turkey.

Tourism is still relatively new to the region, which is certainly a point in its favour. The development of hotels and tourist facilities began in the mid-1960s after the government devised a national plan for tourism, and it's only in the past five years that tour operators have begun to recognize the full potential of the Aegean as a holiday destination.

For a more detailed account of Turkey's past, see pages 129–33.

COMMUNICATIONS

The majority of tour operators use the airport at Izmir to reach resorts in the Aegean region. There is also a smaller international airport at Dalaman, between Marmaris and Fethiye, which gives easy access to the south Aegean. There is a major railway station at Izmir from where it is possible to catch express trains to Istanbul and Ankara. Private coach operators provide cheap and frequent bus services between all the towns on the Aegean, and Turkish Maritime Lines operate frequent services between the main coastal towns.

Most of the tour operators offer excursions arranged through Turkish travel agencies to local places of interest. Some also offer trips to Istanbul, Ankara, Cappadocia and the Greek Islands.

TOURIST INFORMATION

The tourist board's main office on the Aegean is in Izmir at Ataturk Cad. 418 Alsancak (tel: Izmir 220207). Tourism and information offices can be found in all the main resorts.

THE CLIMATE

In general the Aegean climate is warm and dry from April to October. Late spring and early autumn are good times to visit when temperatures are around the mid-70s (20–22°C) and evenings are mild. In the summer the temperature can reach the high 80s (28–30°C), which is great for a beach and watersports holiday but a little oppressive if you plan to do a lot of sightseeing. Winter on the Aegean is mild and fairly dry but there is no real sun after October.

CULINARY SPECIALITIES

Turkish cuisine is a mixture of Mediterranean and Asian-style dishes. In the Aegean region there is, not surprisingly, a detectable Greek taste to the cooking. Moussakas and other dishes which include aubergines, tomatoes, lamb and olives feature on most menus. Grilled fish is another speciality of the Aegean and there is an abundance of good fish restaurants in all the coastal towns. The locals often eat fish while sipping raki (the Turkish equivalent of Pernod).

WHERE TO GO FOR WHAT

Sightseers will particularly enjoy Bergama (the ancient city of Pergamon), Efes and Geyre (which is usually better known as Aphrodisias). Sun-worshippers and swimmers should look out for Kusadasi, Bodrum and Cesme, particularly if you're looking for a lively resort with plenty of nightlife. For quieter beach holidays the Gulf of Edremit is recommended. Here the small resorts of Kucukkuyu, Akcay and Altinoluk offer secluded bays and picturesque harbours. Pamukkale, with its beautiful calcified waterfalls and numerous thermal pools, is a treat for both the sightseer and the health enthusiast. There are also thermal spas near Cesme and Akcay. Izmir is an ideal base for a touring holiday in the Aegean region as it offers easy access to all the main coastal resorts and historic sites.

Traditional Turkish entertainment and a certain amount of nightlife is provided by the festivals which take place throughout the region during the summer months. A few festivals worth noting are: the Ephesus Arts and Culture Festival at Selcuk (29 April–6 May); the Pamukkale Fete at Denizli (25–27 May); the Cesme Sea Festival (3–8 July); the International Bergama Fair (6–8 July); the Troy Festival at Canakkale (10–18 August); and the Bodrum Arts and Culture Festival (1–7 September).

The North Aegean

For the geographical breakdown of the region we have divided the Aegean coast into northern and southern provinces. In the north Aegean we start with Canakkale and work our way down the coast through Ayvalik, Bergama, Manisa, Izmir, Sardis and Cesme, mentioning many smaller towns and resorts en route.

The port of **CANAKKALE** is situated at the end of the Dardanelles Straits (the Canakkale Bogazi) where the Sea of Marmara meets the Aegean. This narrow stretch of water separates Canakkale in Asian Turkey from the port of **ECEABAT** in the country's small European region. Canakkale has been developed around a medieval fortress built by the Ottoman ruler Sultan Mehmet II in the mid-1400s. The fortress is still used today in the defence of the straits and, though it is open to the public, tourists are forbidden to climb to the top of the battlements. Other places of interest close to the town centre include a military museum, a small war museum commemorating Ataturk and the battles of Gallipoli, and a small archaeological museum.

Canakkale itself is not really a holiday resort so you won't find it in any of the package holiday brochures except where it's included as part of a tour. For the independent traveller, however, it's an ideal base for visits to Troy and Gallipoli, and Istanbul is also within easy travelling distance.

Canakkale is certainly not the place to go for a beach holiday, but the pretty resort of Intepe, about 15 kilometres south of the town on the road to Troy, offers one of the most attractive beaches in the area.

As far as hotels and eating places are concerned Canakkale has a reasonable range of accommodation, from fairly expensive motels to very cheap pensions, and an attractive collection of waterfront restaurants, cafés, bars and beer gardens.

If you want to keep it cheap and simple, the **Hotel Bakir** close to the town centre is clean and modestly comfortable and enjoys a view of the straits. There are several cheaper-range hotels in the town centre but the Bakir is one of the few downtown establishments registered with the Ministry of Culture and Tourism. Don't, however, be too wary of hotels which are not registered as this may only mean they don't have a bar; providing you check the facilities before committing yourself you should be safe.

For more luxurious and more expensive accommodation it's necessary to travel out of town towards **INTEPE** where you will find the motels **Mola** and **Tusan**. These establishments provide more in the way of home comforts but they are not really a practical option unless you have a car.

The town is at its busiest in mid-August when it plays host to the Troy Festival. Accommodation is in great demand at this time, and it's advisable to book in advance if possible.

Regular ferry services across the Dardanelles Straits link Canakkale to the port of **ECEABAT** on the narrow peninsula which forms part of European Turkey. The peninsula is known to most of us as **GALLIPOLI**, though it is known to the turks as **GELIBOLU**. A few miles south of Eceabat is the town of **KILITBAHIR**, dominated by a fifteenth-century fortress which can be seen from the eastern shores of the straits. Not far from Kilitbahir there is a giant inscription on the hillside which carries the first words of a poem recalling the battles of Gallipoli during the First World War. In 1915 the Allies, led by Winston Churchill, launched a naval assault on the Dardanelles in a bid to capture Constantinople and penetrate Eastern Europe. In the nine months' fighting which ensued the Turks managed to hold their ground at Gallipoli and Canakkale, but not without massive losses on both sides. Today there are monuments to the Turkish, British and French war dead at SEDDULBAHIR and soldiers from Australia and New Zealand are commemorated at ARIBURNU.

Car ferries operate between Canakkale and Eceabat every hour throughout the day, and there is also a less-frequent motorboat service between Canakkale and Kilitbahir. Day trips to the battlefields of Gallipoli can be booked through some of the Turkish travel agencies in Canakkale and the taxi drivers in Eceabat are normally willing to haggle a fare for a tour of the main sights.

One of the most famous historic sites in the region is the ancient city of **TROY** which is about 20 miles south of Canakkale on the main E24 highway. The city was made famous by Homer, the blind poet from Izmir who gave a detailed account of the Trojan War of 1250 BC in his poem *The Iliad*. According to legend, the Achaean Greeks invaded Troy in order to recapture the beautiful Helen who had been stolen from her husband, the King of Sparta, by the Trojans. The war raged for ten years, and in their most famous assault on Troy the Achaeans gained entry to the city with a wooden horse filled with soldiers.

Up until the last century the city's history was believed to be based on legend alone, but in 1871 an amateur German archaeologist named Schliemann gained permission from the Ottoman government to excavate the site. Schliemann's excavations revealed nine principal levels of occupation between the early Bronze Age and Roman times. The first city of Troy is thought to have been founded around 3000 BC and in the centuries which followed eight more cities emerged, each built on the ruins of the last.

But despite extensive excavation of the site, Troy's legend is still far more interesting than its ruins. If you're a serious archaeologist you'll no doubt enjoy examining the rubble of the ancient cities, but for the average sightseer there isn't much to see. Today the nine cities are numbered Troy I to Troy IX to assist visitors to the site. The most impressive ruins are the towers of Troy I; the ramp and gate of Troy II, which is the world's earliest example of a planned city; and a Roman theatre which formed part of Troy IX. The only other tourist attraction is a replica of the famous Trojan Horse, which is probably the most photographed feature of the site.

Most visitors to Troy are based in Istanbul or Canakkale. The **Mola Motel** and the **Tusan Truva Motel**, which are among Canakkale's better establishments, are conveniently located for the site. Buses which operate along the main route between Canakkale and Izmir pass within two miles of Troy, but the easiest way to get there is by *dolmus* from Canakkale's central bus station.

Further down the coast between Canakkale and Edremit is the archaeological site of **BEHRAMKALE** (the ancient city of Assos). The city, which is little more than a village by today's standards, is almost 3000 years old, and within its crumbling walls there is evidence of Greek, Roman and Byzantine occupation. But Behramkale is notable for its beauty as well as its past. This little fishing village is beautifully positioned between pine woods and the blue water of the Gulf of Edremit, and from the top of the acropolis there is a breathtaking view of the Aegean and the Greek island of Lesbos (also known as Mytilene).

Further round the gulf is the town of **EDREMIT** which is flanked by the pretty beach resorts of **ALTINULOK**, **AKCAY** and **OREN**. These small coastal towns are not really for the fun-seeker, but more for the sun-seeker who likes to avoid the crowds. Akcay is also noted for its numerous thermal springs. Accommodation is easy to find as there is a good range of hotels and pensions dotted along the coastline.

Further south, on the opposite side of the gulf from Behramkale and still within sight of the island of Lesbos, is the beach resort and fishing village of **AYVALIK**. This is reputed to be the prettiest resort on the north Aegean, and it's fast becoming a haven for sun-worshippers. The best beaches can be found two or three miles out of town (on the main bus route) at **CAMLIK** and **SARMISAKLI**. Not far from the beaches is the hilltop known as **SEYTAN SOFRASI** (the Devil's Dining Table) from which there is a spectacular panoramic view of the gulf and the islands.

Throughout the tourist season there are boat trips to the Greek island of LESBOS every day except Tuesday and Thursday. It is also possible to take a boat trip to the island of ALIBEY which is actually linked to the mainland by a causeway. Underwater fishing is popular around Alibey, and it's worth visiting the island if only to sample one of its excellent waterfront fish restaurants.

Eating and drinking in Ayvalik is a pleasant way to spend an evening, especially if you choose one of the small restaurants or beer gardens overlooking the picturesque harbour. Accommodation in the town centre is cheap and plentiful and there are numerous beach hotels on the road between Ayvalik and Sarmisakli.

For the sightseer, a holiday in the north Aegean could not be complete without a trip to BERGAMA, the ancient site of **PERGAMON**. While Bergama is not really a resort in itself, many tour operators offer excursions from Izmir (which is less than two hours' drive away) and it features in many coach tours and classical tours. The E24 coastal road gives easy access to Bergama which is about 20 miles inland, midway between Edremit and Izmir.

The Kingdom of Pergamon was one of the leading centres of culture, learning and medicine in the ancient world, and its extensive ruins are an impressive reminder of its former importance. The kingdom started to flourish under Lysimachus, one of Alexander the Great's generals, after Alexander's death in 323 BC. Its development continued under a succession of kings until 133 BC when the last Pergamese king, the heirless Attalus III, died and willed the kingdom to his Roman allies. When Pergamon became a Roman province in 129 BC it was one of the most powerful kingdoms in Asia Minor.

The site of Pergamon is split into three levels: the Upper City, the Middle City and the Lower City. The focal point of the Lower City, essentially the Roman part of Pergamon, is the **Asclepion**, a huge medical complex dedicated to Asclepios, the Roman god of medicine. Though built by the kings of Pergamon, the centre reached its heyday under the ingenious Roman surgeon Galen, whose medical theories and techniques won world acclaim for the Asclepion. The area around the complex encompasses treatment rooms, pools, a sacred well, a library, a theatre and the temples of Asclepios and Telesphorus.

Pergamon is dominated by the hilltop **Acropolis** (the Upper City) which was built during the third century BC. Close to the Acropolis is the famous **library**, built by the Pergamese kings, which formed the nucleus of Pergamon's cultural development. At one point the library housed more than 200,000 books and was second only to the world's largest library in Alexandria. Few books remain today as the collection was plundered by Marc Antony who gifted many of the books to Cleopatra after the library in Alexandria was destroyed by fire.

Built into the hillside near the Acropolis is a magnificent **amphitheatre** designed to seat more than 10,000 spectators. The theatre is flanked by the **Altar of Zeus**, considered to be one of the finest examples of Hellenic architecture, and the temples of Trajan and Dionysus. Today sightseers can only admire the base of the Altar of Zeus and the rest is kept in the Pergamon Museum in East Berlin.

The road between the Acropolis and the Asclepion passes through the Middle City where the interesting ruins include a massive **gymnasium and school** and the **Temple of Demeter**. The Upper City and the Middle City are linked by the **Agora** (the old market place). The Upper Agora is in the Upper City and the smaller Lower Agora is in the Middle City.

Away from the main sites, Bergama offers other attractions including an **archaeological museum**, an **ethnographical museum** and the **Red Courtyard**, which was a temple built in honour of the Egyptian god Serapis in the first century AD and later converted into a Byzantine basilica. The museums are open to the public every day except Monday. The town centre also has a collection of small restaurants, cafés and tea gardens which are ideal stopping-off points if you need a rest and refreshment between bouts of sightseeing.

Downtown Bergama doesn't have much to offer in the way of accommodation, probably because most tourists spend a day at the ruins and then move on. If you do plan to stay overnight, the **Park Hotel** is recommended for cheap and basic accommodation while the **Tusan Bergama** provides more luxurious motel accommodation. The hotels are normally at their busiest during the second week in July when the International Bergama Fair takes place.

If you're planning a day's sightseeing in Bergama a good camera is recommended and a good pair of walking shoes is essential. The ruins of Pergamon are scattered over 30,000 acres and there are no bus links between the major sites. While it's possible to take taxis between the ruins, a certain amount of hard walking is inevitable.

The coastal road between Bergama and Izmir is dotted with pleasant little resorts and historical sites which make interesting stops for the touring holidaymaker. A few miles south-west of Bergama is the port of DIKILI, a very small resort with only a few hotels and waterfront restaurants. The tranquillity of Dikili is only ever shattered when, from time to time, the cruise liners deposit their passengers at the harbour for excursions to Pergamon.

About 14 miles south of Dikili is the attractive fishing village of **CANDARLI**, the centrepiece of which is a well-preserved thirteenth-century Genoese fortress. The road out of the village takes you past the Hellenic sites of **Gryneion** and **Myrina** which were once bustling Aeolian ports.

One of the prettiest small resorts on this stretch of the coastline is ALIAGA, about 20 miles south of Candarli. Aliaga is particularly interesting because it was built with stones taken from the ruins of the nearby city of **Kyme**, another Hellenic site worth noting. Because of its handy location between Bergama and Izmir, Aliaga is becoming increasingly popular with independent travellers. Hotels to look out for are the **Donmez Hotel**, which is basic but clean, and the **Afacan Motel** which is slightly more up-market.

About ten miles outside Aliaga on the road to Izmir there is a new road which takes you straight to the port of **FOCA**, the ancient Ionian city of Phocaea. In the sixth century BC the inhabitants of Phocaea colonized parts of the Black Sea coast and the French Mediterranean coast, including the ports of Marseille and Nice. Today the tables have been turned and the French have almost taken over Foča with their **Club Mediterranée holiday village**. Guests at the glamorous complex can enjoy windsurfing, sailing, snorkelling and a host of other activities in the idyllic setting of olive groves, white sandy beaches and clear blue waters. If Club Med is a little out of your price range, there is plenty of cheap accommodation in and around the town centre. The **Sultan Hotel** and the **Hanedan Hotel** are worth bearing in mind.

As yet, Foča has been ignored by the majority of British tour operators who prefer to concentrate on the larger south Aegean resorts such as Cesme, Kusadasi and Bodrum. As a result Foča's beautiful beaches are generally quieter than those south of Izmir and accommodation is notably cheaper. From Foča you can visit the nearby ruins of a Genoese fortress and there are regular bus services to Izmir.

Twenty miles north of Izmir on the E24 you arrive at the town of **MENEMEN** where it's possible to take a left turn inland to Manisa, the historic city of **MAGNESIA AD SIPYLUS**. Menemen itself has an interesting past, for it was here that fanatical religious conservatives staged an uprising in 1930 in protest of Ataturk's reforms which sought to replace religious law with the new state law. The hero of the day was one of Ataturk's young officers, Mustafa Kubilay, who was beheaded while attempting to stop the riot. Thereafter, the government swiftly dealt with troublemakers and erected a statue in the town square to commemorate Kubilay.

The attractive city of **MANISA**, with its mixture of new government buildings and numerous old mosques, is located 20 miles east of Menemen off the E24 and 25 miles south-east of Izmir on the main Izmir/Manisa road. Up until the early 1920s the city boasted thousands of examples of Roman, Byzantine, Seljuk and Ottoman architecture, but many of these were destroyed by the Greek armies during the War of Independence (1920–1922). Of the few hundred historic buildings which remain, the most noteworthy are mosques, including the **Ulu Camii**, the **Hatuniye Camii** and the **Muradiye Camii**, part of which houses the city's archaeological museum.

The ruins of Magnesia ad Sipylus, the Byzantine capital during the empire's decline, are located a couple of miles out of the city centre on the road to Izmir. The remains are centred around the thirteenth-century Byzantine citadel which dominates the ancient city from the top of Mount Sipylus. From the summit of the hill there is a wonderful view of the mosques of Manisa and the surrounding countryside.

IZMIR

Izmir is the third largest city in Turkey, with almost two million inhabitants, and the second largest port after Istanbul. As you enter Izmir you suddenly become aware of its modern appearance and an unusual cosmopolitan atmosphere which makes it different from any other town on the Aegean. The city is built on the shores of a large bay and sheltered by the mountains which encircle it from the east. Its palm-lined seafront is dotted with smart shops, restaurants and beer gardens, and its wide boulevards and modern buildings create an impression of newness and orderliness. While Izmir has a long and eventful history, dating back to early Hellenic times, only a few reminders of the past remain. Many historic buildings and antiquities were lost in the Great Fire which destroyed much of the city in 1923, shortly after Turkey's victory over Greece in the War of Independence (a war which Turks are eager to point out was started by the Greeks). The Republic of Turkey was founded in the same year and with the help of the country's new leader, Kemal Ataturk, a new city emerged from the ashes. Today Izmir is a thriving commercial centre, and the presence of NATO's south-eastern headquarters adds to its international ambiance.

As far as the tourist is concerned, Izmir should be thought of as a base for exploration rather than a holiday destination in itself. Thanks to good accommodation and an efficient transportation system, Izmir is an ideal departure point for sightseeing trips throughout the region, and frequent excursions are available to **PERGAMON**, **EPHESUS** and **SARDIS** (the Aegean's greatest archaeological sites). Some tour operators and local travel agencies also run excursions to the thermal spas near **CESME** and the famous calcified waterfalls at **PAMUKKALE**.

Izmir is by no means a great beach resort as its beaches tend to be less attractive and more crowded than those to the immediate north and south. If you're desperate for sand and surf you'll find the best beaches a few miles south-west of the city on the road to Cesme. During the summer months bus services operate between *Konak* (the city centre) and the popular beaches.

The city itself boasts several interesting sights – but only enough to keep you interested for a day or two. The main tourist attractions are the Kadifekale, the Agora, the bazaar and the Kulturpark.

The **Kadifekale** or 'Velvet Fortress' overlooks Izmir from the top of Mount Pagos, the closest of the mountains to the south-east of the city. The fortress was originally built by Alexander the Great in the fourth century BC and later restored by the Romans and the Byzantines. These days tourists can take a *dolmus* to the fortress and enjoy the spectacular view of the city and the Gulf of Izmir. For a truly Eastern experience visit Mount Pagos at dusk as the sun sets on the minarets and muezzins call for evening prayer.

In the city centre you can visit the remains of the **Agora** which was built by Alexander the Great and rebuilt by the Romans following the earthquake of AD 178. The old market place features a number of well-preserved porticoes and the impressive statues of Poseidon, Demeter and Artemis. Only a few streets away you'll find Izmir's colourful **bazaar** with its narrow winding streets and splendid displays of carpets, antiques, jewellery, copperware, clothing and local handicrafts. Outside the bazaar, the majority of Izmir's better shops can be found on the fashionable seafront boulevard (Ataturk Caddesi).

The centrepiece of the city is the huge **Kulturpark**, the venue for the Izmir International Fair which takes place each year from 20 August to 20 September. For eleven months of the year the park simply provides a quiet setting for leisurely walks away from the bustling streets. Within the park you'll find the **Kulturpark Archaeological Museum** and the **Basmane Archaeological Museum** which houses a fascinating collection of Roman artefacts.

Other landmarks in Izmir include the two main city squares. Both are located off Ataturk Caddesi – **Cumhuriyet Meydani** to the north and **Konak Meydani** to the south. At Cumhuriyet Meydani you'll find the famous equestrian statue of Ataturk and the Central Post Office (Merkez PTT). Konak Meydani, the more central of the two squares, is the site of Izmir's elegant Ottoman clock-tower and the attractive Yahli Mosque. It is also one of the city's main departure points for buses and *dolmuses.*

Transport to destinations in and around Izmir is easy to find. From Konak Meydani you can take a bus or *dolmus* to any part of the city for a small fare. Throughout the summer you can take buses to the beaches at Inciralti (about seven miles west of the city) and to Cesme, Kusadasi, Selcuk and Ephesus. Inter-city buses and long-distance services operate from the **Otobus Garaji**, the main bus station in the north of the city. If you're embarking on a long journey you can also go by plane or train – but be warned, the trains are always slow and often uncomfortable. The airport which serves Izmir is about ten miles north of the city at **Cigli**. Turkish Airlines operate internal services from Izmir to all Turkey's main cities, including six daily flights to Istanbul and two daily flights to Ankara. From **Basmane Railway Station**, which is only a short *dolmus* ride away from Konak, there are daily services to Istanbul and Ankara, and thrice-weekly overnight trains to Ankara. Suburban trains to Ephesus and Selcuk run from **Alsancak Railway Station** in the north of the city.

As far as accommodation is concerned Izmir certainly has plenty to offer, though most of it is in the moderate to expensive range rather than the moderate to rock-bottom range. The hotels most favoured by British tour operators are the deluxe **Buyuk Efes Hotel** (sometimes called the Grand Efes) and the middle-of-the-road **Kismet Hotel**. The Buyuk Efes, which is certainly the more expensive of the two, has a swimming pool, a rooftop restaurant and a nightclub which offers an excellent programme of entertainment for both residents and non-residents. It also accommodates a tourist information office. Both hotels enjoy a central location and a good view of the bay. Apart from the Kismet, two other moderately priced hotels worth noting are the **Anba Hotel** and the **Kilim Hotel**. The majority of Izmir's cheap and basic hotels and pensions are scattered around the back streets between Konak and Basmane Railway Station. A few names to look out for are the **Billur Hotel**, the **Kaya Hotel**, the **Atlantik Palas** and the **Karaoglu**. Because of its scarcity, low-budget accommodation is in big demand, so it's wise to book in advance if possible. Alternatively, you can take your tent and head for the **Inciralti Campsite** which is about three miles outside the city on the Cesme road. This site is owned by Kervansaray Mocamp who run the best chain of campsites in Turkey.

The choice of eating places in Izmir is vast. You can eat expensive international cuisine at any of the up-market hotels or fill yourself for less than £1 at the kebab stalls and pastry shops in and around the bazaar. For good-value Turkish cuisine try the seafood restaurants on the seafront and the main boulevards, or the open-air restaurants in the Kulturpark.

During the summer months nightlife centres around the principal hotels and the Kulturpark. Cabaret and oriental dancing can be found at the **Buyuk Efes** and most of the mid-range hotels offer reasonably priced dinner dances which sometimes include Turkish cabaret. From May to October head for the **Mogambo Nightclub** and the **Kubana Nightclub** in the Kulturpark where you can dance the night away, listen to music or enjoy a meal in a pretty outdoor setting.

About 60 miles east of Izmir on the road to Ankara is the ancient city of **SARDIS**, one of the Aegean's best archaeological sites and a popular destination for day-tripping sightseers. In the sixth century BC Sardis was the capital city of the

Kingdom of Lydia, and it was here that coinage was first invented. As a result of the invention Lydia became the wealthiest kingdom in Anatolia with Sardis as its trading centre. The last ruler of Lydia, King Croesus, was known as the 'richest man in the world' in ancient times, and today his name is still synonymous with wealth. The kingdom was first captured by the Persians in 550 BC, then by Alexander the Great in 334 BC and later by the Romans who were left with the task of rebuilding Sardis following the earthquake in AD 178.

The most impressive ruins at Sardis are those of the **Temple of Artemis** which was constructed during the rule of Alexander the Great. With its grandiose columns, the structure is a splendid example of Ionic architecture and one of the largest temples of its kind. Other interesting structures include the gymnasium, baths, theatre and stadium which were built by the Roman emperors, and a well-restored synagogue.

Excursions to Sardis can be booked through any of the large travel agencies in Izmir and many package tour operators organize their own excursions for their clients. Alternatively, you can make your own way there on one of the frequent bus services from Izmir's Otobus Garaji or by train from Basmane Railway Station. The travelling time from Izmir to Sardis is about 1 hour 30 minutes (longer if you go by train). Excursions can also be booked through some travel agencies and tour operators in Cesme and Kusadasi.

If you head west for 50 miles when you leave Izmir you'll come to the pretty port of **CESME**. This popular beach resort and thermal centre is situated at the tip of a peninsula, only six miles away from the Greek island of Chios. Cesme is a sprawling resort made up of several small villages, most of which have their own harbour, their own beach and their own spas. In Hellenic times (1200–600 BC) Cesme was one of the most important medical centres in western Anatolia, and people would travel for miles to 'take the waters' which are said to help in the cure of rheumatic disorders.

In the past the port was dominated by the fourteenth-century Genoese Fortress which was later restored by the Ottomans in the sixteenth century. Today life in Cesme centres around the **Golden Dolphin Holiday Village** which is literally a resort within a resort. The Golden Dolphin (or Altin Yunus in Turkish) is a hotel complex, a health centre and a marina all rolled into one. Its facilities include three hotels (with almost 600 rooms between them), a choice of restaurants offering Turkish and international cuisine, a swimming pool (with a separate pool for small children), shops, bars, a hairdressing salon and a casino. For the sports enthusiast there's tennis, table-tennis, horse riding, mini golf, waterskiing and sailing, and health fanatics can take advantage of genuine thermal pools, saunas, steam baths and a gymnasium. Guests can also obtain special treatment programmes from the centre's dieticians, masseurs and physiotherapists.

A large number of British tour operators who specialize in beach holidays and spa holidays in Turkey now offer Cesme as a destination, and many feature packages at the Golden Dolphin. Cesme is becoming increasingly popular as a family holiday destination because it has gently sloping beaches which provide shallow water for safe swimming.

One of the villages on the outskirts of Cesme which is particularly worth a visit is ILICA which has several thermal springs and one of the best beaches in the area. The road between Cesme and Ilica is dotted with mid-range hotels, some of which offer rooms with private thermal baths. In the centre of Cesme you'll find numerous cheap hotels and pensions which are handy for the independent traveller who wishes to make an overnight stop en route to Chios. In Ilica look out for the **Turban Cesme Hotel**, which is fairly up-market but reasonably priced, and the motels **Balin** and **Motes** which are cheap and modest. In Cesme good accommodation can be found at the **Turtes Motel**, which is modest, and the **Ertan Hotel** which is very basic. For entertainment, nightlife and eating places you need look no further than the Golden Dolphin where you'll find everything under the one roof. If you want a night out away from the crowds try one of the many waterfront restaurants.

Cesme doesn't have much to offer the serious sightseer, but various excursions are available through the package tour operators and local travel agencies. In Cesme itself the main attractions are the **Fortress**, which houses the **Ottoman Museum of Arms** and gives a superb view of the coastline; the sixteenth-century **Caravanserai** with its interesting courtyard and shops; the eighteenth-century Ottoman **Mausoleum**; and two nineteenth-century mosques, **Haci Memis Camii** and

Haci Mehmet Camii, which are still in use today.

Local excursions are available to ancient **TEOS**, the site of the **Temple of Dionysus**, and to **SIGACIK** where you can see the remains of a fortified Genoese port. You can also travel further afield to **IZMIR** or the ancient city of **EPHESUS**. Ferries to the Greek island of Chios operate from April to October with daily services in July and August and twice-weekly services the rest of the season. Cesme is not a good base for far-flung exploration because it is out on a limb – or out on a peninsula to be more precise.

The South Aegean

Fifty miles south of Izmir, just off the E24, is the historic town of **SELCUK** which is adjacent to **Ephesus** (Efes), one of Turkey's most important and best-preserved archaeological sites. Selcuk is generally thought of as a stopping-off point for visits to the ruins at Ephesus but it is also an interesting town in its own right. In ancient times Selcuk and Ephesus were important religious centres and the early rulers of western Anatolia built magnificent shrines in honour of their gods. In the second century BC the Romans established their eastern capital in Ephesus, and in the first century AD the city became one of the most important centres of early Christianity.

There are several places of interest in and around Selcuk which are worth a visit before you head off for the ruins of Ephesus. The **Ephesus Archaeological Museum** will whet your appetite for exploration of the ancient city. The beautifully displayed exhibits are the highlights of more than 100 years' excavation and include the famous many-breasted **Statue of Artemis**, the Greek goddess of fertility. At the top of the hill which overlooks Selcuk there is a **Byzantine citadel** and the newly restored **Basilica of St John** which was built by the Emperor Justinian in the fifth century on the site of the apostle's tomb. At the foot of the hill you can visit the **Isa Bey Camii**, a fourteenth-century Seljuk mosque, and on the outskirts of Selcuk, heading towards Ephesus, you'll find the remains of the **Temple of Artemis**. Built during the rule of Alexander the Great, this splendid temple was once rated among the seven wonders of the world, but today little more than the base remains.

Selcuk is also famous for its Camel Wrestling Festival which is held each year on 15 and 16 January. This unusual spectacle involves large bull camels fighting to the accompaniment of flutes and drums. It's not everybody's cup of tea, but it's certainly authentic Turkish entertainment.

If you want to arrive in Ephesus bright and early for your day's sightseeing, you'll find plenty of modest and comfortable accommodation in Selcuk. In the town centre there's the **Aksoy Hotel** (21 rooms) and a number of small family-run pensions including **Pension Baykal**, **Pension Akbulut** and **Pension Mengi**. **Otel Victoria** (tel: 5451-3203) opened in May '88 by two Turks who previously lived in London. The hotel is situated in a quiet area within 100 yards of the railway station. Excellent value at around 50,000TL a double (room), including breakfast. Just outside Selcuk on the road to Kusadasi there's the **Motel Tusan** which is cheap and within easy walking distance of the ruins. Most of the accommodation in Selcuk is at the lower end of the price scale, so don't expect luxury.

Eating is also a cheap pastime in Selcuk and there are numerous small restaurants and tea gardens. The **Cengiz**, the **Hitit** and the **Yildiz** restaurants are all recommended for pleasant surroundings and value for money.

The hotels and pensions in Selcuk are generally patronized by independent travellers and serious sightseers and archaeologists who wish to be as close to Ephesus as possible. A good one is **Pension Barim**, behind the museum, or **Barim II**, opposite the information office. Otherwise, the majority of tourists who visit Ephesus are based in KUSADASI which is only 12 miles south of the ruins. While accommodation is more expensive in Kusadasi, it does have more to offer in the way of tourist facilities than Selcuk, and its beaches are also a big attraction. Ephesus is also a popular destination for day-trippers based in IZMIR as frequent bus and train services make the ruins easily accessible. You will find that many travel agencies and tour operators in Kusadasi and Izmir offer excursions to Ephesus. If you'd rather make your own way there from Selcuk or Kusadasi a *dolmus* is the best means of transport. *Dolmuses* which operate on the 15-mile stretch between Selcuk and Kusadasi will drop you off at the turning for the ruins near the Motel Tusan. From here you'll have a ten-minute walk to the archaeological site.

In the second century AD when **EPHESUS** was at its most powerful as the eastern capital of the Roman Empire, it was the richest city in the Middle East and one of the busiest ports and trading centres in the Mediterranean. The wealthy Roman emperors adorned the city with temples, theatres, baths, agoras and a host of impressive monuments. Throughout the first century of Roman occupation, the inhabitants of Ephesus worshipped the goddess Artemis, the protector of their city. But in the first century AD, when St Paul was said to have visited western Anatolia, the Ephesians slowly converted to Christianity.

As you approach the ancient city from the Selcuk–Kusadasi road you'll pass the **Gymnasium of Vedius**, built in the first century, and the **Church of the Virgin Mary** which is also known as the Double Church. At the entrance gate there is a cluster of shops and cafés where you can buy refreshments and souvenirs.

From Selcuk you'll enter the archaeological zone through the lower gate which takes you on to the **Arcadian Way**, the city's marble-paved main street. Turn west along the Arcadian Way and you'll arrive at the **old harbour** which has been silted up for centuries; turn to the east and the road leads to the **Grand Theatre** which is undoubtedly the centrepiece of the ruins. With seating capacity of 25,000 the restored theatre provides a dramatic setting for the many folkloric shows which are staged during the annual International Ephesus Festival (29 April–8 May). Just off the Arcadian Way you'll find the remains of the **Lower Agora**, the **Celcius Library** and the **Temple of Serapis**. Further south is the **Curetes Way** where the sights include the **Temple of Hadrian**, the **Trajan Fountain** and the **Upper Agora**.

Ephesus is overlooked by **Mount Pion**, at the top of which you can still see a few remains of the ancient city walls. A footpath on the eastern side of the hill leads to the **Cave of the Seven Sleepers** where, legend has it, seven young Christians became trapped after fleeing Ephesus to avoid persecution by the Romans. Two centuries later when an earthquake hit the area the cave was opened and the youths returned to Ephesus to find it had become a Christian city.

For the average tourist who doesn't wish to explore the ruins in any great depth, a day is ample time to see all the sights. Remember to take a comfortable pair of walking shoes as you'll have to cover a fair bit of ground in order to see the best of the ruins.

If you leave the archaeological site through the upper gate (to the south of the ruins) you'll find yourself on the main road from Selcuk to **MERYEMANA**. Often referred to as The House of the Virgin Mary, Meryemana is an important destination for Christian pilgrims who believe the Virgin Mary spent the last days of her life here. At the beginning of the nineteenth century a German nun named Catherine Emmerich claimed to have had a vision of Mary in her home just before her death. Several years after the nun's death excavations around Ephesus uncovered a small stone cottage which fitted her description of Mary's home to the last detail. A small chapel has been built on the site of the old cottage and every year on 15 August thousands of Christians descend on the small town of Meryemana to celebrate Mary's Assumption into heaven.

To visit the site, catch one of the *dolmuses* which frequently make the five-mile trip from Selcuk to Meryemana.

KUSADASI

Kusadasi is one of Turkey's busiest beach resorts and a popular port of call for cruise liners whose passengers wish to visit nearby historical sites. It is a picturesque port built on the shores of a large and attractive bay and it boasts one of the best-equipped yacht marinas in the country. With its numerous hotels, restaurants, bars, discos, souvenir shops and busy beaches, Kusadasi certainly bears some of the hallmarks of mass tourism, but it is still relatively unspoilt compared to the larger Spanish and Greek resorts. It is not, however, the place to go for a quiet holiday or a typically Turkish experience – as one large coastal resort is very much like another – but it is an ideal destination for the sun-worshipper or socialite who's planning a trip to Turkey. Its proximity to the archaeological sites of EPHESUS, PRIENE, MILETUS and DIDYMA and the Greek island of SAMOS also makes it a good base for sightseeing trips. As a result of commercialization prices in Kusadasi tend to be high by Turkish standards, though still fairly reasonable by Western European standards.

Kusadasi is a perfect example of a package holiday resort: during the day life revolves around the beaches, the tourist shops and the street cafés, and at night entertainment and discos are laid on by the major hotels. An increasing number of British tour operators are offering Kusadasi as a Turkish destination with packages aimed at the young set and young families. It is also a popular centre for watersports and sailing holidays. Many British companies offer packages at **Kustur Holiday Village, Hotel Club Akdeniz** and **Hotel Club Kervansaray**, all lively establishments which attract a young fun-loving crowd. From a historic point of view, the Kervansaray, which is a converted Ottoman Caravanserai now run by Club Med, is undoubtedly the most impressive. Otherwise, all three are equally good with the full range of tourist facilities under one roof. The Kustur Holiday Village and Hotel Club Akdeniz are both a few miles out of town, but transport to and from the hotels is provided for guests. Other popular choices for British holidaymakers are the hotels **Kismet** and **Tusan** and the slightly cheaper hotels **Marti** and **Bellevue**.

Most of the package accommodation offered in Kusadasi is in the moderate to deluxe range, but there are plenty of small, family-run hotels and pensions for the cost-conscious independent traveller. The cheapest accommodation is to be found in the town centre and it fills up very quickly in the high season. A few names to remember are **Hotel Neptun**, **Hotel Ada**, **Hotel Gurkay**, **Pension Akan**, **Pension Sur** and **Pension Istankoy**. These establishments, and many other downtown lodgings, offer very basic but clean accommodation at rock-bottom prices.

There are several campsites within easy travelling distance of Kusadasi, the best of which is the **Mocamp Kervansaray** site which is six miles out of town on the road to Selcuk. The **Onder** campsite and the **Yat** campsite are closer and cheaper and both offer a reasonable standard of facilities.

Because Kusadasi is a tourist trap, eating out can be expensive. As in all Turkish towns, it is possible to eat well for next to nothing, but in Kusadasi you have to look a little harder for the cheap restaurants. If you don't wish to pay over the odds for a mediocre fish dinner steer clear of the restaurants on the harbour-side and the seafront. As you move away from the centre of town you'll find the prices drop and the food is just as good. Only a few minutes' walk from the seafront there are a number of small fish restaurants and kebab houses where you can enjoy a full meal with wine for less than £8. Alcoholic drinks can also be expensive and the best advice is to stick to the local brands. For well-prepared food at reasonable prices try the **Konya Restaurant**, the **Merket Restaurant**, the **Kilis Lokanta** and the **Osman Dundar Kebapci**.

Don't set aside too much time for sightseeing in Kusadasi because there isn't that much to see. If you're really keen to do some sightseeing you'll have to take one of the excursions which can be booked locally through the travel agencies and tour operators.

Kusadasi's main attraction is the pretty 'ISLAND OF BIRDS' from which the resort takes its name. This small, birdless island is linked to the town by a causeway and dominated by a fourteenth-century fortress. The island comes to life after dark when the fortress becomes a nightclub and tourists from the mainland flock to its bars and disco. The town's **Grand Bazaar**, with its colourful stalls and bustling atmosphere, is also worth a visit – even if it is one of the most expensive in Turkey. It doesn't cost anything to walk around and browse, but beware of the skilful traders who are well-practised at parting tourists from their money. The discerning souvenir hunter should be able to find some bargains in jewellery, leatherware and carpets. The only other things worth seeing are the Ottoman **Caravanserai**, an old Turkish resting place which has been tastefully converted into an hotel, and the ancient **Watchtower** in the centre of town which now serves as a police station. Kusadasi's beaches are dotted along a fairly lengthy stretch of coastline to the north and south of the town. The most attractive are those on the outskirts of the resort at ICMELER and YAVANSU.

The *dolmus* is the most common mode of transport for getting to and from the beaches and around the resort. During the peak season it's also possible to get to the beach in one of the horse-drawn carts which can be seen going backwards and forwards along the seafront throughout the day. The main pick-up point for buses and *dolmuses* is the **Otobus Garaji** in Kahramanlar Caddesi, the road which runs inland from the harbour. *Dolmuses* for the beaches to the south of the town leave from the Caravanserai.

With the vast range of facilities on offer in Kusadasi it's possible to have an enjoyable, fun-packed holiday without ever leaving the resort. It would be a shame, however, not to take the opportunity to see some of the great historic sites and other places of interest in the immediate vicinity. The most popular excursions are the cheap day-trips to the three historic sites to the south of the town at PRIENE, MILETUS and DIDYMA. It's possible to travel independently to these places by bus or *dolmus* but the excursion is simpler as it includes visits to all three sites. (A description of these sites is given later in this chapter.) To visit EPHESUS, one of Turkey's most famous archaeological sites, simply catch a *dolmus* at the Otobus Garaji and twenty minutes later you're there. The single fare for the journey is less than 50p. You can also take a day trip to IZMIR if you leave early in the morning and return in the evening. The travelling time from Kusadasi to Izmir is two hours and there are frequent bus services throughout the day. For a little more than £20 you can leave Turkey and spend a day or two on **SAMOS**, the Greek island a few miles across the water from Kusadasi. During the summer months boats leave both ports every morning and every evening and in spring and autumn there are services three or four times a week. The **DILEK NATIONAL PARK** twenty miles south of Kusadasi should feature on the itinerary of any serious nature-lover. The park, which is one of the Aegean's most scenically beautiful areas, is a wildlife reserve and a haven for several rare species of mammals and birds. The park is not covered by the public transport network and can be difficult to reach if you don't have your own transport. You can take a *dolmus* to the pretty beach at **GUZELCAMLI** and then walk or hitch a lift for the remaining three miles. Some travel agencies offer excursions to the archaeological site of **APHRODISIAS** and the thermal resort of **PAMUKKALE**, but these can be somewhat rushed to say the least.

About 150 miles to the east of Kusadasi on the main E24 motorway is the city of **DENIZLI** which is the major connecting point for trips to **PAMUKKALE**, Turkey's most famous thermal resort. Denizli is a fairly modern agricultural city built near the site of ancient **LAODICEA** which is recognized by historians as one of the Seven Churches of the Apocalypse. The ruins of Laodicea are only five miles from the city on the road to Pamukkale, but the large excavated site is pretty meaningless unless you have a special interest in religious history. In fact, Denizli has very little to interest the tourist apart from its proximity to Pamukkale. As there are no direct bus or train links with Pamukkale, many tourists use the services which connect Denizli to the country's major cities. From the Aegean coast you can travel by bus from Izmir via Selcuk or by train from Izmir. Once you arrive in Denizli there will be no shortage of buses and *dolmuses* to take you the remaining 14 miles to Pamukkale. There are plenty of lodgings and restaurants in Denizli which cater for all budgets. While Denizli is a convenient stopping-off point for visitors to Pamukkale, most tourists prefer to stay in Pamukkale itself where many of the hotels and pensions have private thermal baths.

PAMUKKALE, which means 'cotton castle' when translated, is one of Turkey's prettiest and most dramatic natural sites. For thousands of years water flowing from Pamukkale's springs has cascaded down the mountainside on which the town is built leaving a build-up of calcium deposits on the rock-face. The result has been the incredible formation of dazzling white pools, each made of petrified calcium, which overflow with warm water and brilliant stalactites. The pools have formed in a series of terraces down the mountainside, starting fairly shallow and getting deeper as you descend.

In ancient times the spas of Pamukkale, or Hierapolis as it was known in those days, were renowned throughout Asia Minor for their therapeutic powers. It was the Pergamese king, Eumenes II, who first recognized the potential of the warm mineral waters, and in the second century BC he ordered the construction of a major cure centre at Hierapolis. When the centre was destroyed by an earthquake in the first century it was immediately rebuilt by the Romans and the new centre reached its height under Byzantine rule.

Today Pamukkale's three major attractions are its numerous bath houses, its unique natural phenomena and the ruins of ancient Hierapolis. The most impressive of the ruins are the **City Baths** which now house a Roman **archaeological museum**, the **Grand Theatre** with seating for 25,000 spectators and the massive **Necropolis** (burial ground) comprising more than 1000 tombs.

The ruins of the ancient city are now interspersed with the modern motels, restaurants and bath houses of Pamukkale. There are plenty of lodgings and eating places in Pamukkale but if you're operating on a shoe-string budget you'll find prices much cheaper in Denizli which is less of a tourist trap. The cheapest accommodation is provided by **Ali's Rest House**, **Hotel Hierapolis** and the **Paradise Pension**. The **Turizm Motel** is reasonably priced and the **Motels Tusan** and **Koru** are the most expensive. In between, the **Otel Kleopatra** is a modest family hotel, 100 yards from the village centre. Good home cooking and clean rooms. Around 20,000TL a single – meals extra. The best restaurants are to be found in the better motels.

Also within easy travelling distance of Denizli is the famous archaeological site of **APHRODISIAS** which lies south-west of Pamukkale. Built in the 700s BC, the city of Aphrodisias was dedicated to Aphrodite, the Greek goddess of beauty and love. In the second century BC the city became a great centre of art and culture when some of Anatolia's finest artists fled from Pergamon to Aphrodisias to escape the conquering Romans. Today Aphrodisias is one of Turkey's most important archaeological sites because large-scale excavation is still underway and experts believe much of the city has still to be unearthed.

The remains already uncovered include the magnificent **Temple of Aphrodite** which is believed to have been built in the first century BC. In the sixth century AD the Byzantines converted the steamy temple of love into a respectable Christian basilica. The most spectacular and best-preserved of the ruins is the **stadium** with seating capacity of 30,000 and a central arena for chariot races. There is also the **Bishops' Palace** where archaeologists have found numerous religious statues; **Hadrian's Bath**, a Roman health centre with saunas and changing rooms; a crumbling **agora**, and an ancient **odeon** which features a particularly beautiful blue marble stage.

Aphrodisias is situated off the E24 motorway which makes it accessible from Pamukkale and Denizli to the east and Izmir, Selcuk and Kusadasi to the west. Whichever direction you're travelling from, take a bus along the E24 between Izmir and Denizli to the town of NAZILLI and from there take a *dolmus* to the village of GEYRE which is adjacent to the ruins. The journey from Nazilli to Geyre is 38 miles. Alternatively, from Izmir or Selcuk you can catch a bus direct to KARACASU, a small town only six miles north of the ruins. The buses to Karacasu are more convenient but less frequent than buses which run the main Izmir/Denizli route. Some travel agencies in Kusadasi offer excursions to the site, otherwise get a dolmus to Selcuk and take it from there.

If you want an overnight stop within travelling distance of the site, there are one or two modest hotels in Karacasu but don't expect much in the way of tourist facilities.

From the tourist's point of view it's a fortunate coincidence that three of Turkey's finest archaeological sites are within day-tripping distance of one of its most popular beach resorts. The ancient cities of PRIENE, MILETUS and DIDYMA, a few miles south of Kusadasi, have been closely linked throughout history, and yet the remains of each settlement are unique. The three sites are off the beaten-track but can easily be visited in a day, travelling by car or *dolmus* or by excursion from Kusadasi. (Excursions are also available from Bodrum but these tend to be slightly rushed.) *Dolmuses* make frequent trips between the sites and hitch-hiking is also a common practice.

PRIENE was a busy port and an important city in the fourth century

BC when it was the official headquarters for the Federation of Ionian Cities and the venue for regular meetings and festivals. Unlike nearby Miletus, Priene did not undergo major reconstruction when the Romans conquered western Anatolia, and the ruins you can see today are the remains of buildings which were constructed more than 2000 years ago. Built on the slopes of Mount Mycale, Priene holds a commanding position overlooking the River Meander which winds across the plain below. Amidst the rubble and ruins of the archaeological site it's still possible to make out the geometric grid on which the city plan was based. The system of grid planning became popular in the 300s BC and was first implemented during the construction of Miletus.

The first structure you encounter after entering the archaeological zone is the **Bouleterion**, the ornamental council chamber from which the city's official business was conducted. The city's most impressive ruin is the ancient **theatre** which was built in the upper part of the city with the rocky slopes of Mount Mycale forming a dramatic backdrop. This was an intimate little theatre by Hellenic standards, with seating capacity of less than 5000, and much of the structure is still intact. Further up the hill at the highest point of the city is the **Temple of Athena** which can be instantly recognized by the five fluted columns which are now the only reminder of its past grandeur. In its day the temple was considered to be the ultimate example of Ionic architecture and it became a model for many subsequent buildings.

In the lower part of the city the places of interest include a ruined Byzantine church, the remains of a stadium and gymnasium and some well-preserved domestic housing.

About 14 miles south of Priene, still on the coast, is the site of ancient **MILETUS**. As the larger and more important of the two cities Miletus was the target for a succession of ambitious invaders, and, as a result, little remains of its original buildings. The city suffered its worst attack at the hands of the Persian army at the end of the fifth century BC when its population was virtually wiped out. Despite this and numerous other setbacks, Miletus survived as a great centre of learning, philosophy and commerce for almost fourteen centuries (700 BC to AD 700). The city fell into sudden decline when its harbour silted over in the eighth century – the same fate as befell Ephesus.

The most impressive ruins at Miletus are those of the **theatre** which was originally built in Hellenic times and later rebuilt by the Romans. The well-preserved theatre, with seats for 15,000 spectators, overlooks the old harbour and its upper terraces give a glorious view of the site. Other attractions are the **Faustina Baths**, built by the Roman emperor Aurelius for his wife Faustina, and the **Ilyas Bey Camii**, a fifteenth-century mosque built in the Emirate period between Seljuk and Ottoman rule. Not far from the baths there is a small **archaeological museum** which contains artefacts from the site.

Another 14 miles south you come to **DIDYMA**, the site of the magnificent **Temple of Apollo**. Didyma was not built as a city but as a sacred sanctuary to be inhabited only by priests. It was the oracle of Apollo and its famous prophecies which were responsible for Didyma's great prosperity. From the 700s BC to the birth of Christianity the city was respected as a great centre for worship and thousands of pilgrims from Greece and the neighbouring regions paid regular visits to attend the religious festivals held in the temple.

While the Temple of Apollo is Didyma's sole attraction, it is probably the world's best-preserved example of ancient temple architecture and the sheer size of the structure is awesome. Originally built in the early Hellenic period, the temple was partly reconstructed by Alexander the Great after being burned and looted by the invading Persians in the 400s BC. The building you see today is mainly the work of the Romans who undertook the complete restoration of the temple in the fourth century.

Three miles south of the ruins, close to the modern town of **DIDIM**, you'll come to **ALTINKUM PLAJI** (Golden Beach) which is one of the largest sandy beaches in the region. A small resort has developed around Altinkum with a few pensions, hotels, restaurants and shops, but the facilities are rather limited and transport can be hard to come by. If you're travelling independently to the ruins and wish to combine sightseeing with a day on the beach, Altinkum is a pleasant place to stay. The **Ankara Hotel**, **Pension Han Han** and the **Didim Motel** offer cheap, basic accommodation.

Returning to the main coastal road, the next major town to the south is **MILAS** which was known as Mylasa in ancient times. For a direct route to Milas from Kusadasi you must rejoin the main road at **SOKE** and continue south for 40 miles. The pine-clad and mountainous road between Soke and Milas passes several places of interest and takes you through the remote south-western corner of the country. About 25 miles south of Soke, just past the turn-off for Miletus and Didyma, the road passes the southern shores of the beautiful LAKE BAFA where you can break your journey with either a refreshing swim or a refreshing cup of tea from one of the pleasant waterside tea houses. Another ten miles on near the village of SELIMIYE you'll catch a glimpse of the **Temple of Zeus** which is all that remains of the Hellenic settlement of EUROMOS.

Milas itself is one of Turkey's oldest towns, but there is surprisingly little evidence of its long and eventful past. In early Hellenic times (1200 to 600 BC) Mylasa was the capital of the Kingdom of Caria which encompassed the whole of south-western Anatolia. Today Milas is a busy agricultural centre which is noted for the beautiful hand-woven carpets produced by its local craftsmen. The main tourist attraction is the **Gumuskesen Turbe**, a first-century Roman burial chamber which bears a striking resemblance to the famous Mausoleum at Halicarnassus near Bodrum. Other places of interest are the nearby ruins of a **Roman temple** and three fourteenth-century mosques, **Firus Camii**, **Ulu Camii** and **Haci Ilyas Camii**. There are several good pensions in Milas which offer cheap accommodation, including the pensions **Pelit**, **Oguz** and **Yeni**.

Three miles south of Milas on the road to Bodrum is the pretty beach resort of GULLUK where you'll find a small holiday village called the **Gultur** and a few cheap pensions. Gulluk is noted for its attractive beach and its glorious hilltop view of Bodrum to the south.

BODRUM

Bodrum is undoubtedly the prettiest and most popular of Turkey's major holiday resorts. Built on a peninsula with sandy beaches on either side, the town is dominated by an enchanting medieval castle which overlooks two sweeping bays on the southern side of the strip. White-washed buildings, palm-lined streets and brilliant blue waters all add to its charm. In the past few years Bodrum has become a magnet for watersports and sailing enthusiasts, young families, sun-worshippers and socialites, but despite its popularity it appears less crowded and less commercialized than the major resort of Kusadasi. While Bodrum attracts vast numbers of package tourists and independent travellers, its visitors are dispersed among the tiny fishing villages and quiet beaches which adorn the shores of the peninsula. This, and the fact that a large percentage of visitors choose sailing holidays rather than hotel-based holidays, helps Bodrum to retain the friendly atmosphere of a small resort. Known in ancient times as Halicarnassus, Bodrum gained its place in the history books in the fourth century BC when, under the rule of the Persian king Mausolus, it was developed into one of the strongest and most important ports on the Aegean coast. When the Persians invaded Anatolia and captured the kingdom of Caria, Mausolus switched the capital from Milas to Halicarnassus. The king's burial chamber, the **Mausoleum of Halicarnassus**, ranked among the seven wonders of the ancient world.

Bodrum is now *the* place to go for sailing and watersports holidays and you'll find a large percentage of the package deals available are watersports-orientated. Because so many of the tourists visiting Bodrum are accommodated off-shore in yachts and schooners, the hotels in the town are generally small and unobtrusive. The largest hotel complex is the modern **Torba Holiday Village**, six miles outside the centre, which is offered by a number of British tour operators. With 350 rooms, a private beach, a watersports club, a disco, tennis courts, bars, restaurants, pools, saunas and shops, the Torba offers its guests all the facilities they need for a comfortable and action-packed holiday. The smaller **TMT Motel** (170 rooms) is also a popular choice for British holidaymakers and offers a similar range of facilities. Apart from these two large establishments, the majority of lodgings in and around Bodrum are small hotels, pensions, villas and apartments. In the town centre there are literally hundreds of tiny pensions which provide cheap, basic accommodation for the independent traveller. **Hotel Sami, Pension Mylasa, Villa Cem, Villa Karya, Villa Murat**, the **Papiras Apartments** and the **Seckin Konaklar Apartments** are all small, friendly establishments and all are offered by British tour operators. During the summer months, and in September when the Bodrum Festival of Art and Culture is held, the small town-centre lodgings fill up at an incredible rate. Bodrum's campsites are located about two miles outside the town centre at GUMBET BEACH. You'll find several sites here, the best of which are **Baba Camping** and **Ayaz Camping**.

Bodrum is a food-lover's paradise with eating places to suit every taste and every budget. The most popular restaurants are those on the seafront close to the castle, among which you'll find some very good seafood restaurants. Bodrum's fish restaurants are reputed to be the best in the country and you can choose from an interesting selection of dishes. If you're dining out in a group it's a nice idea to order a large fish and share it. Charcoaled chunks of tuna fish go down very nicely with raki or the local wine. The popular seafront restaurants are among the most expensive in the resort, but you'll still be struggling to spend more than £10 a head for dinner with wine. The **Korfez Garden Restaurant**, the **Agli Restaurant**, the **Nese Restaurant**, the **Hey Yarum Hey** and **Orhan's Number Seven** are all recommended for their good Turkish cuisine, pleasant atmosphere and reasonable prices. The cheap restaurants which serve good run-of-the-mill Turkish fare such as kebabs, pastries and stews are concentrated around the market area. If possible, try to avoid the restaurants which open only for two or three months in the summer to make quick money during the tourist season. These are noted for their mediocre food, higher than average prices and can normally be recognized by their fake-Turkish decor and lack of atmosphere.

Nightlife in Bodrum is fairly 'laid-back' compared to some major holiday resorts. While there are plenty of discos (including those laid on by the big hotels), many people opt for the relaxing atmosphere of the music bars which are scattered along the seafront and nearby streets. The open-air theatre in the castle is a great source of traditional entertainment throughout the holiday season, particularly in September when the annual art and culture festival takes place.

If you can set aside a day or two to explore the town there are several places of interest which merit a visit, the castle being the most obvious. **The Castle of St Peter** protected the port of Bodrum from the time of the Holy Wars to the end of the First World War, and it is now the world's finest example of a Crusader castle. It was the Knights of Rhodes who constructed the castle with knights of five nationalities building five different towers which were thus named the German, Italian, Spanish, English and French towers. Within the towers there are various halls, chapels and museums which contain artefacts from archaeological sites around Bodrum. The most interesting museum, and the highlight of a visit to the castle, is the

Museum of Underwater Archaeology which houses a fascinating collection of antiquities recovered from shipwrecks in the Aegean and Mediterranean seas off the shores of Turkey. The **Mausoleum of Halicarnassus** is Bodrum's other claim to fame, but all you see today is an excavated site where the magnificent tomb once stood. A plaster model gives you some impression of the former grandeur of the tomb which stood 150 feet high and featured a pyramid-shaped roof topped with a statue of Mausolus. Bodrum's most famous son was the historian Herodotus, known throughout the world as the 'Father of History' who was born in Halicarnassus in 484 BC. Other tourist attractions in the town centre are the **boatyards** and the **open-air market**. If you walk round the marina on the bay to the west of the castle you can look into the boatyards and catch a glimpse of Bodrum's famous schooners under construction. The bustling market place, which is located between the castle and the bus station as you walk inland from the seafront, operates every Thursday and Friday. Here you can haggle for a wide range of goods including leatherware, hand-made cheesecloths, carpets and rugs, ornaments and jewellery.

On the road from the castle to the bus station you'll also find facilities like the tourist information office, international telephones and the police station (close to the castle) and the post office (close to the bus station). *Dolmuses* and jeeps which are the main mode of transport in and around the resort start out from the bus station.

You can't spend a holiday in Bodrum without visiting some of the fishing villages, beaches, coves and uninhabited islands dotted around the shores of the peninsula. Most of the neighbouring villages have their own beaches, bars and restaurants which means you can leave the resort and enjoy a relaxing day in new surroundings. The closest and most popular beaches are those on the southern shores of the peninsula at the villages of **GUMBET**, **BITEZ** and **BARDAKCI** which are all a short *dolmus*-drive away from the town centre. For quieter beaches catch one of the many boats which leave from the marina in front of the castle heading for the remote spots on the southern coasts and the nearby islands. Some of the prettiest and most interesting villages around the resort are **TURGUT REIS**, **ORTAKENT** and **GUMUSLUK** to the west; **YALIKAVAK**, **GOLKOY**, **TORBA** and **TURKBUKU** to the north; and **GOKOVA** to the east. The most popular islands are **ADA**, **ORAK** and **KARA**, and it's also possible to take a day trip to the Greek island of KOS which is only a few miles from the southern shores. During the summer months boats operate every Monday, Wednesday and Friday, leaving in the morning and returning early evening.

The most interesting archaeological ruins near Bodrum are at the site of ancient MYNDOS which was an important port during the days of Persian rule. Situated at the western tip of the peninsula close to the village of Gumusluk, Myndos is a good day-trip destination because you can combine a morning's sightseeing with an afternoon on the beach. The ruins at Myndos include the remains of the fortified city walls, which were up to nine feet thick in some parts, and a Byzantine basilica. *Dolmuses* heading for Myndos leave the bus station two or three times a day.

If you wish to make a long-distance journey from Bodrum, bus travel is inevitable as rail services stop at Soke, about 80 miles to the north, and the nearest airports are at Izmir, about 190 miles north, and Dalaman which is roughly the same distance south. From the bus station in Bodrum there are regular services to IZMIR, ANKARA, ISTANBUL and MARMARIS which stop at principal towns en route.

The Mediterranean Coast

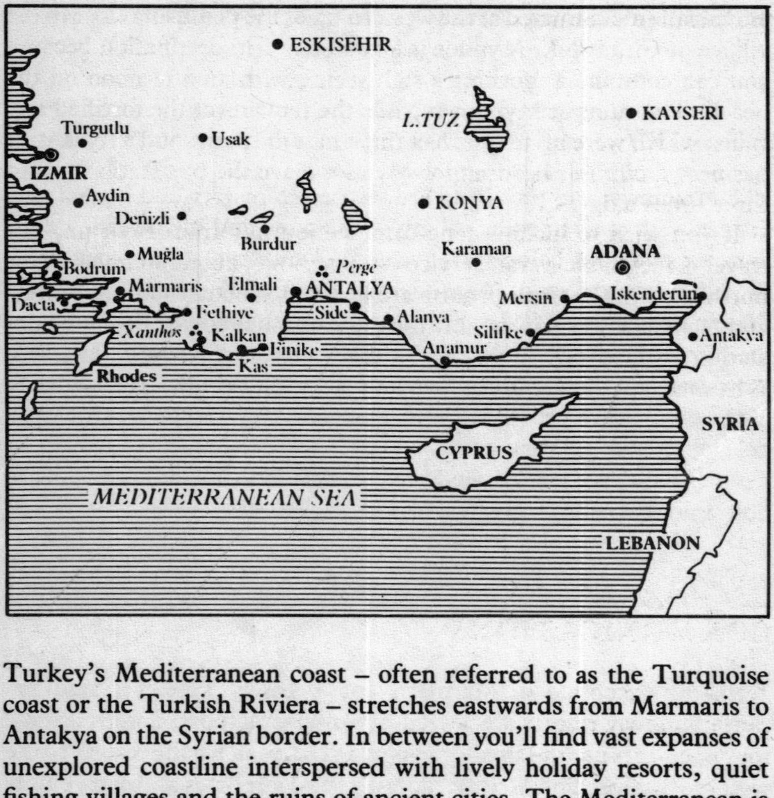

Turkey's Mediterranean coast – often referred to as the Turquoise coast or the Turkish Riviera – stretches eastwards from Marmaris to Antakya on the Syrian border. In between you'll find vast expanses of unexplored coastline interspersed with lively holiday resorts, quiet fishing villages and the ruins of ancient cities. The Mediterranean is an area of great natural beauty and some of Turkey's most breathtaking scenery can be found in the south-western provinces between Marmaris and Kas. At many points along the coastline the snowy Taurus Mountains rise behind the seashores forming an impressive backdrop to the resorts. In fact, if you visit Antalya in spring it's possible to ski in the morning and swim in the warm sea in the afternoon (a claim which the Turkish Tourist Board are very proud of). Up until ten years ago, poor roads made many parts of the Mediterranean coast inaccessible to the tourist, and it's only recently that new road construction has opened up southern Turkey. Despite the major growth in tourism in the past decade, the government has limited development to designated holiday areas in order to protect the coastline's natural assets.

HISTORY

The Mediterranean provinces are steeped in history and legend and littered with ancient ruins. Many of the ports and inland cities were founded by Greek colonists between the tenth and seventh centuries BC and by the armies of Alexander the Great who invaded Anatolia in the fourth century BC. In the centuries which followed the Romans, the Byzantines, the Seljuks, the Crusaders and the Ottomans all made their mark on the coastline. Some of the early cities such as Attaleia (Antalya), Selimiye (Side) and Alexandretta (Iskenderun) were developed and are now principal ports and resorts. Others such as Termessos, Perge and Aspendos were allowed to fall into ruin and are now among Turkey's greatest archaeological sites.

COMMUNICATIONS

With the exception of Marmaris and Fethiye, Turkey's Mediterranean holiday resorts are served by Antalya Airport. Some package tour operators use the smaller airport at Dalaman for the resorts to the west of Antalya. The Mediterranean's third airport is at Adana but its only international flights are to North Cyprus and Syria. Turkish Airlines operate internal flights to the country's major cities from Antalya and Adana. Mersin and Adana are the only Mediterranean cities served by train. A twice-weekly train service from Istanbul to Beirut connects Adana to Istanbul, Ankara and Gaziantep, and there are regular local services between Adana and Mersin. Private bus operators provide cheap and frequent services between all the main towns and many of the smaller towns. In the more mountainous regions of the coastline services can be slow and erratic. In the summer months Turkish Maritime Lines operate services between the main resorts and to some of the Greek islands. There are regular ferries from Mersin to North Cyprus throughout the year.

Whichever resort you go to you'll find excursions to local places of interest. These can be booked through your tour operator or through Turkish travel agencies.

TOURIST INFORMATION

The Tourist Board's main office on the Mediterranean is in Antalya at Cumhuriyet Caddesi 91 (tel: Antalya 11747/15271). Tourist information offices can be found in all the main ports and resorts.

THE CLIMATE

Turkey's Mediterranean coast enjoys a beautiful temperate climate very similar to that of the Aegean. Sunshine is virtually guaranteed from April to October and the winters are pleasantly mild with temperatures rarely falling below 45°F (7°C). July and August are the best months for the sun-seeker when temperatures are in the high 80s (28–30°C). If that sounds a little too hot, try late spring or early autumn when temperatures hover around the mid-70s (20–22°C). If you're planning a winter holiday you'll find the south coast resorts a few degrees hotter than those on the north Aegean coast. While you can sightsee on the Mediterranean all year round, don't expect to do any serious sunbathing after November.

CULINARY SPECIALITIES

Most Turkish dishes are a mixture of Mediterranean and Asian-style cuisine and here, as you might expect, the Mediterranean influence is strongest. You'll come across a lot of charcoaled fish served with interesting side-salads and vegetable dishes. *Sokor*, an unusual but tasty regional fish, will feature on most menus along with sardines, octopus and squid. In the cheaper eating places you'll find the usual lamb-based stews and kebabs. The food becomes spicier the further east you go.

WHERE TO GO FOR WHAT

Sun-worshippers, socialites and watersports enthusiasts will find everything they need at the popular resorts of **MARMARIS**, **ALANYA** and **SIDE**. Apart from their lovely beaches, all enjoy a lively social scene. Alanya and Side are also recommended for family holidays as they both offer a full range of tourist facilities with plenty to keep youngsters amused. If a quiet, relaxing beach holiday is more what you have in mind, the peaceful fishing villages of **KALKAN** and **KAS** offer the full beauty of Turkey's Mediterranean coast without the crowds. **ANTALYA** is an ideal base for a sightseeing holiday because of its proximity to the great archaeological sites of **TERMESSOS**, **PERGE** and **ASPENDOS**. The area to the west of Antalya known as the **LYCIAN PENINSULA** is a haven for nature-lovers. With its pine-clad mountains and lush green valleys, this remote region of Turkey is teeming with wildlife and it offers endless possibilities for walking and trekking.

Traditional Turkish festivals are held throughout the region during the tourist season. Here are some festivals worth noting: the Silifke Festival (20–26 May); the Marmaris Arts Tourism Festival (8–17 June); the Foca Festival of Music, Folklore and Watersports (20–22 July); the Antalya International Arts Festival (1–9 October) and the Mersin International Festival (22 September–12 October).

MARMARIS

It's hard to say exactly where the Aegean coast ends and the Mediterranean coast starts, but the fishing village of Marmaris is generally thought to mark the confluence of the two seas. Built on the shores of a sheltered bay, this popular resort lies 110 miles east of Bodrum and 110 miles west of Fethiye in the south-western corner of the country. Marmaris is by no means a large resort, but it's one of the busiest yachting centres in Turkey. If you enjoy rubbing shoulders with the rich and glamorous this is *the* place to go. Marmaris is fast becoming Turkey's answer to Cannes as more and more of the world's wealthier sailing set are drawn by its picturesque setting and excellent marina. If you don't own a luxury yacht, don't worry – you'll enjoy the cosmopolitan atmosphere and the lively social scene. Despite its fashionable image, Marmaris is no more expensive than any other Turkish resort and you'll find tourist facilities to suit every budget. A large number of British tour operators offer reasonably priced watersports holidays and yacht charters based in Marmaris and independent charters can be booked at the resort. Marmaris is only a short boat trip away from the Greek island of Rhodes, which is another reason for its popularity.

Accommodation is scattered along a ten-mile stretch of the sandy coastline around the bay. The hotels featured in the British holiday brochures are generally the more expensive hotels located on good beaches just outside the village. These include the **Turban Marmaris Holiday Village** and the **Marti Holiday Complex** which offer a high standard of accommodation and a full range of facilities including watersports and sailing. **Hotel Lydia, Hotel Oylum** and the **Poseidon Motel** also offer good accommodation which is convenient for the beaches. Independent travellers looking for cheap accommodation should stick to the town centre where there are dozens of small hotels and pensions offering basic rooms at very low rates. Look out for the hotels **Marmaris, Atlantik** and **Reisoglu** and the pensions **Gokle** and **Oksan**. Also worth considering is **Yulcet Interyouth Hostel**, which has 72 beds and a range of facilities. Bear in mind that the town centre can be fairly noisy, with the sounds of late-night revellers and early-morning muezzins. Independent budget travellers will find several good campsites on the outskirts of the town.

Eating out can be one of the great pleasures of a visit to Marmaris if you stick to the moderately priced harbour restaurants which serve delicious seafood meals in pleasant outdoor surroundings. Expensive meals are served in the restaurants of the major hotels and in the flashier waterfront restaurants. The cheapest eating places are those in the market area of the town which serve grilled meats, stews and pilafs. For a good seafood meal try the restaurants **Karadeniz, Birtat** and **Tilla** on the waterfront, and for cheaper fare try the **Ayyildiz Lokanta** and the **Imran Restaurant** near the bazaar.

In the evenings the whole seafront comes to life as the yachting fraternity and guests from the surrounding hotels descend on the tavernas, open-air music bars, restaurants and discos. The two holiday villages also offer lively programmes of entertainment which include dancing and traditional shows. If socializing and nightlife are high on your list of holiday priorities you should visit Marmaris in June when the annual Festival of Music and Art takes place.

While the area surrounding Marmaris is steeped in history, the resort itself has little to offer in the way of sightseeing. Up until the seventh century BC the prosperous port of Marmaris, known in ancient times as Physcus, was part of the Hellenic Kingdom of Caria and it enjoyed strong trading links with Egypt and Rhodes. The only reminders of the town's past are the ruins of a fifteenth-century **Selar Fortress** and an **Ottoman Caravanserai** which now serves as a small inn and souvenir shop. The most interesting part of the resort is the **Old Town**, between the main harbour and the yacht marina, which gives you some impression of how the town looked before the tourists arrived. Other tourist attractions include the **GUNNUCEK NATIONAL PARK**, only a mile from the centre, which features a small beach and picnic area, and the **shopping bazaar** below the fortress. Beware of being ripped off at the bazaar as several visitors had problems here last year.

Although the resort is spread over a large expanse of coastline, cheap *dolmus* and boat services make all the hotels and beaches easily accessible. The town centre itself poses no problems because all the main tourist facilities (including the post office, bus station, tourist office etc.) are crowded into a few small streets, all within easy walking distance of each other. Throughout the summer the tourist authorities lay on a small train which pulls trailers back and forth along the seafront serving the hotels and popular beaches. Some of the best beauty spots in the vicinity of Marmaris can only be reached by boat so it's a good idea to charter a yacht (which doesn't have to be expensive) or take advantage of the numerous cheap boat trips on offer. Every morning *dolmus* boats leave the harbour destined for the remote beaches and uninhabited islands scattered around the bay. Some of the *dolmus* drivers offer tours of the bay, others offer single destinations.

The beach at **TURUNC**, across the bay to the west of Marmaris, is considered to be one of the most beautiful in the region. Not far from Turunc are the **GOLENYE SPRINGS** which are famous for their therapeutic properties, particularly for intestinal problems. To the east of the resort the attractive beaches of **GUNNUCEK**, **AKTAS** and **ADAKOY** are set amidst pine forests which stretch right down to the seashore. Further round the bay on the Nimara Peninsula you can visit the

ALKAYA CAVES and swim and sunbathe beneath the mountains.

Coach excursions are available to the scenic DATCA PENINSULA and the ancient cities of KNIDOS and CAUNOS (described later in this chapter). During the summer ferries for the Greek island of RHODES leave Marmaris harbour every morning except Sunday and return in the evening. In spring and autumn this service operates two or three times a week. Buses are the only other option for long-distance travel from Marmaris. From the main bus station there are regular services to ISTANBUL, IZMIR, BODRUM and FETHIYE.

The pretty village of DATCA lies on the southern coast of the slender peninsula which juts into the sea to the west of Marmaris. You can visit Datca by boat from Marmaris, but the journey by road is just as captivating. The 55-mile stretch of coastline which separates the two resorts is a succession of lush pine-clad valleys and tranquil blue fjords. Datca's main attractions are its quiet beaches and its proximity to the ancient site of Knidos which is 25 miles to the west. If you wish to stay on the peninsula overnight you can choose from a handful of modest pensions in Datca or Knidos, or simply take a tent and pick your spot. The journey from Datca to Knidos can be made by boat, jeep or *dolmus*.

The ruins of KNIDOS occupy a remote, wind-swept spot at the tip of the peninsula. Founded by the Dorians, the city owed much of its prosperity to the unpredictable winds which swept the neighbouring coastline and forced many ships to seek refuge in its harbour. In the fifth century BC Knidos was one of the greatest centres of art and learning in the ancient world, famed for its magnificent statue of Aphrodite. The statue has long since disappeared and all that remains of Knidos are its crumbling city walls and the ruins of two small temples and a small theatre. In the new town of Knidos, adjacent to the ancient site, there is a tiny museum, a small beach and a few interesting fish restaurants.

The fascinating ruins of ancient CAUNOS lie about 60 miles east of Marmaris just off the main road to Fethiye. To reach the site turn right off the main road at Ortaca and head for the village of Dalyan past Lake Koycegi. From here you can see Caunos, but to visit the ruins you must take a boat trip along the river which connects the lake to the sea. Around the fifth century BC Caunos was a Carian city which stood on the border of the Kingdoms of Caria and Lycia. The site is famous for the Lycian tombs which are cut into the rock-face overlooking the river. It also features extensive Roman remains including a well-preserved theatre and a bath house. A sightseeing trip to Caunos can be fairly long and exhausting but you can break the day with a stop in Dalyan where there are a few teahouses and restaurants.

FETHIYE

About 100 miles east of Marmaris lies the resort of Fethiye (known in ancient times as Telmessos), with a shingle beach about a mile away from the centre. Due to an earthquake in 1958 which razed many of its greatest antiquities to the ground, Fethiye now has a modern, somewhat nondescript town centre. All that remains from the past are some fascinating Lycian tombs and the ruins of a medieval fortress. Fethiye's main attractions are its good beaches and the uninhabited islands which litter its pretty bay. Until recently, Fethiye was a thriving beach resort in its own right, but the nearby town of OLU DENIZ has now stolen much of its limelight. Olu Deniz (Dead Sea) is the picture-postcard lagoon, with white beach and turquoise water, which features on the cover of many a Turkish holiday brochure. Nowadays, many of the tourists who stay in Fethiye use it as a base for Olu Deniz which, as yet, has not been fully developed for tourism.

Fethiye has a good range of accommodation from high-class hotels to cheap pensions and sea-side campsites. The most comfortable and most expensive town-centre establishments are the hotels **Likya** and **Dedeoglu**. **Hotel Sema** and **Hotel Dostlar** are middle-of-the-range and **Hotel Kaya** is cheap. Fethiye has dozens of pensions offering rock-bottom rates, many of which are conveniently located near the waterfront. One of the better pensions is the **Baris**, which offers bed and breakfast for 4000TL. It is clean and comfortable. The tourist information office, which is also on the waterfront, will give you a list of pensions with details of their rates and facilities. If you prefer to camp you can choose from the numerous sites dotted along the ten-mile stretch of coastline between Fethiye and Olu Deniz, some of which also offer basic bungalow accommodation. Good sites near Fethiye include the **Dirlik** and **Seketer** camps and the best sites near Olu Deniz are **Han Camping, Belicekiz Camping** and **Deniz Camping**. Olu Deniz has one hotel, the **Hotel Meri**, which is now being offered by a number of British package tour operators. Hotel Meri has 75 rooms and a good range of facilities, but its rates can be fairly expensive for the independent traveller. **Otel Vizon** (tel: 6151-4424) is situated midway between the bus station and town centre on a quiet wide road. This is an excellent mid-price hotel at around 75,000TL for a double room, including breakfast.

As far as eating out is concerned, you'll get the best value for money if you stick to Fethiye's smaller restaurants. If you choose to dine in the large hotels you'll get a good meal, but you're likely to pay over the odds for it. The best restaurants in the town centre are the **Oh Yaaa**, the **Pasaoglu Restaurant** and the **Rafet Restaurant** which all have outdoor seating areas and good food. Fethiye is not noted for its wild nightlife, but more for its open-air bars and tavernas where you can enjoy live Turkish music and a relaxing atmosphere.

If you can drag yourself off your sun-lounger for long enough, there are several sights in and around the resort which are well worth a visit. Fethiye's most famous sight is the **Necropolis of Telmessos**, a collection of tombs carved into the rock-face overlooking the town. Built around the fourth century BC, the Necropolis is thought to be the world's greatest vestige of the Lycian culture. The most impressive of the tombs is the **Tomb of Amyntas**. From the Necropolis there is a splendid view of the ruined **fortress** built during the age of the Crusades by the Knights of St John. Excursions from Fethiye include day trips to **XANTHOS**, the capital city of ancient Lycia; **KAYA**, a mysterious 'ghost city' deserted by its Greek inhabitants; and **CAUNOS**, the ancient Carian city noted for its rock tombs.

The best beaches in the area are a few miles north-west of Fethiye at **CALIS**, **GUNLUK BAY**, **KATRANCI BAY** and, of course, **OLU DENIZ**. (While Olu Deniz is unequalled for its beauty, it has to be pointed out that the beach is made of fine white pebbles, not sand.) *Dolmuses* from the town centre provide cheap transport to all the beaches and there are numerous daily boat trips to the popular beaches and islands around the Bay of Fethiye.

From Fethiye's central bus station there are several services a day to **MARMARIS**, **KALKAN** and **KAS**. The bus to Marmaris stops at *Dalaman Airport* which is 32 miles west of Fethiye.

The area between Fethiye and Kas, sometimes referred to as the **LYCIAN PENINSULA**, is thought by many to be Turkey's most beautiful region. Here, 42 miles from Fethiye on the main road to Kas, you'll find the ruined city of **XANTHOS**. This was once the capital of the Kingdom of Lycia, and a large and important city in the fifth century BC. The city is now badly ruined but you can still see the remains of the acropolis, a theatre, and a typical Lycian tomb. The interesting ruins of **Sidyma, Letoon** and **Patara** are dotted along the coastline near Xanthos, but they are well off the beaten track and difficult to get to without a car.

The relatively new beach resort of **KALKAN** is situated just off the main road about 30 miles outside Kas. With its beautiful little marina and peaceful bay, Kalkan is claimed to be the perfect example of an unspoilt Turkish fishing village. Unfortunately, things have recently changed and Kalkan can no longer be described as unspoilt, and tourists should beware of being ripped off. In the past few years there have been several new hotel developments and the resort is now being featured in a number of holiday brochures. Despite this, Kalkan is still an ideal place for a quiet beach holiday. The beaches in the town centre are pebbly, but there are plenty of fine sandy beaches in the immediate area. The best beaches are generally those to the west of the resort towards Fethiye, but there is a particularly pretty beach at KAPATUS on the road to Kas. If you want to sunbathe and swim in the town centre you can either brave the pebbles or go to the **Kalamar Beach Club** which has a concrete swimming and diving platform complete with sun-loungers.

Tourist facilities in Kalkan are somewhat limited – which is, of course, part of its appeal. You won't find a tourist office, a travel agency or a swinging nightclub, but you will find a choice of cheap pensions, modest hotels and pleasant restaurants. The pensions **King, Patara** and **Yilmaz** all offer clean, basic accommodation at very low rates. The slightly plusher establishments are those offered by the package tour operators including the **Kalkan Han Hotel** and **Pasha's Inn**.

KAS

If you follow the main road eastwards from Kalkan the next resort you come to is Kaş. Though slightly larger than Kalkan, this sleepy fishing village is one of the Mediterranean's prettiest and most peaceful holiday retreats. Built at the foot of a mountain, Kaş is noted for its natural beauty and its friendly Turkish community. The resort is a popular stopover point for independent travellers and yachting parties and it is starting to feature in British package tour brochures as a get-away-from-it-all destination.

It's difficult to get lost in Kaş because most of the resort's activity revolves around the main square next to the harbour. This is where you'll find the majority of bars, restaurants and teahouses, the police station, the tourist office and a collection of cheap hotels and pensions.

There are some expensive hotels in Kaş but generally accommodation is of the modest variety – though most of it is clean and comfortable. The 'fanciest' place to stay is the **Andifli Motel**, and it won't break the bank. Good cheap pensions (offering good value at about 10,000TL a room) include **Pension Lale, Pension Mini, Pension Kismet** and **Pension Ak Deniz**. If you really want to get to know the locals it's possible to rent a room within a Turkish home, but you'll have to respect the house rules of your host family. The tourist office has listings of the rooms available. Basic camping facilities are available at **Kaş Camping,** a short walk to the west of the centre.

The most popular restaurants in Kaş are those around the main square. All the eating places offer reasonable prices but the quality of food varies. The **Shady Restaurant** and the **Belediye Restaurant** both have a good selection of well-prepared dishes. The **Eris Restaurant** has the plushest surroundings and the most varied menu but the quality of the food leaves a little to be desired. For snack-type meals and simple Turkish fare the **Kebab Restaurant** is recommended.

The shoreline around Kaş is fairly rocky with pebble beaches. If you're keen on swimming and snorkelling the best beaches are those on the peninsula which stretches into the sea opposite the main square to form the far side of the harbour. The water between the peninsula and the village is beautifully warm and calm and teeming with exotic fish. To the east and west of the village there are numerous deserted coves where you can spend an entire day sunbathing without being disturbed. If you're swimming from the remote parts of the coastline be on the lookout for spiky black sea urchins which cling to rocks below the water surface. The beaches closest to the resort are within walking distance of the village and they can also be reached by boat. The local fishermen offer frequent cheap excursions to the quieter beaches.

Sightseeing in Kaş is decidedly limited, but excursions are available to several places of interest nearby. The resort itself has only two noteworthy sights: a well-preserved **Hellenic theatre** to the west of the main square, and a collection of **Lycian tombs** built into the face of the mountain which overlooks the village. The walk up the mountain to the tombs is fairly strenuous and should only be tackled early morning or late afternoon when temperatures are still bearable.

A favourite excursion from Kaş is the three-hour boat trip to the Lycian city of KEKOVA, the ruins of which are partly underwater. The journey east along the coastline is memorable enough, but the city itself is fascinating. The best way to explore Kekova is by swimming with a snorkel. Another popular excursion is the shorter boat trip to the Greek island of KASTELORIZO which is only two miles from Kaş Harbour and clearly visible from the theatre. Excursions are also available to XANTHOS, the capital city of ancient Lycia (described earlier in the chapter), and to the historic towns of DEMRE and MYRA (described later). With some excursions you'll pay a fixed price per person for the round trip, and with others you pay for the boat, and the price per person varies depending on the size of the party.

From the bus station in Kaş there are five direct daily services to DEMRE, KEMER and ANTALYA and four daily services to KALKAN, FETHIYE and IZMIR.

DEMRE is a small, rather nondescript town about 25 miles east of Kas. Despite its dull appearance, the town has a significant place in Turkish folklore, for it was here in the fifth century that the legend of Father Christmas originated. Hundreds of tourists visit Demre to see the **Tomb of St Nicholas**, housed within a beautiful Byzantine basilica, and every year on 6 December a festival is held to commemorate the saint. It is believed that St Nicholas was born in the Mediterranean village of PATARA, west of Demre, and not in the wintry climes of the North Pole as you might expect. As the Bishop of Myra he gained the reputation of a great gift-bearer by giving presents of gold to young girls whose families were too poor to give them a dowry. In order to give the gifts anonymously he would drop bags of coins down the chimneys of their homes. The remains of St Nicholas (who is known to Turkish children as Baba Noel) were stolen from the basilica in the tenth century by Italian raiders. All the Turks have left of him are a few odd bones which are now in safe-keeping at the Antalya Museum.

Apart from the well-restored **Church of St Nicholas** which houses the plundered marble tomb, Demre has two main attractions: its beautiful sandy beach, and its proximity to ancient Myra. The ruins of

MYRA, two miles inland from the basilica, feature some magnificent **Lycian tombs** and the remains of a **Roman theatre**. To reach the ruins you'll have to walk, hitch or pay high taxi fares to the drivers who monopolize the route.

If you wish to stay overnight in Demre you can choose from a few modest pensions, the best of which are the **Myra** and the **Palmiye**. Alternatively, you can pitch a tent on the small campsite next to the beach.

Twenty miles east of Demre is the small port of **FINIKE**, known in ancient times as Phoenicus. This small resort has only a few modest pensions and hotels which are generally patronized by independent travellers and Turkish holidaymakers. **Hotel Sedir**, **Hotel Kosk** and **Hotel Ahmed** are all fairly cheap and basic. **Pension Kale**, **Pension Sirin** and **Pension Esen** offer rock-bottom rates and are even more basic. The town has a handful of equally modest, but very pleasant restaurants including the **Akdeniz Restaurant**, the **Fintur Restaurant** and the **Lezzet Lokanta**.

If you take the main road south from Finike and drive for about 50 miles you'll come to the pretty mountain town of ELMALI built on the shores of the picturesque LAKE KARAGOL. If you've got your own transport, or you're heading south anyway, Elmali is well worth a visit. On the outskirts of Finike as you continue eastwards there's an incredible long white beach of fine pebbles which stretches for almost ten miles to the point where the main road winds up into the mountains. The 45-mile stretch of road between Finike and the coastal resort of Kemer takes you through the BEY MOUNTAINS NATIONAL PARK, an area of great scenic beauty, and passes close to the ancient Lycian cities of PHASELIS and OLYMPOS. Phaselis is the more impressive of the two sites with Roman and Hellenic ruins dating back to the seventh century BC.

The town of **KEMER**, with its miles of sandy beaches, is one of Turkey's newest and fastest-developing holiday resorts. The centrepiece of the resort is a large modern holiday complex called **Club Salima** which has been built under government supervision. The club offers a vast range of facilities, including diving, sports, watersports, entertainment and nightlife, and it has recently started to appear in British holiday brochures. Apart from Club Salima, Kemer offers a good range of accommodation to suit every budget but lacks the authenticity and charm of resorts like Marmaris and Kalkan.

As you follow the coastal road up the Lycian Peninsula, the next resort you come to is the city of **ANTALYA**, about 50 miles south-east of Kemer. With a population of around 170,000, Antalya is a prosperous port, a thriving commercial centre and the principal resort of Turkey's Mediterranean coast. The resort is built on small cliffs which form a crescent-shaped bay overlooking the Gulf of Antalya. This attractive, modern city, with its palm-lined boulevards and new offices, apartments and hotels, has been developed around the ancient city of ATTALEIA which was part of the Kingdom of Pergamon in the second century BC. After the death of the last king of Pergamon, Attaleia was ruled successively by the Romans, the Byzantines, the Seljuks and finally the Ottomans. When the Ottoman Empire was divided up by the Allies at the end of World War One Antalya was promised to Italy, but Kemal Ataturk promptly put a stop to that. Antalya's history and its well-preserved 'old city' now help to make it a popular tourist centre with many cafés and restaurants surrounding the old harbour.

Despite attempts by some tour operators to convince you otherwise, Antalya is not a great beach resort. Admittedly, it does have some fairly good beaches in its immediate vicinity, but there are nicer places to go in Turkey if your main priority is sand, sea and surf. The nearest good sandy beach is about six miles to the east (Lora beach). Antalya is generally used as a base by tourists who wish to see the city's sights and take excursions to the nearby ruins of **Termessos, Perge** and Aspendos.

Antalya's accommodation is dotted around the city and along the bay to the east of the centre. As you might expect, the selection of accommodation is vast, ranging from deluxe hotels to cheap, basic pensions. If you want to splash out for luxurious surroundings the **Talya Hotel** in the city centre is definitely the place to go. The most popular hotels, and those featured most in British package tour brochures, are those in the middle of the price range, including the **Turban Adalya Hotel,** near the old city, and the **Lara Hotel** a few miles to the east of the city. Slightly cheaper are the hotels **Buyuk** and **Yayla**, both of which are central. If you're operating on a really tight budget, stick to the downtown establishments like the pensions **Atlas, Ertan** and **Olympiyat** and the hotels **Tatoglu** and **Kervan**. The **Antalya Motel** east of the centre at Lara Beach also offers cheap lodgings, and the Lara Beach Campsite is just a few miles further on.

Many of the city's favourite restaurants and nightspots can be found within the popular hotels. The Talya Hotel is noted for its excellent but expensive restaurant and it also boasts one of the best nightclubs in town. The restaurants **Mehmet**, **Antalya**, **Teras** and **Sehir** all offer good Turkish menus, friendly surroundings and reasonable prices. The **Mobil Liman Restaurant** by the harbour is recommended for its good fish menu. Many of Antalya's cheapest eating places are located on a small street just off the waterfront boulevard which is normally crowded with tables and chairs and hungry tourists. This is the place to go for kebabs, pastries and tasty quick meals. Antalya's social scene is at its liveliest from 1–9 October when the International Arts Festival fills the city's theatres and streets with music and dancing.

The city's two main beaches are **Konyaalti Plaji**, which is a four-mile stretch of pebbles to the west of the centre, and the sandy **Lara Plaji** which is a short *dolmus* ride to the east. Neither of the beaches are spectacular by Turkish standards, but they are perfectly adequate for a few hours sunning and swimming after a sticky sightseeing trip. Lara Plaji is definitely the prettier of the two beaches, but it's also the most crowded as there are several hotels and pensions along the immediate coastline.

If you're interested in the city's history, Antalya's sights should keep you busy for a day – two days at the most. The city's most celebrated landmarks are the **Yivli Minare**, a fluted minaret built by the Seljuks in the twelfth century, and the equestrian **statue of Ataturk** which is one of the finest in the country. The statue and an old stone **clock-tower** are the main features of the city plaza and the minaret stands nearby.

From the plaza it's only a short walk to the **Old City** which is now a protected historical zone. As you wind your way through the narrow twisting streets you'll pass several interesting sights including the **Ali Pasa Camii**, a twelfth-century Seljuk mosque; the **ancient harbour**, which is thought to date back to the third century BC; some interesting **Ottoman housing**, and the **Kesik Minare** (Broken Minaret). Outwith the old city, Antalya's main tourist attractions are **Hadrian's Gate**, an ornamental marble arch constructed by the Romans in the second century; **Karaali Park**, which overlooks the bay and is full of exotic flowers; the **archaeological and ethnographical museum** and the city **bazaar**.

Most of the sights are within walking distance of each other, but if you want to explore the city in style you can hire a horse-drawn carriage to tour the principal monuments. There are two *dolmus* stations on the eastern outskirts of the city: one which serves the airport and the main city routes, and one which serves the hotels and beaches at Lara.

The most popular excursions from Antalya are those to the archaeological sites of **TERMESSOS**, **PERGE** and **ASPENDOS**. Trips to the individual sites and tours of all three can be booked locally through Turkish travel agencies and the larger British package tour companies. If you prefer to go it alone you can take a *dolmus* to the sites. Excursions are also available to the spectacular **DUDEN WATERFALLS** a few miles east of Antalya, and to the nearby resort of **SIDE** where the modern town is adjacent to the ancient Roman city.

From Antalya you can travel easily to almost any part of the country. Turkish Airlines operate direct daily flights to **ISTANBUL**, **ANKARA** and **IZMIR** from Antalya Airport and there are good bus connections to the major cities and neighbouring provinces. From the main bus station there are overnight services to Istanbul and Ankara and regular services to **ADANA**, **KONYA**, **DENIZLI**, **ALANYA** and **SIDE**.

The ancient fortified city of **TERMESSOS** nestles high in the mountains 20 miles north-west of Antalya. The city was founded by a fearless, warfaring people of Greek origin round about the seventh century BC and its ruins feature some impressive Hellenistic and Roman structures. Before reaching the ruins you enter the Termessos National Park where there is a **museum** housing photographs and archaeological finds, a small campsite and a picnic area. The archaeological zone itself is another six miles into the mountains, but can easily be reached by *dolmus*. Once within the ancient city walls you'll have to explore the site by foot, so remember to take comfortable shoes and try to avoid the hottest times of day.

In the lower part of the city the remains include a large **agora**, the badly ruined **Temple of Hadrian**, a **gymnasium** and a well-preserved **theatre** which is built on the edge of a sheer precipice. The highlight of a visit to Termessos is the **necropolis** which stands at the highest point of the city. This sinister burial ground features numerous open tombs which, through the centuries, have been toppled by earthquakes and plundered by grave-robbers.

If you take the main E24 route out of Antalya the ruins of **PERGE** are 10 miles to the east in the ancient Roman province of Pamphylia. The city was founded by Greek invaders and remained independent until Alexander the Great conquered Anatolia in the fourth century BC. The city prospered under Roman rule, when it was made the principal city of Pamphylia, and fell into decline under the Byzantines.

The extensive ruins of Perge feature some impressive Hellenistic and Roman **city gates**, a long **colonnaded street**, a **theatre** with seating for 15,000 and a magnificent **stadium** which is among the best-preserved of its kind. A climb to the top of the theatre gives an overall view of the site.

Twenty miles east of Perge (30 from Antalya) is the site of ancient **ASPENDOS**, another important Pamphylian city. Most of the ruins at Aspendos date back to Roman times, but the city's history can be traced back to the ninth century BC. Built on the banks of the Eurymedon River, Aspendos was once a busy river port and a prosperous trading centre.

The archaeological zone is dominated by a beautiful **theatre**, which is claimed to be the best-preserved classical theatre in the world, and certainly the finest you'll see in Turkey. Built by the Romans, it survived the rule of the Byzantines, the Seljuks and the Ottomans before Ataturk ordered its restoration. With its 20,000 seats and marvellous acoustics, the theatre is still used for musical and theatrical performances and it is an important venue during the annual Antalya Festival. Other sights at Aspendos include the remains of a **stadium**, an **agora** and the city's ancient **aqueducts**.

The popular resort of **SIDE** lies in the shadow of the Taurus Mountains about 50 miles east of Antalya. Until recently Side was a quiet little fishing port which consisted of a few wooden buildings scattered among the ruins of ancient **Selimiye**. Today it is one of Turkey's busiest tourist centres. In the past decade the development of large hotels, restaurants, nightclubs and bars has transformed a quaint Turkish village into a major resort which virtually bursts at the seams during the summer months. Side's appeal is obvious; it's not everywhere you find a picturesque harbour, two beautiful sandy beaches and a fascinating archaeological site all within a stone's throw of each other. Fortunately, the government has realized that what made Side so attractive to holidaymakers in the first place is now being lost in a concrete jungle of tourist facilities, and plans are afoot to 'undevelop' the resort. This will involve the demolition of some unsightly modern buildings, which will be replaced with new facilities further along the coast, and the preservation and restoration of traditional buildings. While Side is undeniably one of Turkey's most commercialized resorts, it's an ideal destination for young holidaymakers who enjoy sunbathing, sightseeing and dancing the night away.

Despite the vast range of accommodation on offer in Side, empty rooms are very thin on the ground in the height of the tourist season. If you want to avoid fighting for accommodation either book in advance or plan your visit for spring or autumn. A large percentage of visitors to Side are package tourists who are usually put up in the comfortable modern motels along the western beach. The **Motel Cennet** and the **Motel Turtel** are the most popular and both are favoured by British package tour operators. If you're travelling independently you'll find plenty of small hotels and pensions in the village itself, but there's no guarantee you'll find vacancies. Most of the cheaper lodgings are located on the street which runs inland from the waterfront to the bus station. If you're visiting in the summer start with those nearest to the bus station as those near the beach are more likely to be full. **Pension Grup**, **Pension Hermes**, **Pension Sen** and **Pension Huzur** are worth looking out for, though your choice will probably be dictated by availability rather than preference.

There's no escaping the fact that Side is a tourist trap, and it becomes most obvious when the time comes to eat out. The restaurants are generally expensive by Turkish standards and the food is seldom anything to write home about. You're less likely to be ripped off if you steer clear of the waterfront tourist spots and follow the recommendations of your fellow holidaymakers. If you do find a good restaurant it's a good idea to stick to it (then write and tell us about it!). At night time the entire tourist population seems to converge on the waterfront which is lined with restaurants, bars and discos.

Side owes much of its popularity to its history and the ruins which now form part of the resort. The city is believed to have been founded by Greek invaders in the seventh century BC, at which time it was notorious for piracy and slavery. In Roman times it became an important Pamphylian port and most of the city's ruins date back to that era. It was here, on the romantic shores of Side, that Marc Antony first met Cleopatra in the first century AD.

Side's archaeological site is only a few minutes' walk from the main tourist centre. Surrounded by well-preserved city walls, the site's most impressive structures include a large **theatre** built by the Romans on the foundations of a smaller Greek theatre; the ruins of **temples** dedicated to the Greek gods Apollo and Athena; a **Byzantine basilica**; a **Roman bath house** and two **agoras**. There is also an interesting **archaeological museum**, housed within a second Roman bath house, which features some sculptures found on the site including a **bust of Hermes** and some ornamental **stone tombs**.

If you wish to see more of ancient Pamphylia excursions can be booked locally to the ruins of **PERGE** and **ASPENDOS**. The **MANAVGAT WATERFALLS** east of Side on the way to Alanya, provide a pleasant relaxing setting for a picnic if you wish to escape the hustle and bustle of Side for a few hours. There are regular daily bus services between **ANTALYA** and **ALANYA** which stop at Side. Some of the buses will drop you at **MANAVGAT** a few miles inland but there are plenty of *dolmuses* to and from the resort. There are also direct daily services to **ISTANBUL**, **ANKARA** and **IZMIR**.

The next major town on this touristy section of the coastline is the large resort and busy port of **ALANYA**. The town is built at the foot of a rocky promontory and, like Side, is flanked by long sandy beaches. At the top of the promontory, overlooking the resort, is an imposing Seljuk fortress which contains Alanya's most impressive ruins. Despite the recent development of large hotels, restaurants, tourist shops and night-clubs, the town centre has somehow managed to retain its charm and intimate atmosphere. Alanya is a typical sun, sand and surf resort with a handful of historic sights and plenty of nightlife.

Most of Alanya's package tourists are accommodated in the big modern motels a few miles east of the centre. These include the **Panorama Motel**, the **Alantur Motel**, the **Banana Motel** and the **Merhaba Motel**, all of which feature in British holiday brochures. The Alantur is the most luxurious and most expensive, but they all offer a good range of facilities and easy access to the most popular of

Alanya's two beaches. Other hotels favoured by British tour companies are the **Kaptan Hotel**, the **Sultan Hotel** and the **Gungor Hotel** which are located in the town centre. Alanya's cheapest lodging can be found close to the town centre and along the less popular western beach. **Hotel Kent, Hotel Riviera, Yayla Palas** and **Antalya Palas** all offer basic accommodation at low rates. There are camping areas to the east and west of the town but the best campsite is at the **Yeni International Motel** out along the eastern beach.

Eating out can be interesting and inexpensive if you choose your restaurants carefully. For good atmosphere and well-prepared fish dishes treat yourself to a meal in one of the smaller seafront restaurants like the **Sirin Restaurant** and the **Mahperi Restaurant** which are both reasonably priced. You'll find cheaper restaurants serving equally good food further inland. If it's nightlife you're looking for you can choose from the numerous discos and bars in the town centre and in the large hotels to the east.

The sights of Alanya should keep you busy for a day, but it's advisable to confine sightseeing to the mornings before temperatures get too high. Known in ancient times as Korakesion, the town was founded in the fourth century BC and for several centuries it was a haven for the pirate ships which plied the Mediterranean Sea. Most of Alanya's ruins, however, are a legacy from the days of Seljuk rule when it became an important naval base.

The best of the ruins are enclosed within the **twelfth-century fortress** which dominates the town from the top of the promontory. Within its well-preserved double walls you can see the remains of a **covered bazaar**, a **caravanserai**, two **mosques** and a **Byzantine basilica**. The view of the town and the immediate coastline is itself a sight to behold. To see the rest of Alanya's sights, take a walk down to the harbour where you'll find the **old boatyards** which feature some interesting Seljuk architecture and the **Kizil Kule** (Red Tower) which was one of the harbour's main defences in the thirteenth century. The town's **archaeological and ethnographical museum** is located on the western side of the promontory close to the beach. Among the exhibits there are coins, ceramics and examples of regional craftwork, some of which date back to the Bronze Age.

Transport around the town to the sights, hotels and beaches is provided by *dolmuses* and taxis. Alanya town centre is fairly compact and all the main tourist facilities, including the tourist office, the post office and bus station, are only a short walk or *dolmus* ride from each other.

A popular excursion from Alanya is the boat trip which visits the fascinating **caves** dotted around the promontory. Starting from the harbour on either the western or the eastern side of the promontory, visits are made to the **Maidens' Grotto**, where pirates once kept their female captives, the **Lovers' Grotto** and the **Phosphorus Cave** which is noted for its luminous blue rocks. The most famous cave, the **Damlatas Cave**, is on the western side of the promontory and can also be reached by foot from the town. Apart from its multi-coloured stalactites and stalagmites, the cave is famous for its exceptionally high humidity which is said to help sufferers of asthma and other breathing disorders. There is also a boat trip which starts from the western beach. If you wish to explore the region's historical sites, excursions are available to the Roman ruins at SIDE, ASPENDOS and PERGE.

The central bus station on the eastern side of the town links Alanya to Turkey's major cities and the principal towns of the Mediterranean coast. There are daily services to ANTALYA, ISTANBUL, IZMIR, KONYA and MARMARIS and there are several buses a day which serve the route between ALANYA and ADANA stopping in SILIFKE and MERSIN.

The 175-mile stretch of coastline between Alanya and Silifke is particularly pretty as the road rises and falls between mountains and plains. It was this region, known in ancient times as the province of Cilicia, which Marc Antony is said to have gifted to Cleopatra as a wedding present.

About 75 miles east of Alanya there is a town called **ANAMUR** which is noted for its beautiful beach, its medieval castle and its proximity to the ruins of ancient ANAMURIUM. The town itself is nothing to rave about, but it's an ideal place to spend a day if you wish to break the journey to Silifke. Anamur has a few restaurants, a few modest hotels and several camping areas dotted along the beach. The **Karan Motel** and the **Cephe Hotel** both offer cheap accommodation. The well-preserved castle is a short walk from the town on the seashore, but the prettiest stretch of the beach is two or three miles east of the centre. *Dolmuses* ferry tourists to and from the Roman site of Anamurium which is about six miles south-west of the town. The ruins include a **theatre**, a **necropolis**, an **odeon** and some well-preserved **ramparts**.

From Anamur the main E24 route takes you to the town of **SILIFKE**, which has little to offer the tourist except boats to NORTH CYPRUS and buses to MERSIN and KONYA. The city of Seleucia, as it was known in ancient times, was founded in the third century BC by Seleucus, one of Alexander the Great's generals. Today the only noteworthy sights are the imposing castle which overlooks the town and the remains of a Roman theatre and temple.

Most of Silifke's accommodation is located between the town centre and the port of TASUCU, six miles to the west, where you catch the boat or hovercraft to Cyprus. The motels **Tastur** and **Bosak** near Tasucu, and the **Hotel Akdeniz** near Silifke all offer good, cheap accommodation. If you're travelling to Cyprus you can purchase tickets in Tasucu or at the bus station in Silifke where there are plenty of buses and *dolmuses* to Tasucu. Hydrofoil and car ferries make the round-trip from Tasucu to Kyrenia at least twice daily. The trip to Kyrenia takes about two hours by hydrofoil and four hours by boat. From Silifke there are daily bus services to ALANYA, KONYA, MERSIN and ADANA.

There are several places of interest within easy travelling of Silifke. About 20 miles to the north is UZUNCABURC, the Hellenic city of Olba-Diocaesarea, where the impressive remains include the ruined **Temple of Zeus Olbius**. A few miles south of Silifke are the Roman ruins of KAYA which feature a **necropolis** and the **Tomb of St Thecla** who was the first female saint. About fourteen miles east of Silifke on the main road to Mersin there is a turn-off for CENNET VE CEHENNEM (Heaven and Hell) where you'll find some beautiful **caves** and a **ruined Byzantine chapel**. Further along the main road is the tiny resort and ancient site of KORYKOS which is noted for its lovely white **beach** and its **Byzantine castle**. From here the road takes you to KANLIDIVANE and the tombs of ancient Kanytelis.

The modern city of **MERSIN** is the largest port on the Mediterranean coast and Turkey's gateway to Cyprus. Mersin is not a holiday resort but its comfortable hotels are well-patronized by travellers going to and from Cyprus and Syria. The majority of the city-centre hotels are in the moderate to expensive price range. The city's best and most expensive establishment is the **Mersin Hotel** down by the waterfront. The best mid-range hotels are the hotels **Toros, Hosta** and **Nobel** and slightly cheaper rooms can be found at the hotels

Hititer, **Savran** and **Dogan**. The main tourist office on the waterfront will provide information on cheaper lodgings on the outskirts of the city. Mersin has restaurants to suit every budget and most of them can be found along the waterfront and the adjoining streets. Most of the city's tourist facilities, including the post office and the offices of Turkish Maritime Lines and Turkish Airlines, are also located in the harbour area.

Turkish Maritime Lines operate a twice-weekly ferry to **GAZI MAGOSA** and **FAMAGUSTA** in Cyprus and a weekly service to **LATTAKIA** in Syria. The main bus station on the northern edge of the city provides regular daily services to **SILIFKE**, **ALANYA** and **ADANA** and municipal services for the main city routes. From the railway station to the east of the harbour there are daily trains to **TARSUS** and **ADANA**.

Sightseeing around Mersin is certainly limited and the only historic site worth visiting is eight miles west of the city at **VIRANSEHIR**. This is the site of ancient Pompeiopolis which was founded by invaders from Rhodes in the eighth century BC. The ruins of the city feature a spectacular row of **Corinthian columns** and some ancient **aqueducts**, both dating back to Roman times. The main road east of Mersin takes you inland to **TARSUS** which was the birthplace of St Paul 2000 years ago. Apart from a badly ruined **Roman gate** and the remains of a **Byzantine church**, there is little evidence of the town's history.

About 45 miles east of Mersin the main road passes through **ADANA**, Turkey's fourth largest city. With the exception of a few coach tours, very few package tourists ever get this far east. The majority of tourists who visit Adana are independent travellers destined for the eastern provinces. Built on a fertile plain between the Seyhan and Ceyhan rivers, Adana is a prosperous agricultural centre with a thriving cotton industry. The city is not noted for its great historical sights and it has little to offer the tourist apart from the standard facilities of a major city. Its few tourist attractions include the **Roman bridge** spanning the River Seyhan, which was built by the Emperor Hadrian and restored by Justinian; a fourteenth-century Ottoman **mosque**; the remains of a **covered bazaar**, and an interesting **archaeological and ethnographical museum**.

Hotels and restaurants are Adana's strong points. The city has accommodation to suit every budget and a vast selection of pleasant eating places. The deluxe **Divan Hotel** is certainly the best in town, but it's not the place to go if you're counting the pennies. Moderately priced accommodation can be found at the **Inci Hotel**, the **Ipek Palas** and the **Duygu Hotel**. Cheaper rooms are available at the **Agba Hotel** and the **Ener Motel**. As far as eating out is concerned, the **Yildiz Restaurant** is one of the best for atmosphere, good food and value for money. The **Mavi Rose** and the **Muzikhof** restaurants are also recommended.

The nearest beach to Adana is 30 miles south at KARATAS. If you're looking for a pleasant spot to sunbathe and picnic you're as well heading for LAKE SEYHAN to the immediate north of the city. A few miles outside Adana the main road east passes the village of MISIS where there are some interesting Roman ruins including a mosaic which illustrates Noah's Ark.

South-east of Adana is the port of **ISKENDERUN**, the last city on Turkey's Mediterranean coast. Formerly known as Alexandretta, the city took its name from its founder, Alexander the Great. It was on the Plain of Issos, the land between Adana and Iskenderun, that Alexander defeated the Persians in the fourth century BC to gain control of eastern Anatolia and much of Syria. After the First World War Alexandretta became part of the French Protectorate of Syria and it remained in French hands until the dawn of the Second World War. Up until 20 years ago when Mersin was developed as the Mediterranean's principal port, Iskenderun was an important shipping base. Today, it still has a busy harbour but its economy is largely based on commerce.

Despite its interesting history, Iskenderun is off the beaten track of most independent travellers and it doesn't feature often in the package tour brochures. As there is little demand for modern hotels, most of the city's accommodation falls into the modest or basic categories. The best hotel is the comfortable and moderately priced **Hatayli Hotel**. Cheap hotels include the **Guney Palas**, the **Kavakli Pension**, the **Hitit Hotel** and the **Mavi Yal Motel**. If you're eating out try the **Saray Restaurant** on the waterfront.

Thirty miles north of the city is the town of DORTYOL, formerly Issus, where there are several interesting sights from several eras including the remains of a **Turkish bath**, a **bazaar**, an ancient **fountain** and a **mosque**.

Thirty miles south is the inland city of **ANTAKYA** which has strong historical links with Iskenderun. Antakya, the ancient city of Antioch, was founded a century later than Iskenderun by Seleucus, Alexander's top general, following the death of the great conqueror. During Roman times the city became an important centre of Christianity and it was frequently visited by St Peter and St Paul. In the eleventh century Antioch became a Frankish principality, held by the Crusaders, and it remained that way until it fell to the Ottomans in the thirteenth century. Between the First World War and the Second World War the city was part of the French Protectorate of Syria.

Like Iskenderun, Antakya does not do a roaring trade in tourism, but it does have a range of modest hotels the best of which are the **Atahan Hotel** and the **Divan Hotel**. The best eating place in the centre is the **Saray Restaurant**. There are more hotels and restaurants in HARBIYE, a pretty suburb four miles south of the centre.

Antakya's attractions include the **Grotto of St Peter**, where the saint is said to have preached for the first time; the **Hatay Museum** which houses a beautiful collection of **Roman mosaics**; an ancient **Roman bridge** built in the second century, and several **Arabian mosques**.

The Syrian border towns of YAYLADAGI and REYHANLI are only 30 miles from Antakya, but you will not be given entry without a Syrian visa.

The Black Sea

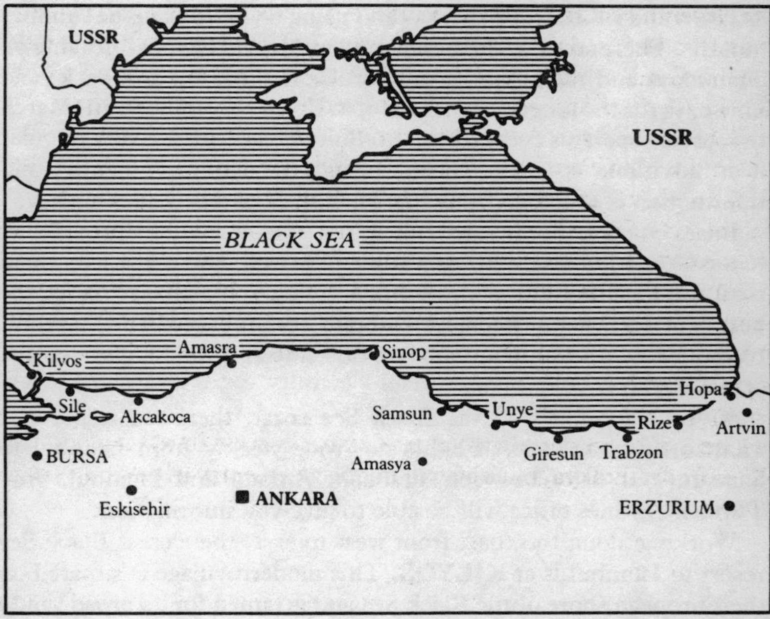

The Black Sea coast is one of the outstanding regions of scenic beauty in Turkey. In contrast to the dry, arid plains of central Anatolia, the climate is warm and humid, ideal for the production of its main crops: maize, tea, tobacco and hazelnuts. The north coast might not have the historical remains and infinite sunshine that the Mediterranean coast offers, but there are charming fishing villages and clean beaches which stretch for miles, and are ideal for campers and family holidays.

The Black Sea coast was first settled in the sixth century BC by the Arcadians and later became the Kingdom of Pontus. It was captured by the Romans and then ruled by the Byzantines under Alexius Comnenus, and remained the last outpost of the Byzantine Empire until Sultan Mehmet II made it part of the Ottoman Empire. At the end of the First World War Ataturk came here from Istanbul to battle for independence.

Some of the beach resorts, **KILYOS** and **SILE** for example, are within easy driving distance from Istanbul for a day trip. A ferry service runs along the coastline from Istanbul to **TRABZON**, calling at **SINOP**, **SAMSUN** and **GIRESUN** on the way and going on to **HOPA** in the summer months. There are boats every week from April to October, leaving on Thursdays and taking six days to cruise to Trabzon and back, and nine days for the longer cruise to Hopa. From November until March the service operates every fortnight. Since these trips are very popular it is advisable to book ahead during the summer months and information is available from any Turkish Maritime Lines agency.

Buses connect all the towns along the coastline with express buses to **SAMSUN** from **KAYSERI**, **ANKARA** and **SIVAS**. There is a very good road from **SINOP** right along to **HOPA** giving you a chance to see the beautiful scenery as it passes through tea, tobacco, and hazelnut plantations with the mountains on one side and the blue sea on the other.

If you want to fly to the Black Sea coast, there are airports at **TRABZON** and **SAMSUN**. Flights go twice weekly from Istanbul to Samsun and daily between Trabzon, Ankara and Istanbul. Any Turkish Airlines office will be able to give you information.

Working along the coast from west to east, the closest Black Sea resort to Istanbul is at **KILYOS**. This modern village is situated on the European shore of the Black Sea and is famed for its broad sandy beaches. It has all the facilities that any European resort might offer, and is well supplied with motels, hotels and campsites.

On the Anatolian shore the holiday village at **SILE** is also within easy driving distance of Istanbul. The town stretches right down to the coastline and is overlooked by the remains of a Genoese castle. There are good beaches, caves and camping facilities. It is well supplied with good restaurants and lively bars.

Further along the coast, the resort town of **AKÇAKOCA** is especially charming. The ruins of a Genoese castle near to the beach are well worth a visit and the town is surrounded by clean beaches, intriguing rock formations and hazelnut plantations. If you are camping, the site at **CAYAGZI VILLAGE** just outside Akçakoca is close to the beach and has restaurants.

AMASRA, a little fishing port, is one of the most beautiful settlements along the coast. As well as a wide beach there are the remains of a **Roman temple and baths** to visit and a **Byzantine church** and **citadel**.

If you are travelling along the coast by boat, your first port of call is **SINOP**. Legend says that the town was founded by the Amazons but though once a busy trading centre, it is now a quiet fishing village. The road from here runs along the coast as far east as Hopa and is particularly beautiful.

The **Tourist Information Office** on Iskele Cad. (tel: 299) can help you with accommodation listings if you want to stay in Sinop. Since Sinop is a fishing village there are of course many fish restaurants around the harbour and it is a good place to stop for a meal.

Sightseers should visit the ruins of the **Temple of Serapis** built by the Hittites and then restored in 1 BC by Mithradates IV, King of Pontus. There are also lots of Seljuk buildings and the thirteenth-century **Alaeddin Mosque** is of particular interest, as is the **Alaiye Medrese** which is the provincial museum.

From Sinop you can head to SEYIT BIAL for a superb view of the tobacco plantations in the area, or the beaches at RUYA and AK LIMAN where the forest grows right down to the sea.

SAMSUN

The next destination for the Turkish Maritime cruise is Samsun. This is the major port for the region and is situated on the fertile deltas of the Kizilirmak and Yesilirmak rivers. Most of the agricultural products of the region are exported through Samsun, making it a busy commercial centre. An agricultural fair is held every June, when beds are hard to find.

The road between Samsun and Trabzon is especially scenic with breathtaking views of the mountains, the pine forests and the coastline, so you might want to fly to Samsun and drive or go by bus from here to Trabzon.

The *airport* is east of the town and a bus service takes passengers into the town centre. The *bus terminal* and *railway station* are about half a mile from Kazimpasa Cad., the main street where the banks, hotels, post office and airline office (tel: 18260) are located. The **Tourist Information Office** is on Irmak Cad. (tel: 11228).

The best hotel is the **Turban Samsun** (tel: 10750) which has a swimming pool and tennis courts; the **Hotel Burc** (tel: 15479) and **Hotel Vindinli** (tel: 16050) are smaller, less costly establishments; both have restaurants. The **Hotel Terminal** (tel: 1551) is conveniently situated beside the bus station.

Samsun does not have any ancient historical sites since it was burnt to the ground in the fifteenth century by the Genoese, however the fourteenth-century **Pazor Camii** and nineteenth-century **Buyuk Camii** are of interest. There is also an **archaeological museum** housing finds from the excavation at Dundar Tepe and Amisos. The statue of Ataturk in the park reminds us that it was from here that Mustapha Kemal set out to defend his country in 1919.

AMASYA

If you travel inland from Samsun, after passing through LADIK, famed for its carpets, you'll arrive in Amasya, one of Anatolia's most attractive towns. Originally the capital of the Pontic Kingdom the town is clustered below a citadel overlooking the valley of the Yesilirmak. It is said that the town was founded by Amasia, Queen of Amazon but the town was captured by a succession of invaders, the Seljuks, the Mongols and then the Ottomans.

The **Tursan Amasya** (tel: 3134) on the banks of the river and the **Saracoglu** (tel: 10783) provide moderately priced accommodation. Budget travellers should try the **Apaydin Hotel** or the **Sehir** which both have basic rooms at low cost.

There are lots of small restaurants in the streets around the market square. The **Cicek Lokantasi** is basic but has an appetizing menu and if you want to take tea it's worth trying the restaurant in the municipal park.

Amasya is an old town with lots to see. A walk across the river takes you out to the interesting old Ottoman houses with their overhanging balconies and vernacular design. The **museum** on the main street is open from 8 a.m.–12 noon and 1.30–5.30 p.m. Tuesdays until Sundays and houses Roman, Pontic, Seljuk and Ottoman exhibits. In the grounds is a tomb where you can see some Seljuk mummies that were found under the thirteenth-century **Burmali Camii** when it was being restored. The fifteenth-century **Sultan Beyazit Camii** is the principal mosque in the town and is worth a visit if you are interested in Islamic architecture, as is the **Gok Medrese Camii** and the **Beyazit Pasa Camii**.

Without doubt the most interesting place for the sightseer to visit are the **rock tombs** cut into the rock on which the citadel stands. They were constructed in 300 BC for the cult worship of dead rulers and are especially impressive when floodlit at night. It is possible to go on up to the citadel at the top of the hill which has a panoramic view of the area.

Back on the coast road, just along from SAMSUN, lies the attractive fishing village of **UNYE**. The beaches in this area are very clean with purple rock formations and hazelnut plantations. It's a good place for campers with numerous sites located beside the sea. The **Kumsal Pansiyon** provides cheap accommodation as does the **Urer**. The motel **Uniye Belediye Camlik** is exceptionally pleasant and inexpensive and is attractively situated in pinewoods, down by the shore.

ORDU 35 miles along the coast is a fishing town and port with some attractive old houses. Situated at the foot of a green hill with steep slopes, it is a pleasant place to stop off for a meal and if you are looking for a beach in this area you've not far to go to reach **Guzelyali**.

The port of **GIRESUN** is crowned by a ruined Byzantine fortress on a cliff overlooking the sea. Another destination for the Black Sea cruise, it was from here that General Lucullus brought the first cherry trees back to Europe. Travelling along the coastal road you'll catch a glimpse of Giresun Island, famed in antiquity for the temple built to Mars by the Amazons.

TRABZON

Trabzon is the next city along the coast, the busiest port in the region. It was founded by the Arcadians in the seventh century BC and developed under Emperor Hadrian. The Byzantine Emperor Alexius Comnenus fled here after the Fall of Constantinople and Trabzon remained the last outpost of the Byzantine civilization until it was captured by the Ottoman Turks in 1461.

There is an *airport* with regular flights to Istanbul and to Ankara and information about flights is available from the Turkish Airlines Office (tel: 13446), on Taksim Cad. just along from the **Tourist**

Information Office (tel: 12722) in the city centre. The *bus station* to the east of the city has a frequent service to Erzurum if you want to travel to eastern Turkey as well as towns along the coast.

For moderately priced accommodation in Trabzon go to the **Hotel Usta** (tel: 12195), but cheaper rooms are to be found at the **Hotel Ozgur** (tel: 11319) and **Hotel Horon** (tel: 11199).

Most of the hotels in Trabzon are situated around Taksim Meydani. The budget traveller should try the **Benli Palas** or the **Turistik Palas** which are fairly cheap.

The rooftop restaurant in the **Hotel Ozgur** is a good place for a meal. Alternatively the **Gaziantep Kebabcisi and Baklavacisi** serve tasty kebabs and snacks.

The most interesting monument in Trabzon is the twelfth-century **Church of St Sofya** which stands on a hill overlooking the bay. The impressive frescoes inside have only recently been uncovered by a team of Scottish archaeologists. The churches of **St Anne** and **St Blaise** are also of interest, as is **Ortahisar Camii** situated inside the citadel. It is worth taking a trip to **Ataturk's Villa** which is situated above the town and commands a superb view.

While in Trabzon don't miss an excursion to the **Monastery of the Virgin** at SUMELA. A taxi will take you up into the mountains and forest above the Black Sea coast to the most important Byzantine monument in the region. The monastery was built to house the icon of the Virgin painted by St Luke and, although that has now been sent to Greece, there are interesting fourteenth-century and eighteenth-century frescoes.

If you have time travel a little further south to the pass of ZIGANA GECIDI. The contrast between the dry Asiatic plain on one side of the pass and the lush, green land of the coast is one of the most striking views you're likely to see. Stop off for lunch at the village of HAMSIKOY which is famed for its excellent cuisine.

The Maritime Cruiser carries on along the coast from Trabzon to **RIZE**. The town is situated on the steep mountain slopes surrounded by one vast tea plantation. It is a typical Black Sea town and the sightseer might like to visit the sixteenth-century **Pasa Islam Camii** and the remains of a Genoese castle.

HOPA is the final destination for the boat trip and those travelling by road. It is a small town about 15 miles from the Russian border and the easternmost Turkish port on the Black Sea. If you want accommodation here you'll find that the **Hotel Papila** is surprisingly comfortable for such a remote town and has an excellent restaurant.

A trip inland from here makes for an exceptional journey of wild and wonderful scenery. An hour's drive into the mountains will bring you to ARTVIN, the capital of the province. The town has archetypal old Turkish houses and a sixteenth-century castle. There is a famous bull-fighting festival every year and, for the more adventurous, white water rafting on the Coruk River.

Central Anatolia

Central Anatolia is a desert-like region of steppeland on a high plateau. It has a harsh climate with extremes of temperature, being extremely cold and rainy in winter but baked dry in the long, hot summers. This was the birthplace of the Hittite civilization, and it is here that some of the most important archaeological sites in Turkey are to be found, in particular at CATALHOYUK, the oldest human settlement in the world. The area has a turbulent history and was subjected to constant foreign domination: from Alexander the Great in the fourth century BC to Tamerlane in the fourteenth century. ANKARA, the heart of the Turkish Republic, is the centre of the region but rather than linger long in the capital, tourists generally move on to see the strange rock formations in the province of CAPPADOCIA, thence to KONYA, the religious centre of the Whirling Dervishes.

This is a good region for the hardy: campers, hikers and those prepared to rough it a bit will get on well here. More traditional coach tours of central Anatolia are run by Metak, Wings and UK Express. However, if you want to visit Cappadocia, Blue Spot and Savile Travel offer tours of a high standard. There are many unusual holidays in Cappadocia; Transglobal Ltd run walking holidays and Birdwatching and Wildlife even operate a donkey trekking holiday. If you want to

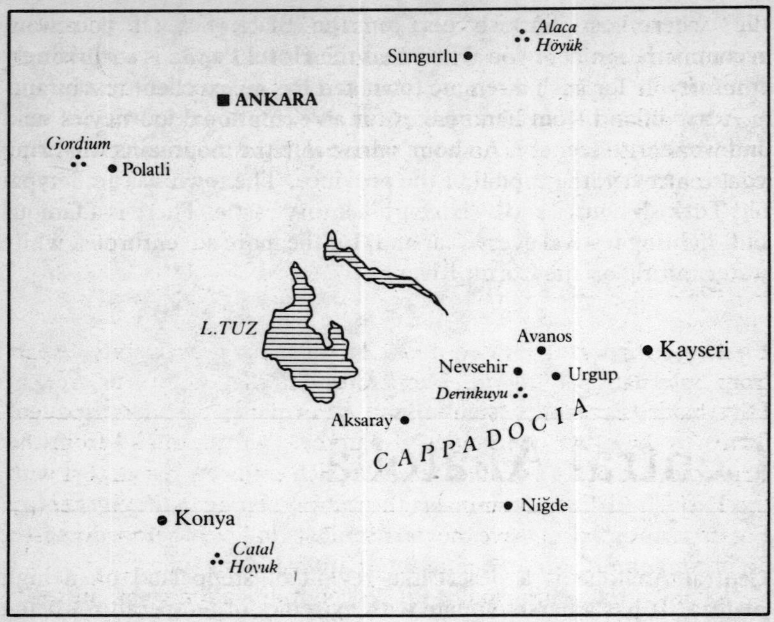

tour Cappadocia, specialized holidays to the region include a Hittite and Phrygian Culture Tour, operated by UK Express, and a holiday to the churches in Cappadocia through Inter-Church Travel.

Ankara

Ankara, the capital of the Turkish Republic, is situated in the centre of the Anatolian plateau. A modern, utilitarian city, it perhaps lacks some of the atmosphere of Istanbul or Konya but it does have some sights worth seeing.

The city lies on the crossroads of the traditional east-west and north–south trade routes and there has been a settlement on this site since before 1200 BC. The original Hatti and Hittite settlements were captured by the Phrygians and then the Romans. Ankyra, the Byzantine city, withstood many Arab and Persian attacks until it was finally captured by the Seljuk Turks in 1071. Under the Ottoman Empire, Ankara was just a quiet provincial town and it was not until

1923 when Ataturk moved the government here that it became a major centre again. He designed a new European-style city unlike any other city in Turkey, with long, wide streets, residential suburbs and modern office blocks, and his name prevails in street names and buildings of today. It is now the financial, medical, educational and legal centre of the Republic.

COMMUNICATIONS

Esenboga Airport is located about 15 miles outside the city. Apart from international flights, it operates internal flights to Adana, Diyarbakir, Erzurum, Istanbul and Izmir daily, with less frequent flights to the other main cities of Turkey. Getting to and from the airport is made easy by a bus service which connects the airport with the Turkish Airlines Terminal at the railway station in the city centre. For departure, buses leave the rail terminal 1½ hours before domestic flight times and 2 hours before international flight times.

Ankara is the central point for all communications, and all roads lead here. From the *bus station* on Hippodrom Cad., buses run frequently to Istanbul and to every city and town of any size in Turkey. It is advisable to book seats in advance and you can do this either at the bus station or at one of the many bus company offices near Kizilay in the city centre.

The *railway station* is on the Hippodrom Cad. not far from the coach terminal. It is fairly convenient and comfortable to travel by train as long as you catch one of the express trains. A service operates between Ankara and Izin, Ankara and Istanbul and Kayseri. (Bear in mind that a coach journey is usually quicker.)

TOURIST INFORMATION

As well as a desk at the airport, the Ministry of Culture and Tourism have an office on Gaza Mustafa Kemal Bul., which is open from 8 a.m.–7 p.m. on weekdays and 9 a.m. until 5 p.m. on Saturdays and Sundays, while in winter it is closed on weekends.

Tourist Information Office
Gaza Mustafa Kemal Bul. 33
Tel: 230 1911/15, 229 2930/95

Esenboga Airport
Tel: 324 2280/81
Open 8 a.m.–7 p.m.

Post Office
Ataturk Bul.
Tel: 25 05 35
Open Mon.–Sat. 8 a.m.–12 midnight. Sunday 9 a.m.–7 p.m.

American Express
Celikkale Sokak 12/B,
Yenisehir

Student Travel Organization
Accommodation
Cumhuriyet Youth Hostel,
Cebeci/Ankara
Tel: 18 99 16/17 77 32

Train Station
Tel: 311 06 20

International Airport
Esenboga Airport
Tel: 312 28 20

Airport Information
At T.A. Terminal,
Railway Station,
Hippodrom, Cad.
Gar Yani
Tel: 312 49 00

Bus Station
Central Bus Station,
Hippodrom, Cad.
Tel: 310 47 47

EMBASSIES

UK
Sehit Ersam Cad. 46/A,
Cankaya,
Ankara
Tel: 127 43 10
Open 9 a.m.–5 p.m.

US
Ataturk Bul. 110,
Kavaklidere,
Ankara
Tel: 126 54 70
Open 8 a.m.–6 p.m.

Canada
Nene Hatun Cad. 75,
Gazi Osman Pasa,
Ankara
Tel: 127 58 03
Open 9 a.m.–6 p.m.

GETTING AROUND

Ankara has a complex system of buses and *dolmuses*. Bus centres are at *Ulus* in the old city and *Kizilay* in the newer part. The most convenient *dolmuses* run along Ataturk Cad. from Ulus to Cankaya.

The city taxis are good value as they are metered and the fares are reasonable.

For information about car hire, see Avis at the airport or at Bestedek Sok. in the city centre.

SIGHTS

Hisar, the citadel dominating the old town of Ankara, is a good place to start a sightseeing tour of the city. It was built in AD 800 by the Byzantine Emperor Michael II and from the towers there is a panoramic view of the city. Close to the gates is the **Museum of Anatolian Civilizations**, a unique collection of exhibits from the Neolithic, Assyrian, Phrygian, Hellenistic and Roman periods which trace the history of the area. Of special interest is the Hittite collection of art and crafts taken from the surrounding excavations. The museum is open from 9 a.m. to 12 noon and 1.30 to 5.30 p.m. but photography is not allowed. From here walk through the bazaar to the thirteenth-century **Aslan Camii**, one of the oldest mosques in the city. Other mosques include the **Alaeddin Camii** built in the twelfth century, and the sixteenth-century **Yeni Camii**.

If you want to visit some Roman ruins head to Nation Square where there are the remains of third-century **Roman baths**; the **Column of Julian**, which celebrates his visit to the city in AD 362, and the **Temple of Augustus**. In front of this is **Hayci Bayran Camii**, a sixteenth-century mosque built with marble from the Roman ruins nearby.

Those interested in history should visit the **War of Salvation Museum** and the **Republic Museum**. Open from 9 a.m.–12.30 p.m. and from 1.30–5.30 p.m. these provide insight into the development of a democratic state from the autocracy which existed. Another museum to see is the **Ethnographic Museum** in the modern part of the city, which has exhibits of folklore weapons and musical instruments. While in this area you might like to head to the **Youth Park**, a pleasant place to walk and picnic.

ACCOMMODATION

The most luxurious hotel in the city is the **Buyuk Ankara** (tel: 134 4920) on Ataturk Bul. With 1180 rooms, 14 suites and 3 restaurants; a heated swimming pool; tennis courts and a garage, it ranks as five star. Slightly less expensive, the **Dedeman Hotel** on Buklum Sok. (tel: 117 62 00) has 252 rooms, a swimming pool and a rooftop nightclub while the **Marmara** (tel: 231 301) outside the city on Ataturks Fam. has been recently opened and is a smaller hotel in a lovely setting. The **Etap Mola** (tel: 133 90 65) and the **Kent Hotel** (tel: 131 21 11) are among Ankara's best hotels and the Kent has an especially good restaurant and an oriental coffee salon.

More moderately priced accommodation can be found at the **Apaydin Hotel** on Bayindir Sok. (tel: 133 3135–7), with 50 air-conditioned rooms, the **Bulvar Palas** (tel: 1342180) which has 177 rooms, or the new **Ergen Hotel** on Karamfil Sok. (tel: 117 5906). The budget traveller should try hotels in Ulus which tend to be less expensive. The **Paris** (tel: 324 1283) and the **Efes Hotel**, both on Denizuler Cad. are recommended, as are the **As Hotel** (tel: 310 3999) on Ruhgarli Cad. and the **Oba Hotel** (tel: 105 879) just off Ataturk Bul.

Student accommodation is available from 1 July to 31 August at the **Cumhuriyet Student Hostel**, Cebeci (tel: 19 36 34) and there is a campsite 22 km outside Ankara on the Istanbul road at **Kervansaray Susuzkay Mocamp**.

EATING

The restaurants in the big hotels serve an international menu. The Buyuk Ankara has a good but expensive rooftop grill while Turkish specialities are served at the **Marmara**, the **Kent** and **Bulvar Palas**. The **R.V.**, **Milka** and **Pizza Pino** are more moderately priced restaurants but for good seafood go to the **Liman**. For those travelling with a family the **Set Kafeterya** is a self-service restaurant in a department store or in summer eat outdoors at **Merkez Lokantasi**.

If you are really on a low budget you'll find the Turkish food at **Urfali Rest** excellent value for money or any of the kebab shops, most of which are clean and serve tasty food.

The hotels offer lively but expensive entertainment at night. **Mon Amour**, **Gar Gazinosu** and the **Bastikent** are all worth trying, as are the less sophisticated **Pino**, **Sehrazat**, **Kulup Fergman** and the **Tuna**. The **Set** is open at night in Kizilay Highrise with music or go to the **Youth Park** where there are outdoor performances in the cafés.

There is an opera house in Ankara so if you like more highbrow entertainment you may like to spend an evening here.

EXCURSIONS

The historian or archaeologist will want to take an excursion to **BOGAZKALE**, the Hittite city of Hattusas. You can drive there on the way to the Black Sea, or take a bus to Sungurlu and hire a taxi to take you to the site itself. It is true to say that most of the interesting finds have been shipped to Ankara but the site itself is of interest. The vast **Great Temple of the Storm God** dates from the fourteenth century BC. It was one of the five temples in the area and the fortified acropolis on Buyukale was the residence of the Hittite kings and queens. Be sure to visit the **Sphinx Gate** and the **Lion Gate**, built to frighten away evil spirits and invaders.

One mile north-east of Bogazkale is the sanctuary of **Yazilkaya**, one of the most holy temples in Turkey. Here you can see reliefs depicting the various Hittite gods, and of special interest is a well-preserved carving of a Hittite king dressed as a high priest.

AKALHOYUK is yet another Hittite site, though little remains to be seen to the untrained eye. There is a **Sphinx Gate** here which was the main entrance to the ancient city, and other finds from the site are displayed in a small museum with impressive exhibits from the Hatti civilization that flourished here 1000 years before the Hittites arrived.

Some 50 miles to the west of Ankara lies **GORDION**, one of the most important archaeological sites in Anatolia. Dating from 3000 BC, here eighteen settlements lie on top of one another, but the Phrygian remains are the most interesting. The burial chamber in the centre of the mound is said to be that of King Midas and it can be entered through a passageway.

Konya

Konya is the fourth largest city in Turkey and a destination for many coach tours of Anatolia. One of the world's most ancient cities, the original settlement dates as far back as 7000 BC and legend has it that Konya was the first city to emerge after the Flood. It was first a Hittite town; later it became a notable Roman city – visited by St Paul and St Barnabas – however, in the twelfth century it was captured by the Seljuk Turks and it became their capital.

At this time Mevlana Rumi (1207–73) founded the religious sect of the Whirling Dervishes and Konya became an important religious centre. Poet, scholar and philosopher, Mevlana was one of the world's greatest humanists advocating infinite tolerance, sexual equality and the pursuit of good, in an age when the rest of Europe was relatively uncivilized. During the Ottoman Empire the Dervishes had a great deal of influence, but in 1925 Ataturk disbanded the order. Each year in December the Whirling Dervishes perform the *Sema*, a dance devised by their founder, who believed that in dance each person abandoned himself to the love of God and thus attained divine unity. The dancers wear long white robes representing shrouds and tall hats like tombstones, and they whirl and rotate around the floor with arms outstretched, the right hand pointing upwards to communicate with God and the left hand down towards the earth. If you visit Konya between 9 and 17 December, during the annual Festival of Mevlana, there are performances at 8 p.m. each evening. Hann Overland (see section on tour operators) run a trip to Konya to coincide with the Dervish Festival.

COMMUNICATIONS

There is no *airport* in Konya, but for information about flights from Kayseri, the nearest airport, there is a Turkish Airlines Office at Mevlana Cad. (tel: 12032). The *bus station* is to the north of the city (tel: 11223) and a frequent service connects Konya with Ankara, Antalya, Side and Cappadocia. To get from the coach terminal into the city centre, take the minibus marked 'Mevlana' or alternatively try one of the three-wheeled *dolmuses* unique to the area.

Trains run to Istanbul from the railway station at the end of Istaysyon Cad. but there is no direct route to Ankara, so if you want to make this journey you'll have to go by bus.

TOURIST INFORMATION

Maps of the area and accommodation listings are available from the **Tourist Information Office** at Mevlana Cad. 21 (tel: 11074). It is open from 8 a.m. until 7 p.m. daily in the summer. (This office in particular has the knack of arranging for you to attend a Turkish wedding at no extra charge.)

ACCOMMODATION

The **Yeni Sema Hotel** (tel: 13279) is perhaps the most comfortable hotel, but it is outside the city. Alternatively try the **Kaymah Park Hotel** (tel: 33770) near to the bus station. It has 90 air-conditioned rooms and a restaurant. Less expensive rooms are offered by the **Hotel Seljuk** (tel: 11259) which has 50 rooms and is situated in a quiet part of the city, close to many restaurants. The **Hotel Dergah** has a central position, 43 modern rooms and a restaurant (tel: 11197). The budget traveller might try any one of these for a good deal on accommodation.

For those camping there is a campsite at **Sehir Stadi**, the sports complex to the east of the railway station.

EATING

Konya does not have the formal restaurants that Istanbul and Ankara boast but there are many clean establishments with good menus. The local speciality is *firin kebab*, oven-roasted mutton, and it is well worth trying. The **Fuar** is a reasonable outdoor restaurant but for simple cheap food try the **Derya Kebab Salonu** or the licensed **Kosem Restaurant**, which has especially good *meze* and *pide*. The **Catal Lokantasi** and the **Konak Lokantasi Merkez** are simple and charge low prices, though they have no licence. For food to take away, try **Kenanlar Pasta Salonu** on Alaattin Bul. which serves breakfast and snacks.

SIGHTS AND EXCURSIONS

The most striking feature in Konya is the beautiful Seljuk architecture, notably the very impressive doorways in the city centre. However, the most visited sight is without doubt the **Monastery and the tomb of Mevlana** which is open Tuesday until Sunday from 9 a.m.–12 noon and from 1.30–5.30 p.m. A green tiled building on Mevlana Cad., it was made a museum in 1927 after Ataturk dissolved the order of the Whirling Dervishes, although it does still remain a place of worship. The interior decoration is magnificent with carved wood, rich fabrics, beautiful rugs and ornate gold and silver work. In the Koran reading-room there is an exhibition of calligraphy and manuscripts, and you can also see collections of musical instruments and the strange garments worn by the sect. Most interesting, however, are the tombs of great disciples and in particular that of Mevlana.

Just opposite Mevlana's Museum is the **Selimiye Camii** built in 1558 by Selim, governor of the city. Konya's other main attractions are on Alaetti Cad. where the **Alaettin Camii**, a mosque of unusual Syrian style, and the **ruins of a Seljuk palace**, are to be found. Opposite the palace is **Karatay Medrese**, a thirteenth-century theological school which is open Tuesdays till Saturdays from 9 a.m. to 5 p.m. as a **Museum of Ceramics**, and further along the **Ince Minare Medrese** is today a **museum of stone and wood carving**.

Also of interest is the thirteenth-century **tomb of Sahip Ata**, and close to it the **Archaeological Museum** houses some interesting third-century Roman exhibits as well as some impressive sarcophagi.

From Konya you can take an excursion 30 miles south to **Catalhoyuk**, one of the first settlements in the world and the most important archaeological site in Turkey. The **Tourist Information Office** will be able to arrange a guided tour of the area and, although most of the cult figurines have been removed, the site is still worth seeing.

About an hour's drive from Konya on the route to Aksaray is the **Sultanhan**. An oasis surrounded by barren steppe-land, this Caravanserai was built by Alaeddin Keykubat in 1229 and is the largest and most magnificent in Anatolia. The building is an impressive sight with ornately carved gates and elaborate towers and buttresses.

On the Konya road on the way to Cappadocia you'll pass the village of IHLARA. About 25km south of the main road, it is located at the head of the Peristrema Valley, a gorge 7 miles long whose sides drop vertically some 3773 feet. A guide will take you to the Byzantine churches and monasteries which stand along the top part of the gorge, or alternatively hikers might take a mini-expedition along the valley floor through the poplar and olive trees.

Cappadocia

The region of Cappadocia is situated between the towns of KAYSERI, NEVSEHIR and NIGDE, and with its spectacular landscape of strange cones and 'fairy chimneys', it is one of the most visited areas in Turkey. The unusual geographic features here were caused by the eruption of three volcanoes, Erciyes Dag, near Kayseri, Melendiz Dag and Hasan Dag, both near Nigde, which covered the whole region with a layer of mud, ashes and lava. This hardened to form a soft, porous rock called tuff, which has since been eroded by wind, sand and water into the crags, canyons and unearthly shapes that you see today.

The earliest people to live here literally dug into the rock to build dwellings, and later, when Christianity came to Cappadocia, churches and monasteries were constructed, the inspiration of St Basil of Kayseri. At DERINKUYU and KAYMAKLI whole cities were developed under ground as a hideaway from Arab raiders. There is also another underground city at OZKONAK, 21 kms north of Avanos which is open to the public too.

The dry, sunny climate makes Cappadocia a popular destination all year round and there are tours from specialist church pilgrimages to the monasteries in the GOREME NATIONAL PARK to birdwatching, camping and even donkey trekking trips. (See tour operators directory.)

URGUP is the main tourist destination in the area and is a most convenient place, along with Göreme, to base yourself to explore the countryside. It is a picturesque village, situated at the foot of a cliff riddled with rock dwellings, and is typical of the settlements in the province. The **Tourist Information Office** at Kayseri Cad. (tel: 1059) is open from 8 a.m. until 7 p.m. daily, and, as well as providing you with maps of the area, they can help set up a taxi tour of the region so that you can see the sights comfortably, and for a moderate price.

There are several good hotels in Urgup but since many tour operators use accommodation here, it can be difficult if you haven't booked in advance. There are spectacular views from the **Buyuk Hotel** (tel: 1060) which has 40 rooms and a swimming pool, while not far from the village the modern **Turban Motel** (tel: 1490) offers 160 mini suites and also a swimming pool. For cheaper accommodation, try the **Sinasos** or any one of the numerous pensions – the **Efes**, **Europa**, **Goreme**, or **Turist** – which are for the most part clean and good value for money. **Cimenli Tepesi Camping** provides campers with a large swimming pool and a restaurant.

From Urgup take a trip out along the Nevsehir road to **ORTAHISAR**, a village clustered around a huge rock needle. You can climb up to the top of the pinnacle and look over the landscape. Head on to **GOREME**, which is inside the **NATIONAL PARK** where the most interesting grottoes and Byzantine churches and an open air museum are to be found. The park is open from 8.30 a.m. until 5 p.m. every day and tickets can be purchased from a kiosk in the car park if you want to visit the churches. Goreme itself is a village whose old name was Avcilar. There are approximately 35 pensions and many restaurants. Try **Köse Pension**, which is in the centre of the village and famous for its scrambled eggs. It's run by a Scottish woman and her Turkish husband. You could also try the **Peri** and **Goreme Pensions**. One of the best restaurants in the village is the Maccan, also in the centre.

Dolmus tours go daily from Goreme to Zelve. **ZELVE** is a city of rock dwellings which was excavated in the 1950s because of erosion and is a popular spot with tourists.

The monastic rock complex is full of churches and shrines but the most interesting are: the twelfth-century **Elmali Kilise**, which contains frescoes of the life of Christ; the eighth-century **Barbara Kilise**, the smallest of the churches; the **Yilanli Kilise** with its vivid frescoes of St George and Theodore killing the dragon, and the **Kiranlik Kilise** which has a refectory nearby with benches and tables carved from the stone. Unfortunately, the church itself is being restored and is closed for the moment. The **Cariki Kilise** and the **Tokali Kilise** with its detailed frescoes of saints are also of interest.

Situated at the foot of a hill, below a fifteenth-century Seljuk fortress, **NEVSEHIR** is the largest town in the region and is easily accessible by major roads. It has plenty of accommodation and is another good centre for tourists, though it is not as attractive as Urgup or the other villages in the area. It is the centre of the region's local transport, with buses to Ankara, Konya, Istanbul, Mersin, Izmir, Antalya and Kayseri.

The **Tourist Information Office** in Lale Cad. (tel: 1137) will arrange transport and tours to Goreme National Park and is open from 8 a.m. to 7 p.m. daily in summer, and in winter Monday to Friday between 8.30 a.m. and 5 p.m. With 80 rooms and a swimming pool, the **Orsan Cappadocia** on the Urgup road (tel: 1035or 2115) is the most comfortable hotel in town. The **Hotel Goreme** (tel: 1706) provides less expensive rooms and has a central position while the **Hotel Lale** (tel: 1799) or the **Hotel Vira** (tel: 1326) offer budget accommodation. Campers might try the **BP Mocamp** or the more sophisticated **Goreme Mocamp** which has water and electricity.

You might consider an excursion 10 miles south of Nevsehir on the Nigde road to DERINKUYU and KAYMAKLI – fascinating underground cities, with tunnels, rooms, water systems and ventilation shafts.

For a good view of the whole area, drive to UCHISAR which is located on the edge of the erosion basin. The village is particularly interesting with its houses decorated with sculptures. Club Med run the **Hotel Kaya** which is partly built into the rock-face and has yet another spectacular view and an excellent restaurant.

Travelling north towards AVANOS, you'll pass a valley of pink-tinged cones called 'fairy chimneys'. These are formed by boulders of hard stone trapped in the tuff which protects the tuff directly beneath from further erosion, and the result is a column or cone with a boulder on top. Avanos has long been famed for its onyx carving and the traditional red pottery from the clay of the Red River. Now it is full of tourist shops selling the local pottery and carpets, the other speciality industry of the province. In the town centre, there is a **Tourist Information Office** (tel: 60) in the **Hotel Venessa** beside the river. Accommodation is also provided at the **Tuscan Kilim Motel** (tel: 49).

KAYSERI

The town of Kayseri is on the northern edge of the province of Cappadocia. Situated at the foot of Erciyes Dag, the earliest traces of settlement here, are Hellenistic, though this was originally Hittite country. This is the birthplace of St Basil, the founder of the first monastic complex in the Goreme Valley, and it was here that he established a charitable institution for the poor and the sick. The Seljuks took the city in 1243 and held it until the Mongols arrived, then later it was captured by the Ottoman Turks.

There is an *airport* at Kayseri with flights twice a week to Istanbul costing around 30,000 TL (tel: 13947). The *railway station* is on Istasyon Cad. (tel: 12314) and a service operates daily to Ankara, Adana, Siras and Erzurum, though once again buses are often quicker.

The *bus station* is on the west side of Kayseri and there are frequent buses making the 4½-hour trip to Ankara, as well as *dolmuses* connecting Kayseri with other towns in Cappadocia. There is a useful bus service to Goreme about every hour run by the Nevtur and Goreme Turizm bus companies.

For **Tourist Information** go to Kagni Pazari Honat, Camii Yani 61 (tel: 11 190), open 8 a.m.–6 p.m., for accommodation listings and sightseeing brochures.

Sights in Kayseri include the **citadel** (Hisar), an impressive building of black volcanic rock built in AD 500 under Emperor Justinian, and the early Seljuk **Ulu Camii**, Kayseri's greatest mosque, which is situated close to the **covered bazaar**. There are many theological schools: the **Sahibiye Medrese** is now a museum, but perhaps the most interesting is the **Cifte Medrese**, the first medieval school of anatomy which joins the **Kursunlu Cami** with its distinctive lead-covered dome. The **Hatun Camii** complex to the east of the citadel comprises a mosque, a Turkish bath and the tomb of Sultan Keykubat's wife. There is also an **Archaeological Museum** which houses finds from the excavations at KULTEPE, the site of ancient Kanesh, as well as Roman, Greek and Hittite statuary.

For accommodation in Kayseri try the **Hattat Hotel** (tel: 19331) or the **Turan**, both of which have 70 rooms and a restaurant, while the smaller **Terminal** has 18 rooms, 10 with showers.

Culinary specialities in Kayseri include *pastirma* – a sun-dried beef with herbs – *sucuk*, *salami* and *tulum penir* – hard cheese cured in goat skin and honey (*bal*).

If you want to *ski*, there is a ski resort on ERCIYE DAG, 15 miles from Kayseri. It is open from November until May and has a ski lodge which sleeps 120, and qualified instructors offer tuition for all levels. However, only very limited ski hire is available and there are only two lifts. A trip here at any time of the year will offer you spectacular scenery and there is a mountain hut half-way up for serious *mountaineers*.

While in Kayseri it's worth taking an excursion to SULTANHAN, a thirteenth-century Seljuk royal Caravanserai built by Alaein Keykubat, one of the most beautiful of its kind. KARATAY HAN which was once on the main East/West trade route and has now been extensively restored.

The town of NIGDE is in a green valley surrounded by volcanic peaks at the south of Cappadocia. Originally called Nahita, a Hittite settlement, it flourished in the thirteenth century under the Seljuk Turks. Sights here include **Dis Camii**, three-domed **Alaettin Camii** built by Keykubat, and another interesting mosque with Gothic features – the **Sungur Bey Camii**. The **Hudavend Hatun Turbesi** is a most impressive mausoleum with ornate stone carvings, and those interested in archaeology should head for the **Ak Medrese**, which is now an archaeological museum.

Eastern Turkey

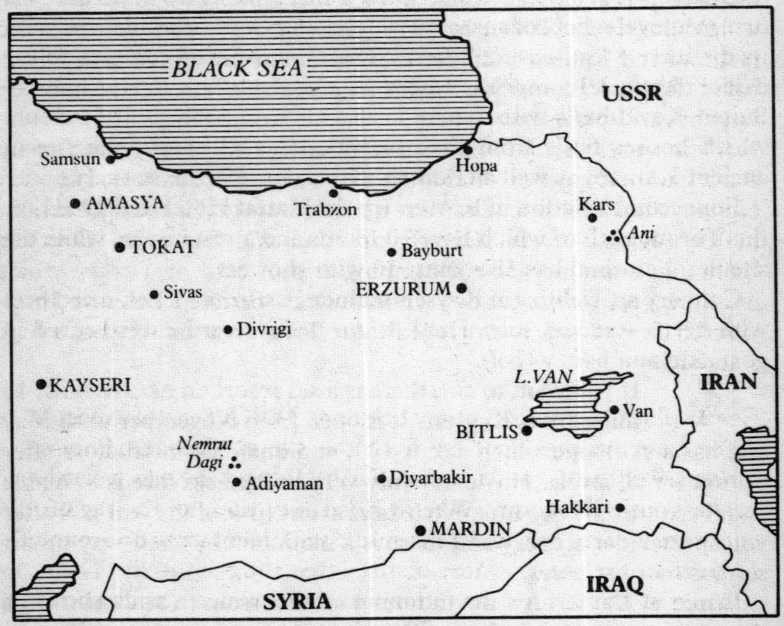

Eastern Turkey is very different in both appearance and character to the rest of Anatolia. The variety of landscape will surprise travellers: there are the fertile valleys around **KARS**; the dusty plateau of **ERZURUM**; the great peaks of **NEMRUT DAGI** and **MOUNT AGRI**, and the turquoise waters of LAKE VAN in the east. The region is not yet accustomed to tourists, consequently few facilities exist for them, but for the more adventurous traveller eastern Turkey offers a fascinating experience.

The best time of year to visit eastern Turkey is between May and September as winters are very severe and travel is virtually impossible from October until April. The summer is hot and dry, especially in south-eastern Turkey, but even then it can get quite chilly at night, particularly at high altitudes.

The quickest way to get out to eastern Turkey is to fly from Ankara to one of the provincial capitals – VAN, ERZURUM or DIYARBAKIR. Turkish Airlines have flights three times a week to Van and daily to Erzurum and Diyarbakir. There is a good train service linking Istanbul, Erzurum and Kars; and another linking Istanbul and Van which crosses Lake Van by ferry. Alternatively buses run between Istanbul and Ankara and Tokat, Sivas, Erzurum, Adiyaman, Diyarbakir, Bitlis, Van and Kars with an especially fast service between Istanbul and Erzurum.

If you would prefer to visit eastern Turkey with an organized group some tour operators do offer tours to the east. UK Express, Highway Holidays and Blue Spot Travel run coach tours to the main attractions in the region – Urfa, Diyarbakir, Van and Erzurum. Overseas Camping Tours organize a camping trip of eastern Turkey which might appeal to the hardy, while on the specialist holidays Inter-Church Travel and Swan Hellenic Art Treasures run tours of a high standard.

Geographically eastern Turkey begins at **TOKAT**, situated about 70 miles from Amasya, not far from the site of **Comana Pontica**, a sanctuary of the Great Anatolian Earth Mother who was worshipped in the Pontic Kingdom. When Christianity came to the region this cult worship died out, and a Byzantine settlement grew up around the fortress to the south. Most of the interesting sights in Tokat are situated at the foot of the Ottoman citadel which stands above the town on a twin-peaked rock. The **Gok Medrese** is the most notable building. It was built in 1270 as a school of Koranic theology but now houses archaeological finds from the area, and from Comana Pontica in particular. At the **Hatuniye Medrese**, constructed in the fifteenth century under Sultan Beyaszit, note the beautiful, ornate doorway, and whilst in the town the **Ali Pasa Camii** and **Garifler Camii** are also worth visiting.

An hour's journey by bus to the south lies the town of **SIVAS**, a Hittite settlement which developed into a Roman trading centre due to its strategic location on the crossroads of the caravan routes from Baghdad and Persia. Sivas was one of the principal cities of the Sultanate of Rum during the Seljuk period. More recently, it was here where in 1919 Mustafa Kemal held a congress to set in motion his plans for the liberation of Turkey. The hall where he held this historic meeting has since been made the **Inkilap Museum** (the Museum of the Revolution).

The **Tourist Information Office** at Vilayet Konagi (tel: 12 850) will provide you with brochures on Sivas and help with accommodation. Sights of the town include the **Cifte Minare Medrese**, built in 1271, which has a most impressive doorway and two minarets; and across the street the **Sifayiye Medrese**, one of the most elaborately constructed institutions ever built by the Seljuks. Of the many mosques to be found in Sivas, the oldest one, the **Uli Camii**, dates from 1197 and is perhaps the most interesting, though **Yeni Cami** is a close contender.

For accommodation try the hotels **Kosk Oteli** (tel: 1150) on Ataturk Cad. or the **Sultan Oteli** (tel: 2986) on Belediye Sokak which are both inexpensive and offer facilities as good as will be found in this area.

If you are travelling from Sivas to Erzurum by train you'll pass through the attractive and historic town of **DIVRIGI**. The town is little known on the tourist circuit but it certainly is worth getting to, even if it is difficult to reach by road. The architecture in the town is quite exceptional, especially the elaborate inscriptions and decoration on the thirteenth-century **Ulu Camii** and, next to it, the **Darussifa Hospital** which was built in 1228.

ERZURUM is the largest city in eastern Turkey. Originally a Byzantine city, it has subsequently been held by the Arabs, the Armenians, the Seljuks and most recently by the Russians in 1916. Now it is the cultural, commercial and academic centre of the east.

It is the transfer point for most travellers coming to eastern Turkey. There is an airport with daily flights to Istanbul and Ankara. Flight information is available from the Turkish Airlines Office on Hasteneler Cad. (tel: 18530/11904/13409). Express trains link Erzurum with Istanbul, Kars and Ankara, but once again buses are often quicker. A bus service operates between Erzurum and all of the major towns in the area. Maps of the area and accommodation listings can be obtained from the **Tourist Information Office** at Cemal Gusel Cad. (tel: 15697) which is open 8 a.m.–12 noon and 1.30–5 p.m. Monday–Friday and from 8 a.m.–4 p.m. on weekends.

There are some fine Turkish buildings in Erzurum. The twelfth-century **Ulu Camii** is huge but very simple in design. It has a beautiful courtyard with colonnades characteristic of the early Seljuk period. Close to it the **citadel** is noted for the Greek inscriptions and its unusual minaret which now has been converted into a clock tower. There are two important theological schools; the thirteenth-century **Cifte Minare Medrese**, which has two minarets and an ornate doorway, and the **Yakutiye Medrese**, a Mongol seminary, constructed in the thirteenth century with a tiled minaret (entry to this mosque is forbidden). Of the many mausoleums in Erzurum the three tombs in the **Uc Kumbet** are the most interesting, in particular the **Emir Sultan Turbesi**, the largest one. Those interested in archaeology might want to visit the **Archaeological Museum** which has exhibits from several millennia.

Good accommodation can be found in Erzurum. The **Hotel Oral** on Terminal Cad. (tel: 19740) is the largest hotel in the city and provides moderately priced accommodation. Other inexpensive hotels are the **Hotel Efes** on Tahticilar Cad. (tel: 17081) and the **Polat Hotel** on Kazim Karabekir Cad. (tel: 11623). The budget traveller might try the **Cihar Hotel** on Ayazpasa Cad. (tel: 13580), the **Behara Hotel** (tel: 15096) or the **Hotel Kral** (tel: 17783) on Erzinean Kapi, which are all inexpensive.

There is a **ski centre** at Palandoken, about four miles outside Erzurum, with some of the best skiing conditions in Turkey and some of the most difficult runs. It is a ski resort with a ski lodge, sleeping 100, and the facilities for a skiing holiday – restaurants, a ski lift and ski instructors.

Most visitors to eastern Turkey will want to see the huge statues in the open-air temple on the summit of **NEMRUT DAGI**. The statues of lions, eagles and gods stand nearly 30 feet high on a ledge cut out of the mountain 8200 feet above sea level. The inscriptions in the temple tell how in 80 BC Mithradates Callinicus established the capital of the Commagenes in Arsemia, which is now the village of ESKI KAHTA (see below), and how his son Antiochus ordered the building of the temple.

The most novel (and expensive) way to get up Nemrut Dagi is by helicopter from Adiyaman, but a cheaper alternative is a minibus from Adiyaman or Kahta which will take you almost to the top, and you can climb the rest of the way quite easily. Not surprisingly there is a spectacular view from the mountain top, particularly at sunset.

If you plan to visit Nemrut Dagi, **ADIYAMAN** is about 50 miles away and has the most comfortable accommodation in the area. The **Motel Antiochos** (tel: 1240 and 1184), on Menderis Cad. is moderately priced and has camping facilities as well. Alternatively try the **Motel Arsemia** on Bahcelievler mah. **Nemrut Yolu** (tel: 2122 and 3131), which is situated near the bus station. The **Tourist Information Office** is on Hukumet Konagi (tel: 1008). They will help arrange excursions including one to NEMRUT DAGI.

An alternative base is at **KAHTA**, at the foot of Nemrut Dagi. The **Hotel Merhaba** (tel: 98 139) is very pleasant indeed but it is advisable to book in advance as it is very popular with tour groups. For budget travellers, there is the **Kommagene Pension** on Eski Kahta Yolu (tel: 92). Good camping facilities are to be found at the **Nemrut Camping** on Adiyaman Kata.

From Kahta you can also arrange a trip to ESKI KAHTA, the ancient Commagene capital of Arsemia. Here there are impressive stone reliefs; one of Mithradates shaking hands with Hercules, and also the longest Greek inscription ever discovered. On the top of the hill the foundations of the capital city can be seen: the palace with a mosaic floor; and the sanctuary. It is the perfect place to stop off for a picnic on your way back from Nemrut Dagi.

Three miles from Eski Kahta, the village of **DAMLACIK** is the best place to stay if you are travelling on a very tight budget. The **Bahceli Restaurant and Camping** on the Nemrut road has basic but adequate facilities.

The famed River Tigris flows close to the black basalt walls of **DIYARBAKIR**. The site was first inhabited in the Bronze Age, making the city one of the oldest in southern Anatolia. Diyarbakir has been fought over by a succession of conquerors and was dominated by the Urartians, the Assyrians, the Persians, the Greeks, the Romans and the Arabs. This fascinating city still has a distinctly Arab feel to it, perpetuated by both the people and the architecture.

There is an *airport* to the south of the city. For information about flights contact the Turkish Airlines Office on Izzet Pasa Cad. in the **Denir Hotel** (tel: 10101). The *railway station* is at the end of Istasyon Cad. and has connections to Van. A bus service runs from all major Turkish towns to the *bus station* on Elazig Cad. which is in the new part of the city, outside the walls. The **Tourist Information Office** is also to be found in this area on Lise Cad. (tel: 12 173) and is open from 8 a.m. until 6 p.m. Monday–Friday.

Without doubt the **city walls** are the most impressive sight in Diyarbakir. They stretch intact for almost three miles. A good way to see them is to hire a horse-drawn carriage and take a trip right round them, stopping off to see the reliefs and inscriptions. Be sure to visit the more interesting city gates of which the **Harput Kapisi** and the **Urfa Kapisi** are the best preserved.

Diyarbakir has many mosques worth visiting, but perhaps the most interesting of these is **Ulu Camii**. Originally constructed in 1091, it was restored in 1155 after it had been damaged by fire. Unlike **Nebii Camii**, which is of typical Ottoman design, Ulu Camii is of unusual Arab design. Close to the mosque the **Zinciriye Medrese**, a medieval school of theology, is now the **archaeological museum**. It is open from 8.30 a.m.–12.30 p.m. and 1.30–5.30 p.m. with exhibits covering a period of almost four thousand years.

Accommodation in Diyarbakir is simple but adequate. The **Demir Hotel** (tel: 12315) and the **Sarac Hotel** (tel: 12365), both on Izzet Pasa Cad., provide inexpensive rooms. Alternatively, on Inonu Cad. the **Buyuk Diyarbakir** (tel: 12444) and the **Denya Hotel** (tel: 14966) are worth trying, as is the **Turistik Hotel** (tel: 12662) on Ziya Gokalp Bul, which has a pleasant restaurant situated around a fountain. The **Hotel Ertem** (tel: 12972) on Izzet Pasa Cad. is recommended for those really counting the pennies.

About 70 miles south-east of Diyarbakir, towards the Syrian border, is the city of **MARDIN**. It has one of the most impregnable citadels in Turkey and has withstood the attacks of great conquerors such as Saladin and Tamerlane. Inside the walls of the **fifteenth-century citadel** there are the ruins of a **mosque** and a **royal residence**.

It's worth going up to the summit for the spectacular view of the city and of the Syrian plain.

Also of interest are: the **Latife Camii**, founded in 1371, and the twelfth-century **Ulu Camii** with its unusual fluted dome. However, perhaps the most important Seljuk monument in Mardin is the **Isa Bey Medresi**. It is situated on the hill leading up to the citadel and has an unusual design and ornate decoration.

From Mardin, it is worth taking a trip to the borderlands of Turkey and Syria, an area that is now the centre of Jacobite Christianity. There are several monasteries where Aramaic is still spoken. The most famous of these is **Der Zaferan**, the ancient patriarchal seat of the Syrian Orthodox Church. Situated about four miles east of Mardin, this makes an interesting excursion.

The town of **BITLIS** lies about a hundred and fifty miles north-east of Mardin. This historic old town lies in a narrow, deep valley and has several Seljuk monuments which are worth visiting. The **Ulu Camii** is one of the oldest Seljuk Great Mosques. Other sights include the sixteenth-century **Serefiye Camii**, the **Gokmeydani Camii**, the **Sa a Han**, a Caravanserai built in the fifteenth century, and the **Byzantine fortress** which overlooks the town.

It is only about ten miles from Bitlis to **LAKE VAN**, one of the highlights of Turkey. Lake Van is Turkey's largest lake, covering about six times the area of Lake Geneva. The view is spectacular – turquoise-blue waters mirroring the mountain peaks that surround the lake. It was formed when a volcano near Tatvan erupted and blocked off the exit for the spring waters. The water has a high mineral concentration which makes it rather unusual to swim in, though not unpleasant.

A trip to **AKDAMAR ISLAND** is certainly not to be missed if you are in this area. The island is situated about a mile from the southern shore of Lake Van and you can take a boat across from Gevas, on the shore road between Tatvan and Van. Akdamar is uninhabited but the reason for visiting it is the tenth-century Armenian Church. The **Church of the Holy Cross** is all that remains of the palace and monastery built here in 921 by Gagik Artzruni, King of Vaspurakan. It is a small building of pink sandstone and the interior walls are decorated with some of the great masterpieces of Armenian art. There are friezes of animals, birds and men and, among the many Biblical scenes, the most notable are of Jonah being cast into the whale's mouth, David slaying Goliath and Adam and Eve about to eat the Forbidden Fruit.

If you come across you'll need to bring your own food since there is no restaurant on the island. However, it really is a superb location to picnic and to swim in the lake.

The city of **VAN** is located inland from the lake shore. It was once the site of Tushpa, the capital of the Urartian civilization, but the old city which was situated below the Rock of Van was destroyed during the First World War and only a few ruins remain. Van is now a modern city and a market centre for the local tribesmen who live in the mountains of south-east Turkey and come here to sell hand-woven rugs and bags.

Van has an *airport* with flights three times a week to Istanbul and Ankara. The Turkish Airlines Office on Cumhuriyet Cad. (tel: 1241) will be able to provide information about flights. The railway line that runs from Ankara to Iran passes through Van and there are two *railway stations; Sehir Istasyon* to the north of the city centre; and *Iskele Istasyon* at the dockside. The *bus terminal* is at the northern end of Cumhuriyet Cad. and at the other end of the street is the **Tourist Information Office** (tel: 2018), which is open from 8 a.m.–12 noon and 1.30–5.30 p.m. and can provide listings of accommodation as well as brochures and maps of the area.

The most famous sight in Van is the **Rock of Van** which stands on the lakeside a little to the west of the city. The walls and towers of the **citadel** on the Rock of Van were originally built by the Urartians but have been restored and expanded by the Armenians, the Seljuks and the Ottomans. There are numerous cuneiform inscriptions from as far back as 800 BC, some in the caves which were apparently built as burial chambers for early Urartian kings. Looking south from the summit of the rock the foundations of the ancient city of Tushpa can be seen and looking west from the citadel there is a spectacular view of Lake Van.

The other sight in Van is the new **Archaeological and Ethnographic Museum**. The archaeological exhibits include some impressive Urartian jewellery and there are some pots from the Old Bronze Age of 5000 BC. The ethnographic display has superb kilims, the flat woven mats made by the local villagers and tribesmen. The museum is open 9.30 a.m.–12.30 p.m. and 1.30–5.30. p.m.

Van has the most modern accommodation in eastern Turkey. The **Hotel Akdamer** (tel: 3036) on Kazim Karabekir Cad. is very comfortable, as is the **Tekin Hotel** (tel: 3010) on Kucuckcamii Civari. For cheaper rooms try the **Bayram Hotel** (tel: 1136) near the bus station, the **Kent Hotel** (tel: 2404) on Isbankasi Arkasi or the **Caldiran Hotel** (tel: 2718) on Sihke Cad., all of which are good value for money.

You might consider a trip to the town of **HAKKARI** while in this region. Hakkari is situated about 130 miles south of Van and the road to the town passes through the Zap Valley which has some of the most breathtaking scenery in Turkey. This region is deep in the mountains, is surrounded by peaks almost 12,000 feet high and has its own language and culture. Hakkari is a small town and although there is not much of interest the medieval **fortress**, which dominates the town, is worth a visit as is the **medrese** which is close to it.

On the road north from Van you'll pass through the town of Agri and then travel east to **DOGUBAYAZIT**. Dogubayazit is located on the edge of a dusty plain with the famed Mount Ararat – or Agri Dagi as it is called in Turkish – standing behind it. It is a good place to stop off and admire the view. The snow-capped volcano is almost 17,000 feet high and rising up out from the plain, the sight is even more majestic. Legend says that it is the resting place of Noah's Ark and over the years there have been several reports of sightings of a boat shape on the mountain. If you want to climb the mountain you need written permission from the authorities although Trek Travel and Metro Tourism in Istanbul do organize group climbs. However, most tourists are content just to view the mountain and the best time to do this is at sunrise or early morning before it becomes obscured by cloud.

The best place to stay in Dogubayazit is the **Hotel Istahan** (tel: 1139). Previously known as the **Hotel Ararat**, it has simple rooms (ask for no. 504) and a good restaurant. The main attraction in Dogubayazit is the **Isak Pasa Complex**. This mosque and palace complex is situated five miles outside the town and can be reached by *dolmus*. Construction began here in 1685 under the orders of Isak Pasa, the enormously wealthy governor of the province; however, the palace was not completed until 1784. The result is a highly original building that is a curious mixture of different architectural styles. The mosque is still used for prayers and it is still possible to climb up into the minaret which has a panoramic view of the region.

About a hundred and sixty miles north-west of Dogubayazit is the town of **KARS**. The town has been besieged by a succession of armies who have marched along this invasion route between Anatolia and Russia: the Seljuks, the Byzantines, the Mongols, the Turks and most recently the Russians. The proximity to the Soviet border has led to Kars resembling its neighbour who occupied the town from 1877 until 1920. Nowadays Kars is surrounded by pastureland, the centre of a farming community famed for its dairy produce.

The train service from Erzurum comes through Kars en route to Moscow and the *railway station* is at the southern end of Istasyon Cad. The *bus station* is on Karadag Cad. and a bus service links Kars with Ankara, Diyarbakir, Erzurum, Istanbul, Kayseri, Konya and Sivas. For **Tourist Information** go to the office on Faik Bey Cad. (tel: 2724) which is open from 8 a.m.–12 noon and 1.30–5.30 p.m. on weekdays and 8.30 a.m.–4 p.m. on weekends.

The **twelfth-century fortress** is not open to the public but you can visit the **Church of the Holy Apostle** next to it, which served as the cathedral of Kars until Ottoman times when it became a mosque. When the town was occupied by the Russians it was used as a church and then in 1920 became a mosque once more.

The most interesting sight in Kars is the **museum**. Open 8 a.m.–12 noon and 1.30–5.30 p.m. from Tuesdays until Sundays, it houses artefacts from the Bronze Age through the Greek, Roman, Seljuk and Ottoman Empires. There is also an ethnographic exhibition with some fine kilims, carpets and costumes.

Accommodation in Kars can be described as basic at best. The **Yilmaz Hotel** (tel: 1074) on Kucukkazimbey Cad. and the **Temel Palas Hotel** (tel: 1376) on Pazar Cad. provide moderately priced rooms. The **Hotel Bal** on Ataturk Cad. is the best of the cheaper hotels.

From Kars you might consider an excursion to picnic at LAKE CILDAR or head to the *ski resort* at SARIKAMIS. This is a modern ski resort with a ski lodge, ski lift and instructors and if you want to ski here the best time to come is between January and March.

Almost all tourists who come to Kars do so to visit the medieval ghost town of **ANI**. Since it is necessary to get police permission to visit the site, due to its position on the Russian border, it is best to arrange a trip through the Tourist Information Office who will help find a *dolmus* or taxi driver to take you out to the site.

The abandoned city which has been uninhabited for six centuries is most impressive. Once the capital of an Urartian state, it became the capital of an Armenian Bagrahd kingdom between 953 and 1045. Later it was captured by the Byzantines and then dominated by a succession of invaders until the Mongols occupied the city in 1239 and then abandoned it.

The remains of the **city walls** are more than half a mile in length and enclose the ruins of eight churches, a convent and a citadel. There were originally four gates to the city, and you enter by the **Arslan** or **Lion Gate**, so named because of the design on the inner wall of the gateway. The **cathedral** is the largest and most impressive building. It was built between 989 and 1010 when the city was held by Armenian Catholics and was changed from church to mosque to church depending on who occupied the city. Other buildings of interest include: the eleventh-century **Church of the Holy Saviour** and the thirteenth-century **Church of St Gregory of Tigran Honent**, which has well-preserved friezes and a very dramatic clifftop position.

The Language

English is not widely spoken in Turkey but you'll find most Turks will try their utmost to understand you and make themselves understood. In the major cities and resorts there are Turks who speak a little bit of everything, and a basic knowledge of French or German often comes in handy. Language rarely poses a problem in the resorts as most tourist offices, hotels etc. have at least one member of staff who can speak English. In the more remote regions you'll usually find someone in the village who can translate if you run into difficulty. Wherever you're going, a good English/Turkish phrasebook will be invaluable and your efforts to speak the language will be appreciated.

It's difficult to compare Turkish to any other language – because there's no other language quite like it. Over the centuries the alphabet, pronunciation and dialects have been influenced by several languages including classic Arabic, Latin and Mongolian. You can't hope to grasp much of the language in a few weeks but you can learn a few essentials. Here are some basic words and phrases which will be useful for your trip. (Remember, ş is pronounced 'sh', ç is 'ch', c is 'j' and i is 'ee'.)

English	*Turkish*
Yes	Evet
No	Hayir
Hello	Merhaba
Please	Lütfen
Thank you	Tesekkür ederim

Good morning	Günaydin
Good afternoon	Tünaydin
Good day	Iyi günler
Good evening	Iyi akşamlar
Goodbye (when leaving)	Allahaismarladik
(when staying)	Güle Güle
Excuse me	Affedersiniz
Where is/are?	Nerede?
When?	Ne zaman?
What?	Ne?
How?	Nasil?
Who?	Kim?
Why?	Nicin/Neden?
I understand	Anliyorum
I don't understand	Anlamiyorum
Do you speak English?	Ingilizce biliyor musunuz?
Can I have . . . ?	. . . rica edebilir miyim?
I would like . . .	. . . istiyorum
a single room	Tek yatakli bir oda . . .
a double room	Çift yatakli bir oda . . .
a room with a bath	Banyolu bir oda . . .
a room with a shower	Duşlu bir oda . . .

What is the price per night?	Bir gecelik ücret ne kadardir?
What is the price per week?	Bir haftalik ücret ne kadardir?
It is . . .	O . . . dur
It isn't . . .	O . . . degildir
Is there/are there . . . ?	. . . var mi?
There is/there are . . .	. . . var
Good/bad	Iyi/kötü
Cheap/expensive	Ucuz/pahali
Big/small	Büyük/küçük
Where can I get a taxi?	Nereden bir taksi bulabillirim?
Take me to this address please	Beni bu adrese götürün
Where's the nearest bank please?	En yakin banka neredир?
Can you change a traveller's cheque please?	Şahsi banka ceki bozdurabilirim lütfen?
Can you show me on this map where I am?	Haritada nerede bulundugumu gösterir misiniz?
I'm lost	Kayboldum
I would like my bill, please	Lütfen hesap istiyorum
Where's the ladies' toilet?	Bayanlar tuvaleti nerede?

Where's the gents' toilet?	Baylar tuvaleti nerede?
Can I use your telephone?	Telefonunuzu kullanabilir miyim?
It's urgent	Aceledir
Get an ambulance	Ambülans çağirin
Get a doctor	Doktor çağirin
Get the police	Polis çağirin
One	Bir
Two	Iki
Three	Üç
Four	Dört
Five	Beş
Six	Alti
Seven	Yedi
Eight	Sekiz
Nine	Dokuz
Ten	On
Sunday	Pazar
Monday	Pazartesi

Tuesday	Sali
Wednesday	Çarşamba
Thursday	Perşembe
Friday	Cuma
Saturday	Cumartesi
Today	Bugün
Tomorrow	Yarin
Yesterday	Dün

Index

European City Breaks

'Weekend' Escapes to Europe's 20 Major Cities

Katie Wood

As flight times decrease and air fares tumble, and with the approaching reality of the Channel Tunnel, the cities of Europe are becoming as accessible for short breaks – of three or four days, or maybe even a week – as those of Britain. Now, within a matter of hours you can escape the rigours of everyday life and find yourself strolling up the Champs-Elysées or dining in Budapest, rapt in the Rijksmuseum, shopping in Munich or having a drink in St Mark's Square.

Full of advice on how to get there, which tour operators to use, where to stay and eat and what there is to see and do, this is an invaluable handbook for every enthusiastic traveller. Whether you want to wander in your own way, cram in culture, arrange a romantic weekend or visit two cities in a week, *European City Breaks* – the result of several years of research – will help you decide where to go and when, and tells you all you need to know both before you go and when you're there.

Covers every city break operator for:

Austria – Innsbruck, Salzburg, Vienna; **Belgium** – Bruges, Brussels; **Czechoslovakia** – Prague; **France** – Nice, Paris; **Great Britain** – London; **Hungary** – Budapest; **Ireland** – Dublin; **Italy** – Florence, Milan, Rome, Venice; **Netherlands** – Amsterdam; **Portugal** – Lisbon; **Spain** – Madrid; **West Germany** – Munich, West Berlin

FONTANA PAPERBACKS

The Winter Sun Guide

The Best Holidays Round the World from October to April

Katie Wood and George McDonald

A blistering sun glistening on silvercrested waves; long, cool drinks in the shade of softly fringed palm trees; the red glow of sunset shimmering over tropical landscapes: holidaying abroad is the ideal way to escape the icy clutches of a cold and gloomy winter at home.

The Winter Sun Guide highlights over fifty of the world's most popular destinations and explores the exciting bargains on offer from October to April, the inexpensive long-term holidays and how to get the best out of them. Whether you're looking for the colourful nightlife of the Greek islands or that enticing blend of ageless culture and modern sophistication in Morocco, the lush paradise of the Seychelles and Maldives or the exotic splendour of India, *The Winter Sun Guide* provides the vital facts to help you discover that winter break with a difference.

★ Which resort to pick

★ Comprehensive guide to the best tour operators

★ Wide choice of accommodation and how to book it

★ How and when to travel – package or independent

★ What to see and do, with a look at specialist holidays

★ Easy to read, objective, well researched and up to date

FONTANA PAPERBACKS

Katie Wood and George McDonald

The Round the World Air Guide

The long haul travel market is dramatically expanding and for little more than the price of a return flight to Australia you can now circumnavigate the globe. *The Round the World Air Guide* has been written specifically for the new breed of serious traveller and whether you are on a round the world ticket or using conventional long haul options, it will guide you to the best places and the best prices. It is the only book which covers all you need to know to plan and book your trip *and* acts as a practical guide to the world's fifty major destinations.

Full of essential information on:

* How to cut costs and get the most out of your ticket
* Stop off possibilities and side trips
* Airport facilities around the world
* Where to go and what to see
* Where to sleep and what to eat
* Dining out and nightlife

No frequent traveller can afford to take off without it!